Cavendish
Publishing
Limited

COMMERCIAL LAW

Professor Michael Furmston
TD, MA, BCL, LLM, Barrister
Bencher of Gray's Inn
Professor of Law
The University of Bristol

Peter Shears, BA, LLB, LLM
Director of Legal Studies
University of Plymouth

First published in Great Britain 1995 by Cavendish Publishing
Limited, The Glass House, Wharton Street, London WC1X 9PX
Telephone: 0171-278 8000 Facsimile: 0171-278 8080

British Library Cataloguing in Publication Data

Furmston, MP
Commercial Law – (Lecture Notes Series)
I Title II Series
344.2067

ISBN 1-874241-66-X
Cover photograph by Jerome Yeats
Printed and bound in Great Britain

Preface

Commercial law is one of the great contributions of English law to the legal systems of the world. Yet it is curiously difficult to know what its boundaries are and what should be taught within a university course on commercial law. The emphasis in this book is on those parts of the subject which are concerned with, and facilitate, transactions in the goods. It is hoped, however, that most of the material here will be found in most of the courses which readers are studying in their universities. The purpose of the work is to reduce the burden of note-taking and thus enable students to concentrate on what the lecturer is actually saying and to provide a framework into which the students' own notes and thoughts can be incorporated.

I am particularly grateful to Peter Shears for producing the section on consumer credit. Margaret Baillie has provided invaluable help with the production of the text and Jo Reddy has provided an ideal combination of admonition and encouragement.

Michael Furmston
University of Bristol
August 1995

Contents

PART I – SALE OF GOODS

PART II – LAW OF AGENCY

PART V – CONSUMER CREDIT

Table of Cases

Table of Statutes

PART I

SALE OF GOODS

Chapter 1

Introduction to Sale of Goods

Many sale of goods cases are decided by the application of the rules of general contract law. For instance, the rules as to whether there is a contract at all (offer and acceptance, consideration and so on) are basically the same for all contracts. There is, however, a body of rules which is peculiar to sale of goods transactions or which is applied by analogy to transactions like hire-purchase or hire. One problem is to tell which questions are answered by contract law and which are answered by sales law. It is not easy to answer this question but, for the moment, do not worry about it. Be aware as you are going along that the problem exists. When you have finished the course you will usually be able to see what the answer is in any particular situation.

Another problem arises from the fact that, whereas the law of contract consists of principles which have to be culled from the cases, the law of sale of goods is to be found in a single statutory code. In 1893 Parliament passed the Sale of Goods Act. This Act was designed to *codify* the common law on sale of goods: that is, to state the effect of the decisions of the courts in a succinct statutory form.

Judges have repeatedly said that in deciding the meaning of a codifying statute like the Sale of Goods Act 1893, the cases on which it was based should not normally be consulted. The most famous statement is that of Lord Herschell in *Bank of England v Vagliano Brothers* (1891) (a case decided in reference to the Bills of Exchange Act 1882, another codifying statute) where he said:

> '... the purpose of such a statute surely was that on any point specifically dealt with by it, the law should be ascertained by interpreting the language used instead of, as before, by roaming over a vast number of authorities in order to discover what the law was, extracting it by a minute critical examination of the prior decisions.'

So, as a rule, reference to pre-1893 cases should not be necessary. There have been many cases since then and it is often only possible to discover the accepted meaning of sections in the 1893 Act by careful examination of those cases. In addition, the 1893 Act was amended a number of times and in 1979 Parliament passed a new Sale of Goods Act. This was a *consolidating* measure which simply brought together in a tidy

1.1 Nature of the subject

form the 1893 Act as it had been amended between 1893 and 1979 and made no changes in the law. With only a couple of exceptions – indeed the section numbers of the 1893 and 1979 Acts are identical.

The law of sale of goods is for the most part, therefore, an exposition of the effect of the Sale of Goods Act 1979. In most universities nowadays, you will be allowed to take a copy of the Sale of Goods Act 1979 into the examination or will be provided with a copy in the examination room. This means that you do not need to learn the sections off by heart. You do, however, need to know your way round the Act so that you should not look at it for the first time in the examination room. The key to doing well is knowing the organisation of the Act and in which sections the answers are to be found. The 1979 Act has been amended by three further Acts; the Sale of Goods (Amendment) Act 1994; the Sale and Supply of Goods Act 1994. and the Sale of Goods (Amendment) Act 1995. These Acts insert a number of new provisions or varied provisions into the 1979 Act. This book incorporates the changes made by the 1994 Act.

1.2	**Is the Sale of Goods Act a complete code?**

It seems likely that Sir MacKenzie Chalmers intended the Sale of Goods Act 1893 to contain all the special rules about the sale of goods. He was certainly well aware of the problems discussed in the last section and dealt with them by providing in s 62(2) that:

> '... the rules of the common law, including the law merchant, save in so far as they are inconsistent with the provisions of this Act, and in particular the rules relating to the law of principal and agent and the effect of fraud, misrepresentation, duress or coercion, mistake or other invalidating cause, apply to contracts for the sale of goods.'

In *Re Wait* (1927) Atkin LJ clearly took the view that where a matter was dealt with by the Act, the treatment was intended to be exhaustive. He said 'The total sum of legal relations ... arising out of the contract for the sale of goods may well be regarded as defined by the code.' The question in that case was whether the buyer could obtain specific performance of the contract. Section 52 of the Sale of Goods Act says that a buyer may obtain specific performance of a contract for the sale of specific or ascertained goods. (These terms are explained below, para 1.6.3.) The Act does not expressly say that specific performance cannot be obtained where the goods are not specific or ascertained but Atkin LJ thought that s 52 should be treated as a complete statement of the circumstances in which specific performance should be granted for a contract of sale of goods. On the other hand, in the more recent case of *Sky Petroleum Ltd v VIP Petroleum Ltd* (1974) Goulding J thought that he had jurisdiction to grant specific performance in such a case, though the views of Atkin LJ do not appear to have been drawn to his attention.

The problem was discussed again, though not decided, in *Leigh and Sullivan Ltd v Aliakmon Shipping Co Ltd* (1986) where Lord Brandon of Oakbrook stated that his provisional view accorded with that expressed by Atkin LJ in *Re Wait*.

1.3 Domestic and international sales

Most of the cases discussed in this part will concern domestic sales: that is, sales where the buyer, the seller and the goods are all present in England and Wales. Obviously there are many international sales which have no connection at all with English law. However, there are many international sales which are governed by English law, either because English law is the law most closely connected with the transaction or because the parties have chosen English law as the governing law. It is in fact common for parties expressly to choose English law because of a desire to have the transaction governed by English law or for disputes to be litigated or arbitrated in England. So, many transactions in the grain or sugar trades will be subject to English law by reason of the parties' choice although neither the seller nor the buyer nor the goods ever comes near England.

In general where an international sale transaction is subject to English law, it will be subject to the provisions of the Sale of Goods Act. However, in practice a solution which makes good commercial sense for domestic sales may make much less good sense for international sales and vice versa. So although the Act says that risk *prima facie* passes with property, a rule which is often applied in domestic sales, in practice it is extremely common in international sales for risk and property to pass at different moments. Furthermore, most international sales involve use of documents, particularly of the bill of lading, and often involve payment by letter of credit which is virtually unknown in domestic sales. The law of international sales is discussed more fully in Part IV.

1.4 Commercial and consumer sales

The Sale of Goods Act 1893 was predominantly based on Chalmers' careful reading of the 19th century cases on sales. These cases are almost entirely concerned with commercial transactions, particularly relatively small-scale commodity sales. Few consumer transactions, except perhaps sales of horses, figure in this body of case law. It is true that the 1893

Act has some provisions which only apply where the seller is selling in the course of a business but these provisions do not discriminate according to whether the buyer is buying as a business or as a consumer. For the most part this is still true though the modern consumer movement has meant that we now have a number of statutory provisions which are designed to protect consumers either in circumstances where it is assumed that businesspeople can protect themselves or that they need less by way of protection. These developments are particularly important in relation to defective goods and exemption clauses.

1.5   Types of transaction

1.5.1   Non-contractual supply

This section considers the different ways in which the act of supplying goods may take place.

Usually where goods are supplied there will be a contract between the supplier and the receiver of the goods. A contract is not essential.

The most obvious case where there is no contract is where there is a gift. In English law, promises to make gifts in the future are not binding unless they are made under seal (for example, covenants in favour of charities) but a gift, once executed, will be effective to transfer ownership from donor to donee provided that the appropriate form has been used. So, in principle, effective gifts of goods require physical handing over.

In some cases a donee may have an action against the manufacturers. So if I give my wife a hair dryer for her birthday and it burns her hair because it has been badly wired, she will not have an action against me except in the unlikely case that I knew of the defect. In most cases the retail shop which supplies the goods would be in breach of their contract with me but I would not have suffered the loss, whereas my wife, who has suffered the loss, has no contract with them. However, she could sue the manufacturer if she could prove that the hair dryer had been negligently manufactured.

It can be surprisingly difficult to decide whether or not a transaction is a gift. Many promotional schemes make use of so-called gifts; can customers complain if they do not receive the gift? Often the answer seems to be yes. The question was examined by the House of Lords in *Esso Petroleum v Customs and Excise* (1976).

Even where it is clear that money will change hands, the transaction is not necessarily contractual. An important example is the supply of prescribed drugs under the National Health Service. Although for many patients there is now a substantial charge, the House of Lords held in *Pfizer Corpn v*

Minister of Health (1965) that there is no contract. The basic reason for this is that a contract depends on agreement, even though the element of agreement is often somewhat attenuated in practice. The patient's right to the drugs and the pharmacist's duty to dispense do not depend on agreement but on statute.

Section 2 of the Sale of Goods Act 1979 defines a contract of sale of goods as 'a contract by which the seller transfers or agrees to transfer the property in goods to the buyer for a money consideration called the price'. It follows that this is essentially a transaction in which one side promises to transfer the ownership of goods and the other pays the price in money. This therefore excludes cases where there is no money price and situations where what is sold is not goods but land or what is often called intangible property, that is property interests which cannot be physically possessed such as shares, patents, copyrights and so on.

1.5.2   Sale of goods

It is one of the features of English law that quite different regimes apply to contracts for the sale of land and the sale of goods. So, for instance, while sellers of goods are under extensive implied liability as to the quality of these goods, sellers of land are liable only for their express undertakings as to quality. Usually there is no difficulty in deciding whether the contract is one for the sale of land or for the sale of goods but there are some borderline problems in relation to growing crops or minerals under the land. Under s 61(1) of the Sale of Goods Act 1979, a contract for crops or minerals is a contract for the sale of goods if they are to be severed from the land either 'before the sale or under the contract of sale'. On the other hand a contract for the sale of a farm would normally be treated as a contract for the sale of land even though there were growing crops, but compare *English Hop Growers v Dering* (1928).

1.5.3   Exchange

The requirement in s 2 of the 1979 Act that there must be a money price in a sale means that an exchange of a cow for a horse is not a sale. For most purposes this makes no great practical difference because the courts are likely to apply rules similar to the Sale of Goods Act by analogy. Between 1677 and 1954 contracts for the sale of goods worth £10 or more needed to be evidenced in writing. This requirement was never applied to exchanges so that many of the older cases arose in this context. Straightforward exchange or barter does not appear to be very common in domestic trade though it is increasingly common in international trade because one of the parties is short of hard currency. On the other hand part exchange is very common, particularly in relation to motor cars. This raises the question of the correct classification of an agreement to exchange a new car for an old one plus £2000. In practice this is often solved by the way the parties write up the contract. In many cases they will price each car so that the natural analysis is that there are two sales with an agreement to pay the balance in cash. This was how the transaction was approached in *Aldridge v Johnson* (1857) where 32 bullocks valued at £192 were to be transferred by one party and 100 quarters of barley valued at £215 were to be transferred by the other.

Exchange is usually discussed in relation to transfer of goods by each party but the same principles would seem to apply where goods are transferred in exchange for services.

1.5.4 Contracts for work and materials

Many contracts which are undoubtedly contracts of sale include an element of service. So if I go to a tailor and buy a suit off the peg, the tailor may agree to raise one of the shoulders since one of my shoulders is higher than the other. The contract would still be one of sale. Conversely if I take my car to the garage for a service, the garage may fit some new parts but such a transaction would not normally be regarded as a sale. In both these cases the parties could, if they wished, divide the transaction up into two contracts, one of which would be a contract of sale and the other a contract of services, but in practice this is not usually done.

It is clear that there are many contracts in which goods are supplied as part of a package which also includes the provision of services. Some are treated as contracts of sale, others are treated as a separate category called contracts for work and materials.

In some cases it is possible to say that the property transfer element is so predominant that the contract is clearly one of sale; in others the work element is so large that it is obviously work and materials. This approach seems to work with the off-the-peg suit (sale) and car service (work and materials) examples above, but what is the position where there is a substantial element of both property transfer and work?

Unfortunately in the two leading cases the courts adopted different tests. In *Lee v Griffin* (1861) a contract by a dentist to make and fit dentures for a patient was said to be a contract of sale on the ground that at the end of the day there was a discernible article which was to be transferred from the dentist to the patient. On the other hand in *Robinson v Graves* (1935) it was said that a contract to paint a portrait was one for work and materials because 'the substance of the contract is the skill and experience of the artist in producing a picture'. These tests appear irreconcilable.

Where the contract is classified as one for work and materials, the supplier's obligations as to the quality of the goods will be virtually identical to those of the seller since the terms to be implied under the Supply of Goods and Services Act 1982 are the same as those to be implied under the Sale of Goods Act 1979. It is worth explaining, however, that the supplier's obligation as to the quality of the work will often be substantially different from that concerning the quality of the materials. This can be illustrated simply with the everyday case of taking a car to a garage for a service. Let us suppose that during the service the garage supplies and fits a new tyre to the car. As far as fitting is concerned, the garage's obligation is to ensure that the tyre is fitted with reasonable care and skill. However, it may be that the tyre though fitted carefully contains a defect of manufacture not apparent to visual inspection which leads to a blow-out when the car is being driven at speed on the motorway. The garage will be liable for this defect because the tyre was not merchantable or reasonably fit for its purpose and this liability is quite independent of any fault on the part of the garage owner.

In most respects a contract with a builder to build a house is very like a contract with a tailor to make a suit. In both cases, property in the raw materials will pass but the skills deployed in converting the raw materials into the finished product appear to make up the greater part of the transaction. There is one obvious difference, however. A contract to buy a ready made suit is clearly a contract for the sale of goods but a contract for a house already built is a contract for the sale of land. This has meant that the seller of a house does not undertake the implied obligations as to the quality of the product which are undertaken by the seller of goods.

However, although English law treats sales of off-the-peg suits and houses quite differently, it treats the contract to make suits and build houses very similarly since it will imply into a contract to build a house terms as to the quality of the materials and workmanship. So in *Young and Marten Ltd v McManus Childs Ltd* (1969) a contract for the erection of a building required the builders to use 'Somerset 13' tiles on the roof. They obtained a supply of these tiles (which were only made by one manufacturer) and fixed them with reasonable skill. Unfortunately the batch of tiles proved to be faulty and let in the rain. The House of Lords held that the builders were in breach of their implied obligations as to fitness for purpose.

Under a hire-purchase contract the customer agrees to hire the goods for a period (usually two or three years) and has an

1.5.5 Construction contracts

1.5.6 Hire-purchase

option to buy them at the end of this period, usually for a nominal additional sum. The economic expectation of the parties is that the customer will exercise this option and indeed the rate charged for hire will be calculated on the basis of the cash price of the goods plus a handsome rate of interest and not on the market rate for hiring them. Nevertheless the customer does not actually contract to buy the goods and the House of Lords held in *Helby v Matthews* (1895) that the contract was not one of sale and that a sale by the hirer before all the instalments had been paid did not operate to transfer ownership to the sub-buyer. The effect of this decision was that although economically and commercially a contract of hire-purchase had the same objectives as a credit sale, its legal effect was fundamentally different.

A further oddity of hire-purchase is that, particularly in the case of motor cars, the finance does not actually come from the supplier but from a finance company: that is, a body whose commercial purpose is to lend money and not to supply goods. The supplier will sell the goods to a finance company which will then enter into a contract with the customer. The supplier will usually have a supply of draft contracts so that all the paperwork can be done at once in the supplier's office but the customer's contract is actually with the finance company.

1.5.7   Hire

In practice whether the contract is one for sale, exchange, work and materials or hire-purchase the customer will end up as the owner of the goods. However, the customer may be more concerned with the use than the ownership of the goods. One reason for this could be that only short-term use is intended: for example, a car which is hired for a week's holiday. But there may be other reasons. Many British families choose to rent rather than buy a television.

A contract in which goods are transferred from the owner to a user for a time with the intention that they will be returned later is a contract of hire. It is an essential part of such a contract that the possession of the goods is transferred. So a number of transactions which would colloquially be described as hire are not accurately so called. For instance, one might well talk of hiring a bus for a school outing but this would not strictly be correct if, as would usually be the case, the bus came with a driver. In that case the owner would remain in possession through the driver and the contract would be simply one for use of the bus. The position is the same in a commercial context where a piece of plant such as a bulldozer or a crane is supplied with an operator except where, as is often the case, the operator is transferred with the equipment and becomes for the time being the employee of the hirer. In

In recent years it has been common for contracts for the use of goods to be made and described as 'leases'. So a car may be 'leased' rather than bought, as may major items of office equipment or computers. There can be a number of advantages in this from the customer's point of view. One is that such transactions appear to be of an income rather than a capital nature so they will not show up in the company's balance sheet as a capital purchase. This can be attractive as it may make the company's financial position look better. Nor is this necessarily a cosmetic benefit since there can be perfectly good business reasons for wishing to avoid tying up capital in equipment, particularly where it has to be borrowed at high rates of interest. Apart from these financial advantages, there may also be tax benefits for a business in leasing equipment rather than buying it.

Although the term 'lease' is very commonly used to describe such transactions there is at present no separate legal category of leases of goods, unlike leases of land which have been recognised from the 12th century. Therefore in law most leases will simply be contracts of hire. In some cases, however, there may be an understanding that at the end of the period of the lease the customer may or will buy the goods. This may amount to no more than a non-binding arrangement, in which case it will have no effect on the legal nature of the transaction. If, however, the customer has an option to buy the goods at the end of the lease, the transaction will in substance be one of hire-purchase. If the customer has agreed to buy the goods at the end of the lease then it would seem that the contract is actually one of sale.

It is worth noting that in many 'leases' the 'lessor' is not the supplier but a bank or finance house. In such cases the supplier sells the goods to a bank which then leases them to the customer. This produces a triangular relationship like that in a hire-purchase contract.

1.5.8   Leases

The Sale of Goods Act divides the meaning and types of goods as follows:

* existing and future goods;

* specific and unascertained goods:

* sales and agreements to sell

1.6   Meaning and types of goods

Section 61(1) of the Sale of Goods Act 1979 states that goods:
'Includes all personal chattels other than things in action and money, [and in Scotland all corporeal moveables except money] and in particular "goods" includes

1.6.1   The definition of goods

> emblements, industrial growing crops, and things attached to or forming part of the land which are agreed to be severed before sale or under the contract of sale.'

The words in brackets reflect the different legal terminology of Scotland and may be ignored for present purposes.

So 'personal chattels' mean all forms of property other than 'real property' (freehold interests in land) and 'chattels real' (leasehold interests in land). 'Things in action' are those forms of property which cannot be physically possessed so that they can only be enjoyed by bringing an action. This includes such things as shares, patents, copyrights, trademarks, rights under bills of exchange and policies of insurance. The exclusion of 'money' presumably means that a contract to purchase foreign exchange is not a sale of goods.

| 1.6.2 | Existing and future goods |

The Sale of Goods Act 1979 contains two explicit sets of subdivisions of goods. One is existing and future goods and the other specific and unascertained goods. Section 5(1) says that:

> 'The goods which form the subject of a contract of sale may be either existing goods, owned or possessed by the seller, or goods to be manufactured or acquired by him after the making of the contract of sale, in this Act called future goods.'

Future goods are also defined by s 61(1) as:

> 'goods to be manufactured or acquired by the seller after the making of the contract of sale.'

It will be seen that goods which are in existence may be future goods, for example, where the seller has agreed to sell goods which at the time of the contract are owned by someone else. A typical example of future goods would arise where the seller was to make the goods, but the category would also appear to include things which will come into existence naturally as where a dog breeder agrees to sell a puppy from the litter of a pregnant bitch. In such a case there is an element of risk that things will not turn out as the parties hope; for instance that all the puppies die or that the buyer had contracted for a dog puppy and all the puppies are bitches. In such a case the court will have to analyse the agreement to see whether the seller's agreement was conditional on there being a live puppy or a puppy of the right sex.

| 1.6.3 | Specific and unascertained goods |

Section 61(1) defines 'specific goods' as 'goods identified and agreed on at the time a contract of sale is made'.

Unascertained goods are not defined by the Act but it is clear that goods which are not specific are unascertained. It is important to emphasise that the distinction relates to the position at the time the contract of sale is made. Later events will not make the goods specific but they may, and often will, make them ascertained.

The distinction between specific and unascertained goods is of particular importance in the passing of property between seller and buyer. Unascertained goods may be of at least three different kinds. One possibility is that the goods are to be manufactured by the seller. Here they will usually become ascertained as a result of the process of manufacture though if the seller is making similar goods for two or more buyers some further acts may be necessary to make it clear which goods have been appropriated to which buyer. The second possibility is that the goods are sold by a generic description such as '500 tons Western White Wheat'. In such a case the seller could perform the contract by delivering any 500 tons of Western White Wheat (provided that it was of satisfactory quality, etc). If the seller was a trader in wheat he might well have more than 500 tons of wheat but would not be bound to use that wheat to perform the contract; he could and often would choose to buy further wheat on the market to fulfil the order. Where there is an active market-sellers and buyers may be entering into a complex series of sales and purchases according to their perception of how the market is moving and leaving who gets what wheat to be sorted out later. Obviously this is particularly likely where the sales are for delivery at some future date rather than for immediate despatch. In this situation the seller may form plans to use a parcel of wheat to deliver to buyer A and another parcel to buyer B. Usually the forming of these plans will not make the goods ascertained until the seller makes some act of appropriation which prevents a change of mind.

A third and perhaps less obvious possibility is that the goods may be part of an undivided bulk. So if the seller has 1,000 tons of Western White Wheat on board the SS *Challenger* and sells 500 tons to A and 500 tons to B, these are sales of unascertained goods since it is not possible to tell which 500 tons has been sold to which purchaser. In this situation the goods become ascertained only when it can be established which part of the cargo is appropriated to which contract. The legal effect of such a sale is altered by the Sale of Goods (Amendment) Act 1995 (see para 4.8).

Section 2 of the Sale of Goods Act 1979 draws a distinction between sales and agreements to sell. Section 2(4) provides:

1.6.4   Sales and agreements to sell

'Where under a contract of sale the property in the goods is transferred from the seller to the buyer the contract is called a sale.'

Section 2(5) states:

'Where under a contract of sale the transfer of the property in the goods is to take place at a future time or subject to some condition later to be fulfilled, the contract is called an agreement to sell.'

The reason for this distinction arises from an ambiguity in the word 'sale' which may refer either to the contract between buyer and seller or to the transfer of ownership from seller to buyer which is the object of the agreement. In English law it is possible in principle for ownership to pass from seller to buyer simply by agreement, without either delivery of the goods or payment of the price.

Introduction to Sale of Goods

This chapter considers a number of preliminary topics. These include:

- the relationship between sales law and general contract law;

- the distinction between sale of goods and other similar transactions such as exchange or hire-purchase;

- the meaning and types of goods.

Chapter 2

The Price

In a contract of sale the irreducible minimum of obligations is for the seller to deliver the goods and the buyer to pay the price. This chapter considers the rules about the ascertainment of the price and Chapter 3 describes the rules about payment of the price and delivery of the goods.

Sections 8 and 9 of the Sale of Goods Act 1979 deal with the price. Section 8 provides:

'(1) The price in a contract of sale may be fixed by the contract, or may be left to be fixed in a manner agreed by the contract, or may be determined by the course of dealings between the parties.

(2) Where the price is not determined as mentioned in sub-section (1) above the buyer must pay a reasonable price.

(3) What is a reasonable price is a question of fact dependent on the circumstances of each particular case.'

Section 9 states:

'(1) Where there is an agreement to sell goods on the terms that the price is to be fixed by the valuation of a third party, and he cannot or does not make the valuation, the agreement is avoided; but if the goods or any part of them have been delivered to and appropriated by the buyer he must pay a reasonable price for them.

(2) Where the third party is prevented from making the valuation by the fault of the seller or buyer, the party not at fault may maintain an action for damages against the party at fault.'

These sections do not in fact appear to cover all the difficulties that can arise and in practice resort is also made to the general principles of contract law.

The fact that no price has been agreed might be good evidence that the parties had not completed a contract, but it is clear that in practice people often make binding contracts without having agreed on the payment terms. In such a case it is clear that there is a contract to buy at a reasonable price (s 8(2)).

Section 8(3) of the Sale of Goods Act 1979 says that what is a reasonable price is a question of fact. If the seller

2.1   Introduction

2.2   The parties say nothing about the price

is in business, evidence of his or her usual prices will be good evidence of what is a reasonable price but, in theory at least, it is not decisive.

Where the seller is not in business or not in the business of selling goods of the kind sold, there will be no seller's standard price to appeal to and the court will have to do the best it can with such evidence as the parties present to it.

2.3 The parties fix the price in the contract

This is the simplest and probably most common situation. Obviously the parties may fix the price in a number of different ways. I may sell my car for £3,000 but if I take the car to the filling station I would ask for as much petrol as was needed to fill the tank at 55p a litre; in the first case a global price and in the second a unit price.

2.4 The price is left to be fixed in a manner agreed by the contract

Section 8(1) of the Sale of Goods Act 1979 clearly contemplates that the contract may leave the prices to be fixed later in an agreed manner. One such manner would be third party valuation but this is expressly dealt with by s 9. The Act is silent on other methods of price-fixing.

One possibility is that the contract may provide for the price to be fixed by the seller (or the buyer).

In *May and Butcher Ltd v R* (1934) Lord Dunedin said 'With regard to price it is a perfectly good contract to say that the price is to be settled by the buyer.'

In *Lombard Tricity Finance Ltd v Paton* (1989) this was assumed to be correct by the Court of Appeal and applied to a contract which entitled a lender to change the interest rate unilaterally.

Rather than leave the price to be fixed by one party, the parties may agree that the price shall be fixed by agreement between them later. This is a common but potentially dangerous course. There is no problem if the parties do agree on a price but difficulties arise if they do not. It might be thought that in that case s 8(2) would apply and a reasonable price would be due. However, in *May and Butcher v R* the House of Lords held otherwise. In that case there was a contract for the sale of tentage at a price to be agreed between the parties. The parties failed to agree and the House of Lords held that there was no contract. The argument which was accepted was that s 8(2) only applied where there was no agreement as to the price so that its operation was excluded where the parties had provided a mechanism for fixing a price which had not worked. This decision had never been overruled and is still in theory binding. Nevertheless the courts have not always followed it.

In *Foley v Classique Coaches* (1934) the plaintiffs sold land to the defendants who agreed as part of the same contract to buy all their petrol from the plaintiffs 'at a price to be agreed between the parties in writing and from time to time'. The transfer of the land was completed and the defendants later argued that the agreement to buy the petrol was not binding as the price was uncertain.

There is therefore a good chance that a court will hold, where the parties do not agree, that they intended the price to be a reasonable one. This is particularly likely where the goods have actually been delivered and accepted by the buyer. Nevertheless it remains imprudent for the parties to make such an agreement, granted that courts sometimes hold such agreements to be inadequately certain. These dangers can be avoided entirely by providing machinery for dealing with those cases where later agreement proves impossible or by simply providing that the price 'shall be such as the parties may later agree or in default of agreement a reasonable price'.

Price-fixing by third party valuation is dealt with by s 9 of the Sale of Goods Act 1979 (see 2.1 above). The provisions are reasonably straightforward. Price-fixing by third party valuation, is valid but dependent on the third party actually undertaking the valuation. If one party prevents the valuation that party is said to be liable to an action. Presumably it would be the seller who would usually prevent the valuation by not making the goods available. It is worth noting that the result of such obstruction by the seller is not a contract to sell at a reasonable price, as is the case where the goods are delivered and no valuation takes place, but an action for damages. This may not make much difference in practice since what the buyer has been deprived of is the chance to purchase the goods at the price the valuer would have fixed and a court would almost certainly hold this to be the same as a reasonable price.

An important question is what, if anything, sellers can do if they think the valuation is too low, or buyers if they think it is too high. No doubt the valuation is not binding if it can be shown that the valuer was fraudulently acting in concert with the other party. Apart from this instance it would seem that the valuation is binding as between seller and buyer. However, the party who is disappointed with

2.5   Fixing the price by third party valuation

the valuation will have an action against the valuer if it can be shown that the valuation was negligent. This was clearly accepted by the House of Lords in *Arenson v Casson* (1977), a case involving the sale of shares in a private company at a price fixed by valuation.

The Price

This chapter considers the legal effect of the various ways in which the parties may fix the price.	**Introduction**

Sections 8 and 9 of the Sale of Goods Act 1979 deal with the price.

Where the parties say nothing about the price, s 8(a) provides that the buyer must pay a reasonable price. What is a reasonable price is a question of fact (s 8(3)): if the seller is in business, his or her usual prices will be evidence of what is a reasonable price; if the seller is not in business, the court will have to do the best it can with such evidence as the parties present to it.	**The parties say nothing about the price**

Parties usually fix the price in the contract. They may do so in a number of ways, such as agreeing to sell a car for £8000 (a global price) or agreeing to buy as much petrol as was needed to fill the tank at 55p a litre (a unit price).	**The parties fix the price in the contract**

Section 8(1) of the Sale of Goods Act 1979 contemplates that the contract may leave the prices to be fixed later in an agreed manner. One possibility is that the contract may provide for the price to be fixed by the seller (or the buyer) (*May and Butcher Ltd v R* (1934)).	**The price is left to be fixed in a manner agreed by the contract**

Problems have arisen, however, where rather than leave the price to be fixed by one party, the parties agree that the price shall be fixed by agreement between them later. In *May and Butcher v R* (above), the parties failed to agree and the House of Lords held that there was no contract on the basis that s 8(2) only applied where there was no agreement as to the price so that its operation was excluded where the parties had provided a mechanism for fixing a price which had not worked.

Price-fixing by third party valuation is valid but dependent on the third party actually undertaking the valuation. If one party prevents the valuation that party is said to be liable to an action for damages (s 9(2)).	**Fixing the price by third party valuation**

Chapter 3

Payment, Delivery and Acceptance

Section 27 of the Sale of Goods Act 1979 provides:

'It is the duty of the seller to deliver the goods and of the buyer to accept and pay for them in accordance with the terms of the contract of sale.'

Section 28 states:

'Unless otherwise agreed, delivery of the goods and payment of the price are concurrent conditions, that is to say, the seller must be ready and willing to give possession of the goods to the buyer in exchange for the price and the buyer must be ready and willing to pay the price in exchange for possession of the goods.'

This chapter considers the legal problems arising from the duty of the seller to deliver the goods and of the buyer to accept and pay for them.

Section 28 states that, unless otherwise agreed, payment and delivery are concurrent conditions. This means that they should take place at the same time. Obviously the parties may have agreed expressly or by implication that payment is to precede delivery or the other way round. In practice, payment and delivery cannot take place simultaneously without the willing co-operation of both parties. This means that the seller who complains that the buyer has not paid must show that he was ready and willing to deliver and conversely a buyer who complains of the seller's failure to deliver must show that she was ready and willing to pay the price. In practice this is often done by tendering the goods or the price respectively.

In commercial sales it is often agreed that goods will be delivered on usual trade terms, such as payment within 30 days or payment within 30 days of receipt of invoice. The effect of such an agreement is that the seller must deliver first and cannot subsequently have a change of mind and insist on payment on delivery.

For the same reason a seller cannot refuse to deliver because the buyer has been late in paying on an earlier contract. Sellers often think they are entitled to do this and frequently do but it is clear that this is wrong. In *Total Oil v Thompson* (1972) a petrol company entered into a typical contract to supply petrol to a filling station. The contract provided for delivery on credit terms but the filling station owner turned out to be a bad payer and the petrol company attempted to change to a cash-on-delivery basis. It was held that they were not entitled to do this. A seller is entitled to change the payment terms in respect of future contracts.

Questions may arise about the form of payment. The starting point is that in the absence of contrary agreement the seller is entitled to be paid in cash but the parties are free to make other agreements.

In many cases it would be relatively easy to infer that payment by cheque was acceptable. Usually payment by cheque is said to amount only to a conditional discharge, that is the buyer is discharged only when the cheque is paid. This means that if the buyer's cheque bounces, the seller has a choice either to sue on the cheque or on the underlying transaction of sale. In the same way it has been held that a buyer who pays by banker's letter of credit is conditionally discharged only by the opening of the credit. So in *ED & F Man Ltd v Nigerian Sweets and Confectionery Co Ltd* (1977) the buyer had arranged a credit with a bank which went into liquidation before paying the seller. It was held that the buyer was liable for the price.

3.3   Delivery

'Delivery' bears a meaning in the Sale of Goods Act 1979 quite different from its colloquial meaning. If I say that a grocer will deliver, this would usually be taken to mean that the groceries will be brought to the house of a customer. In the Sale of Goods Act the word does not have any necessary connotation of taking the goods to the customer and refers simply to the seller's obligation to hand over the goods. In the basic case the seller performs its obligations by making the goods available to the buyer at its (the seller's) place of business.

3.3.1   The meaning of delivery

Section 61(1) of the Sale of Goods Act 1979 states that delivery means 'voluntary transfer of possession from one person to another'. This is slightly misleading, as it suggests that delivery necessarily involves the seller handing the goods to the buyer. Although the typical case is undoubtedly that of the seller making the goods available to the buyer at the place and time set out in the contract, there are many cases where this does not happen.

In some cases the buyer will already have been in possession of the goods. A typical example would be where goods were being acquired on hire-purchase and the customer exercised an option to buy the goods at the end of the period of hire. It would be absurd to require formal delivery and re-delivery of the goods.

Conversely the goods may be delivered even though the seller stays in possession if the capacity in which he is in possession changes. An example would be the position of the dealer in the standard hire-purchase car triangle. The dealer sells the car to the finance company but the car is never physically transferred to the finance company. It goes straight from dealer to customer. Physical transfer to the customer is a sufficient delivery to the finance company.

In some cases it may be sufficient to transfer the means of control. So delivery of a car may be made by transfer of the keys and delivery of goods in a warehouse in the same way.

Section 29(4) of the Sale of Goods Act 1979 deals with the case of goods which are in the possession of a third party. It provides:

> 'Where the goods at the time of sale are in the possession of a third person, there is no delivery by seller to buyer unless and until the third person acknowledges to the buyer that he holds the goods on his behalf; nothing in this section affects the operation of the issue or transfer of any document of title to the goods.'

The most common example of this would be where the seller had put the goods into the hands of someone whose business it is to store other people's goods, such as a warehouseman. Obviously the seller could tell the warehouseman to deliver the goods to the buyer but the buyer might wish to leave the goods in the hands of the warehouseman. Again it would be absurd to require a formal delivery and re-delivery but here agreement between seller and buyer will not be sufficient to effect delivery. The common practice is for the seller to give the buyer a delivery order, that is a document instructing the warehouseman to deliver to the buyer. The buyer can present this to the warehouseman and ask that the goods be kept on the buyer's behalf. Delivery takes place when the warehouseman recognises that the buyer is the person now entitled to the goods (this is technically known as an 'attornment').

This rule does not apply, as s 29(4) of the 1979 Act states, where there is a document of title involved. The notion of a document of title can best be explained by considering the most important example, a bill of lading. A bill of lading is the document issued by the master of a ship to a person who puts goods on board the ship for carriage. The bill has a number of functions. It operates as evidence of the terms on which the goods are to be carried and also as a receipt for the goods. In the days of sail, goods might be put on board a ship for carriage and the bill of lading sent ahead by a faster ship. The practice grew up of dealing in the bills of lading and by the late 18th century the courts had come to recognise the bill of lading as having a third function of being a document of title to the goods on board ship. So if the owners of goods put them on a ship and received a bill of lading made out to themselves or 'to order', they could endorse the bill by writing on its face a direction to deliver the goods to someone else and that would transfer to that person the right to receive them from the ship's master. In other words, the shipowner is required to deliver to whoever holds a bill of lading properly endorsed. In the case of commodity cargoes where trading is very active, the goods may be transferred many times while they are on the high seas.

The principal difference between the warehouseman and the ship's master is that because the bill of lading is a document of title the transfer is effective at once without the need for any attornment. In some cases it is not possible to transfer the bill of lading, for instance, because only part of the goods covered by the bill of lading is being sold. In this situation the seller may issue a delivery order addressed to the master but since the delivery order is not a document of title, delivery will not be effective until the master attorns.

Finally, delivery to a carrier may be a delivery to the buyer. This is dealt with by s 32.

It should be emphasised that the rule that delivery to the carrier is delivery to the buyer is only a *prima facie* rule and can be rebutted by evidence of a contrary intention. So in the case of sea carriage, if the seller takes the bill of lading to its own order, as would usually be the case, then this is evidence of a contrary intention. Further if the seller sends the goods off in her own lorry this will not be delivery to a carrier for this purpose, nor probably if the carrier is an associated company.

3.3.2 Place of delivery	In many cases the parties will expressly agree the place of delivery or it will be a reasonable inference from the rest of their agreement that they must have intended a particular place.

If there is no express or implied agreement then the position is governed by s 29(2) which provides:

> 'The place of delivery is the seller's place of business if he has one, and if not, his residence; except that, if the contract is for the sale of specific goods, which to the knowledge of the parties when the contract is made are in some other place, then that place is the place of delivery.'

3.3.3   Time of delivery

It is very common, particularly in commercial contracts, for the parties expressly to agree the date for delivery. This may be done either by selecting a particular calendar date, for example 1 May 1996, or by reference to a length of time, such as six weeks from receipt of order. In this respect it is worth noting that the law has a number of presumptions about the meaning of various time expressions, so that a year *prima facie* means any period of 12 consecutive months; a month means a calendar month; a week means a period of seven consecutive days and a day means the period from midnight to midnight (the law in general takes no account of parts of a day).

The parties might agree that delivery is to be on request. This could happen, for instance, where the buyer can see the need for considerable volume over a period of time and does not wish to risk having to buy at short notice. If the buyer lacks storage facilities he may leave the goods with the seller and call them up as required. A typical example might be a builder who is working on a housing estate and can see how many bricks, doors, stairs, etc will be needed but does not want to store them for long periods on site. In this situation the seller must deliver within a reasonable time from receiving the request and since the goods should have been set on one side, a reasonable time would be short.

The parties may completely fail to fix a date. The position will then be governed by s 29(3) of the Sale of Goods Act 1979 which provides:

'Where under the contract of sale the seller is bound to send the goods to the buyer, but no time for sending them is fixed, the seller is bound to send them within a reasonable time.'

It is normally a breach of contract for the seller to deliver late. The major exception to this rule would be where the contract gives some excuse for late delivery such as a *force majeure* clause. The buyer is entitled to damages to compensate for the loss suffered as a result of late delivery. In many cases, however, the buyer will not be able to show that any significant loss has been suffered as a result of the delay and the damages will only be nominal.

3.3.4   Effect of late delivery

In some cases the buyer will be entitled to reject on late delivery, depending on whether 'time is of the essence'. However if, but only if, time is of the essence a late delivery can be rejected. Time can be of the essence for three reasons:

(a) because the contract expressly says so;

(b) because the court characterises the contract as one where time is inherently of the essence. This is essentially a two-stage process. In the first stage, the court will consider whether the contract is of a kind where prompt performance is usually essential. The second stage is to consider whether there are particular circumstances which justify departure from the usual classification. Applying this approach courts have consistently held that the time of delivery is normally of the essence in commercial sales;

(c) because although time is not initially of the essence, the buyer may 'make' time of the essence. What this slightly misleading expression means is that if the seller does not deliver on time, a buyer may call on her to deliver within a reasonable time on pain of having the goods rejected if this does not happen. Provided the court later agrees with the buyer's assessment of what was a reasonable further time of delivery, such a notice will be effective.

Buyers are not obliged to reject late delivery and indeed will often have little commercial alternative but to accept the goods because they are needed and not readily obtainable elsewhere. There is an important practical difference here between a buyer who purchases goods for re-sale and one who purchases goods for use. A buyer who accepts late delivery of the goods waives any right to reject for late delivery but does not waive the right to damages.

| 3.3.5 | Rules as to quantity delivered |

Section 30 of the Sale of Goods Act 1979 contains a number of rules which deal with problems which arise where the seller delivers the wrong quantity. The basic rule is that the buyer is entitled to reject if the seller fails to deliver exactly the right quantity. Section 30(1) deals with the simplest case and provides:

> 'Where the seller delivers to the buyer a quantity of goods less than he contracted to sell, the buyer may reject them, but if the buyer accepts the goods so delivered he must pay for them at the contract rate.'

At first sight it seems obvious that the buyer is not bound to accept short delivery but there is an important practical consequence of this rule and the rule that the seller cannot deliver in instalments unless the contract expressly provides for delivery in that manner. It follows that if the seller delivers part of the goods and says that the balance is following the buyer is entitled to reject. What happens in this situation if the buyer accepts the part delivery? It is probable that he has waived the right to reject but that this waiver is conditional on the seller honouring the undertaking to deliver the balance. If the seller fails to do so, it seems probable that the buyer can reject after all. If he has meanwhile sold or consumed the part delivery, it will not be possible to reject since rejection depends on returning the goods.

Sections 30(2) and 30(3) deal with delivery of too much and provide:

'(2) when the seller delivers to the buyer a quantity of goods larger than he contracted to sell, the buyer may accept the goods included in the contract and reject the rest, or he may reject the whole.

(3) where the seller delivers to the buyer a quantity of goods larger than he contracted to sell and the buyer accepts the whole of the goods so delivered he must pay for them at the contract rate.'

It will be seen that buyers are entitled to reject not only if sellers deliver too little but also if they deliver too much. In this case, therefore, buyers have three alternatives: they may reject the whole delivery; they may accept the contract amount and reject the balance; or they may accept the whole delivery and pay pro rata.

Section 30(4) of the Sale of Goods Act 1979 provides:

'Where the seller delivers to the buyer the goods he contracted to sell mixed with goods of a different description not included in the contract, the buyer may accept the goods which are in accordance with the contract and reject the rest, or he may reject the whole.'

It will be seen that the rules stated in s 30(1)–(4) of the Sale of Goods Act 1979 impose a very strict duty on the seller to deliver the correct quantity of goods. It is open to the parties to modify this and this is expressly recognised by s 30(5) which provides:

'This section is subject to any usage of trade, special agreement, or course of dealing between the parties.'

Section 30 is amended by s 4 of the Sale and Supply of Goods Act 1994 which adds a new section (2A) which provides:

'(2A) A buyer who does not deal as consumer may not

(a) where the seller delivers a quantity of goods less than he contracted to sell, reject the goods under subsection (1) above, or

(b) where the seller delivers a quantity of goods larger than he contracted to sell, reject the whole under subsection (2) above,

if the shortfall or, as the case may be, excess is so slight that it would be unreasonable for him to do so.'

So the buyer's right of rejection is now qualified in the case of non-consumer sales, where the shortfall or excess is so slight that it would be unreasonable for the buyer to reject. It seems that there are two stages: first the court decides that the shortfall (or excess) is slight; second, it decides that in the circumstances it would be unreasonable to allow the buyer to reject.

3.3.6   Delivery by
         instalments

Section 31(1) of the Sale of Goods Act 1979 provides:

'Unless otherwise agreed, the buyer of goods is not bound to accept delivery of them by instalments.'

The Act does not expressly say so but it must surely also be the case that the buyer is not entitled to call on the seller to deliver by instalments, unless otherwise agreed.

It seems desirable to say something here about defective performance of instalment contracts. Either party can bring an action for damages for loss resulting from a defective performance in relation to one instalment. The critical question is whether faulty performance in relation to one instalment entitles a party to terminate the contract. In other words, can a seller refuse to deliver a second instalment because the buyer has not paid for the first one or, conversely, can the buyer treat the contract as at an end because the goods delivered under one instalment are faulty?

Where there are a series of separate contracts it is not possible to refuse to perform a second contract because the other party failed to perform the first. This rule does not apply to a single contract performable in instalments even where the contract provides 'each delivery a separate contract' since the House of Lords held in *Smyth v Bailey* (1940) that these words did not actually operate to divide the contract up.

In the case of instalment contracts it is undoubtedly open to the parties explicitly to provide that defective performance by one party in relation to any one instalment entitles the other party either to terminate or at least to withhold performance until that defect is remedied. Even if the parties do not explicitly so provide, defective performance in relation to one instalment may still have this effect because of s 31(2) of the Sale of Goods Act 1979 which provides:

'Where there is a contract for the sale of goods to be delivered by stated instalments, which are to be separately paid for, and the seller makes defective deliveries in respect of one or more deliveries, or the buyer neglects or refuses to take delivery of or pay for one or more instalments, it is a question in each case depending on the terms of the contract and the circumstances of the case whether the breach of contract is a repudiation of the whole contract or whether it is a severable breach giving rise to a claim for compensation but not to treat the whole contract as repudiated.'

This sub-section does not expressly cover all the things which may go wrong with instalment contractors. Nevertheless these situations seem to be covered by the test laid down which is that everything turns on whether the conduct of the party in breach amounts to a repudiation by that party of his obligations under the contract. In practice the courts are very reluctant to treat defective performance in relation to a single instalment as passing this test. An accumulation of defects over several instalments may do so, as in *Munro v Meyer* (1930) where there was a contract to buy 1,500 tons of meat and bone meal, delivery at the rate of 125 tons a month. After more than half had been delivered the meal was discovered to be defective. It was held that the buyer was entitled to terminate and reject future deliveries.

The case of *Regent OHG Aisenstadt v Francesco of Jermyn Street* (1981) revealed that there is a conflict between s 30(1) and s 31(2) of the 1979 Act. In this case the sellers were manufacturers of high-class men's suits and contracted to sell 62 suits to the buyers. Delivery was to be in instalments at the seller's option. The sellers in fact tendered the suits in five instalments. For reasons which had nothing to do with this contract, the parties fell out and the buyers refused to accept delivery of any of the instalments. This was clearly a repudiation and the sellers would have been entitled to terminate. In fact the sellers did not do so and continued to tender the suits. Shortly before tendering the fourth instalment the sellers told the buyers that because a particular cloth was not available the delivery would be one suit short. This shortfall was not made up in the fifth and final delivery so that the sellers ended up by tendering 61 suits instead of 62. It was clear that if the contract had been for a single delivery of 62 suits the case would have been governed by s 30(1) and the buyer would have been entitled to reject delivery which was one suit short. Equally clearly, however, the seller's conduct did not amount to repudiation within the test laid down by s 31(2) for delivery by instalments. It was held that in so far as there was a conflict between ss 30(1) and 31(2) the latter must prevail and that the buyer was accordingly not entitled to reject.

3.4   Acceptance

Section 27 of the Sale of Goods Act 1979, quoted in para 3.1 above, refers to the seller's duty to deliver the goods and the buyer's duty to accept. At first sight one might think that the buyer's duty to accept is the converse of the seller's duty to deliver, that is the duty to take delivery. However, it is quite clear that although acceptance and taking delivery are connected, they are not the same thing. In fact 'acceptance' is a sophisticated and difficult notion.

Section 35(1) provides:

'The buyer is deemed to have accepted the goods when he

intimates to the seller that he has accepted them, or (except where section 34 above otherwise provides) when the goods have been delivered to him and he does any act in relation to them which is inconsistent with the ownership of the seller, or when after the lapse of a reasonable time he reclaims the goods without intimating to the seller that he has rejected them.'

This section does not so much define acceptance as explain when it happens. It is implicit in the section that acceptance is the abandonment by the buyer of any right to reject the goods. (This by no means involves the abandonment of any right to damages.) The buyer may be entitled to reject goods for a number of different reasons; for instance (as we have already seen) because the seller delivers too many or too few goods or, sometimes, delivers them late. Other grounds for rejection, such as defects in the goods, will be dealt with later.

Section 35 of the Act tells us that buyers can abandon the right to reject the goods, that is 'accept' them in a number of different ways. Before examining these it is worth noting that buyers cannot be under a duty to accept in this sense since they would be perfectly entitled to reject the goods in such cases. Buyers can only be under a duty to accept when they have no right to reject. In s 27 therefore the word 'accept' must mean something different from what it means in s 35, that is, something much closer to a duty to take delivery.

The reason for the elaboration of s 35 is that in this area the law of sale appears to be slightly different from the general law of contract. The buyer's right of rejection is analogous to the right of an innocent party to terminate in certain circumstances for the other party's breach of contract. Under the general law of contract it is not usually possible to argue that a party has waived the right to terminate unless it can be shown that he knew the relevant facts which so entitled him, but in the law of sale the buyer may lose the right to reject before knowing he had it. This is no doubt hard on the buyer but probably justified on balance by the desirability of not allowing commercial transactions to be upset too readily. So the buyer loses the right to reject not only by expressly accepting but also by failing to reject within a reasonable time or by doing an act which is inconsistent with the ownership of the seller, such as sub-selling.

A key question here is what is a 'reasonable time'? In *Bernstein v Pamson Motors Ltd* (1987) the plaintiff sought to reject a new motor car whose engine seized up after he had owned it for three weeks and driven it only 140 miles. Rougier J held that the car was not of merchantable quality but that a reasonable time had elapsed and the right to reject had been lost. He took the view that the reasonableness of the time did not turn on whether the defect was quickly discoverable but on:

> 'What is a reasonable practical interval in commercial terms between a buyer receiving the goods and his ability to send them back, taking into consideration from his point of view the nature of the goods and their function, and from the point of view of the seller the commercial desirability of being able to close his ledger reasonably soon after the transaction is complete.'

Although the buyer may lose the right to reject quite quickly it would be very harsh if the buyer lost the right to reject before there had been a chance to examine the goods, since in many cases the buyer will not be able to tell at the moment the goods are delivered that they are defective. So s 34 of the 1979 Act provides:

> '(1) Where goods are delivered to the buyer, and he has not previously examined them, he is not deemed to have accepted them until he has had a reasonable opportunity of examining them for the purpose of ascertaining whether they are in conformity with the contract.
>
> (2) Unless otherwise agreed, when the seller tenders delivery of goods to the buyer, he is bound on request to afford the buyer a reasonable opportunity of examining the goods for the purpose of ascertaining whether they are in conformity with the contract.'

It is important to note that s 35 is made subject to s 34 so that a buyer does not lose the right to reject by failing to do so within a reasonable time or by doing acts inconsistent with the seller's ownership if he has not had a reasonable opportunity of examination. Suppose, for instance, that A sells goods to B and B sub-sells the same goods to C and that B tells A to deliver the goods direct to C. The goods delivered by A are defective and C rejects them. If s 35 stood alone B would not be able to reject because the sub-sale was inconsistent with A's ownership; however, the overriding effect of s 34 means that B can reject in this situation because there has not been a reasonable opportunity to examine the goods. B will not be able to reject unless C has rejected since otherwise he will not be able to return the goods, but it is precisely C's rejection which is the event that will make B wish to reject.

Both s 34 and s 35 have been amended by the Sale and Supply of Goods Act 1994. Set out below are both the 1979 and 1994 versions, underlining the new words in the 1994 version and indicating deletions from the 1979 version by striking through in the text of the 1994 version:

Sale of Goods Act 1979

34 Buyer's right of examining the goods

(1) Where goods are delivered to the buyer, and he has not previously examined them, he is not deemed to have accepted them until he has had a reasonable opportunity of examining them for the purpose of ascertaining whether they are in conformity with the contract.

(2) Unless otherwise agreed, when the seller tenders delivery of the goods to the buyer, he is bound on request to afford the buyer a reasonable opportunity of examining the goods for the purpose of ascertaining whether they are in conformity with the contract.

35 Acceptance

(1) The buyer is deemed to have accepted the goods when he intimates to the seller that he has accepted them, or (except where section 34 above otherwise provides) when the goods have been delivered to him and he does any act in relation to them which is inconsistent with the ownership of the seller, or when after the lapse of a reasonable time he retains the goods without intimating to the seller that he has rejected them.

Supply and Sale of Goods Act 1994

34 Buyer's right of examining the goods

(1) Where goods are delivered to the buyer, and he has not previously examined them, he is not deemed to have accepted them until he has had a reasonable opportunity of examining them for the purpose of ascertaining whether they are in conformity with the contract.

—   Unless otherwise agreed, when the seller tenders delivery of goods to the buyer, he is bound on request to afford the buyer a reasonable opportunity of examining the goods for the purpose of ascertaining whether they are in conformity with the contract, and, in the case of a contract for sale by sample, of comparing the bulk with the sample.

35 Acceptance

(1) The buyer is deemed to have accepted the goods when he intimates to the seller that he has accepted them, or (except where section 34 above otherwise provides) when the goods have been delivered to him and he does any act in relation to them which is inconsistent with the ownership of the seller, or when after the lapse of a reasonable time he retains the gods without intimating to the seller that he has rejected them subject to subsection (2) below -

(a) when he intimates to the seller that he has accepted them, or

(b) when the goods have been delivered to him and he does any act in relation to them which is inconsistent with the ownership of the seller.

(2) Where goods are delivered to the buyer, and he has not previously examined them, he is not deemed to have accepted them under subsection (1) above until he has had a reasonable opportunity of examining them for the purpose -

(a) of ascertaining whether they are in conformity with the contract, and

(b) in the case of a contract for sale by sample, of comparing the bulk with the sample.

(3)   Where the buyer deals as consumer or (in Scotland) the contract of sale is a consumer contract, the buyer cannot lose his right to rely on subsection (2) above by agreement, waiver or otherwise.

(4)   The buyer is also deemed to have accepted the goods when after the lapse of a reasonable time he retains the goods without intimating to the seller that he has rejected them.

(5)   The questions that are material in determining for the purposes of subsection (4) above whether a reasonable time has elapsed include whether the buyer has had a reasonable opportunity of examining the goods for the purpose mentioned in subsection (2) above.

(6)   The buyer is not by virtue of this section deemed to have accepted the goods merely because -

(a) he asks for, or agrees to, their repair by or under an arrangement with the seller, or

(b) the goods are delivered to another under a sub-sale or other disposition.

(7)   Where the contract is for the sale of goods making one or more commercial units, a buyer accepting any goods included in a unit is deemed to have accepted all the goods making the unit; and in this subsection "commercial unit" means a unit division of which would materially impair the value of the goods or the character of the unit.

(2)   Paragraph 10 of Schedule 1 below applies in relation to a contract made before 22 April 1967 or (in the application of this Act to Northern Ireland) 28 July 1967.

(2)(8) Paragraph 10 of Schedule 1 below applies in relation to a contract made before 22 April 1967 or (in the application of this Act to Northern Ireland) 28 July 1967.

Under the 1994 version, all three of the grounds for acceptance are subject to the buyer's right to examine the goods. This is done by moving the right to examine the goods from s 34(1) to s 35(2) and by making acceptance under s 35(1) subject to s 35(2). So, even if the buyer tells the seller that he has accepted the goods, this is not binding until he has had a reasonable opportunity of examining them.

There are a number of other changes. Section 35(3) is important in view of the widespread practice of asking consumer buyers to sign acceptance notes. Consumer buyers will not lose their right to rely on not having had a reasonable opportunity to examine the goods because the delivery man got them to sign a note of acceptance. It should be noted that it is the right to examine which cannot be lost by 'agreement, waiver or otherwise'. This does not mean that the right to reject cannot be lost by 'agreement, waiver or otherwise' once the right to examine has been exercised. So, if defective goods are delivered to a consumer buyer who examines them, decides that they are defective but decides to keep them, he will not later be able to say that he has not accepted them. However, this is also qualified by the change in s 35(6). A reasonable buyer will often wish to give the seller a chance to make the goods work. A disincentive to doing this was that one might be advised that giving the seller a chance to repair was an acceptance, thereby preventing a later rejection of the goods if the repair was ineffective. This is not the case now.

Is *Bernstein v Pamson Motors Ltd* (1987) reversed by the 1994 Act? The wording in the latter part of s 35(1) of the 1979 version now appears in s 35(4) in the same terms. However, s 35(4) is now qualified by s 35(5) and it may be argued that this has had the effect of altering the notion of a reasonable time. However, the defect in *Bernstein v Pamson Motors* was one which could not have been discovered by any kind of examination. It was an internal defect in the engine which made it certain that the engine would seize up but could only be discovered when the engine in fact seized up. Although the decision in *Bernstein v Pamson Motors* has been widely criticised, it is far from clear that the Act has reversed it.

Instead of waiting for the seller to tender delivery and then refusing to accept, the buyer may announce in advance that he will not take the goods. Usually this will amount to an 'anticipatory breach' and will entitle the seller to terminate the contract though he may choose instead to continue to tender the goods in the hope that the buyer will have a change of mind and take them.

A difficult problem arises where buyers announce in advance that they will not take the goods and later seek to argue that they would have been entitled to reject the goods in any case because they were defective. The general rule in the law of contract is that a party who purports to terminate for a bad reason can usually justify the termination later by relying on a good reason which has only just been discovered. The buyer will often have great practical problems in establishing that the goods which the seller would have delivered would have been defective. This is probably the explanation of the difficult and controversial case of *British and Benningtons v N W Cachar Tea* (1923) where the buyer had contracted to buy tea to be delivered to a bonded warehouse in London. There was no express date for delivery and delivery was therefore due within a reasonable time. Before a reasonable time had elapsed the buyers said that they would not accept delivery. The ships carrying the tea had been diverted by the shipping controller and the buyers seem to have thought that this would prevent delivery within a reasonable time. (The buyer and the court took different views of what time would be reasonable.) The House of Lords held that the buyer had committed an anticipatory breach and that the seller could recover damages. The best explanation of this result seems to be that at the time of the buyer's rejection, the seller had not broken the contract and although he could not prove that he would certainly have delivered within a reasonable time, the buyer could not prove that the seller would not have delivered within a reasonable time. The position would be different if the seller had committed a breach of contract so that it could be said for certain that he would not be able to deliver within a reasonable time.

Payment, Delivery and Acceptance

The primary duty of the seller is to deliver the goods and the primary duty of the buyer to accept and pay for them. This chapter considers these duties. In particular it considers the meaning of delivery, the effect of delivering too little, too much or late; and the rules about delivery by instalments. It also explains the complex and important concept of 'acceptance'.

Introduction

Payment and delivery are concurrent conditions (s 28). This means that they should take place at the same time. Obviously, the parties may have agreed expressly or by implication that payment is to precede delivery or the other way around.

Payment

'Delivery' refers simply to the seller's obligation to hand over the goods and the seller performs his or her obligations by making the goods available to the buyer at the seller's place of business. It is common, particularly in commercial contracts, for the parties expressly to agree the date for delivery. Note the new rules as to the quantity delivered. Section 30 is amended by s 4 of the Sale and Supply of Goods Act 1994, which adds a new section (2A): the buyer's right of rejection is now qualified in the case of non-consumer sales where the shortfall or excess is so slight that it would be unreasonable for the buyer to reject.

Unless otherwise agreed, the buyer of goods is not bound to accept delivery by instalments (s 31(1)). In the case of instalment contracts, it is open to the parties to provide that defective performance by one party in relation to any one instalment entitles the other party either to terminate or at least to withhold performance until that defect is remedied. Even if the parties do not explicitly so provide, defective performance in relation to one instalment may still have this affect because of s 31(2).

Delivery

It is implicit in s 35 that acceptance is the abandonment by the buyer of any right to reject the goods (this by no means involves the abandonment of any right to damages). Section 35 provides that buyers can abandon the right to reject the goods (that is 'accept' them) in a number of different ways. It should be noted that the buyer may lose the right to reject before knowing he had it: by s 35, the buyer loses the right to reject

Acceptance

not only by expressly accepting but also by failing to reject within a reasonable time or by doing an act which is inconsistent with the ownership of the seller, such as sub-selling.

It is important to note that s 35 is made subject to s 34 so that a buyer does not lose the right to reject by failing to do so within a reasonable time or by doing acts inconsistent with the seller's ownership if he has not had a reasonable opportunity to examine.

Chapter 4

Ownership

The primary purpose of a contract for the sale of goods is to transfer ownership of the goods from the seller to the buyer. This chapter deals with a series of problems which arise in this connection. The first involves the nature of the seller's obligations as to the transfer of ownership; the second concerns the moment at which ownership is transferred; and the third, the circumstances in which a buyer may become owner of goods, even though the seller was not the owner.

The Sale of Goods Act does not in general talk about ownership. It does talk a good deal about 'property' and 'title'. Both of these words can, for present purposes, be regarded as synonyms for ownership. The Act uses the word 'property', when dealing with the first two questions above and 'title' when dealing with the third. A distinction is sometimes drawn between the 'general property' and the 'special property'. Here the words 'general property' are being used to describe ownership and the words 'special property' to describe possession, that is physical control without the rights of ownership.

4.1 Introduction

The seller's duties are set out in s 12 of the Act which provides:

'12 (1) In a contract of sale, other than one to which subsection (3) below applies, there is an implied condition on the part of the seller that in the case of a sale he has a right to sell the goods, and in the case of an agreement to sell he will have such a right at the time when the property is to pass.

(2) In a contract of sale, other than one to which subsection (3) below applies, there is also an implied warranty that –

(a) the goods are free, and will remain free until the time when the property is to pass, from any charge or encumbrance not disclosed or known to the buyer before the contract is made, and

(b) the buyer will enjoy quiet possession of the goods except so far as it may be disturbed by the owner or other person entitled to the benefit of any charge or encumbrance so disclosed or known.'

4.2 The seller's duties as to the transfer of ownership

It will be seen that these two subsections set out three separate obligations. Of these, by far the most important is that set out in s 12(1), under which the seller undertakes that he has the right to sell the goods. It is important to note that the seller is in breach of this obligation, even though he believes that he is entitled to sell the goods and even though the buyer's enjoyment of the goods is never disturbed.

4.3 Meaning of 'right to sell'

Section 12(1) talks about the right to sell and not about the transfer of ownership. There are cases where the seller has no right to sell, but does transfer ownership because it is one of the exceptional cases where a non-owner seller can make the buyer owner. In such cases, the seller will be in breach of s 12(1). In most cases the seller will be entitled to sell, either because she is the owner or the agent of the owner or because she will be able to acquire ownership before property is to pass (as will be the case with future goods). Perhaps surprisingly it has been held that even though the seller is the owner, she may, in exceptional circumstances, not have a right to sell the goods. This is well illustrated by the leading case of *Niblett v Confectioner's Materials* (1921) where the plaintiffs bought tins of milk from the defendants. Some of the tins of milk were delivered bearing labels 'Nissly brand', which infringed the trademark of another manufacturer. That manufacturer persuaded Customs and Excise to impound the tins and the plaintiffs had to remove and destroy the labels, before they could get the tins back. It was held that the defendants were in breach of s 12(1) because they did not have the right to sell the tins in the condition in which they were, even though they owned them. This was clearly reasonable, as the plaintiffs had been left with a supply of unlabelled tins which would be difficult to dispose of.

4.4 To what remedy is the buyer entitled if the seller breaks his obligation under s 12(1)?

The buyer can certainly recover, by way of damages, any loss which he has suffered because of the breach. Further, the seller's obligation is stated to be a condition and the buyer is generally entitled to reject the goods when there is a breach of condition. In practice, however, it will very seldom be possible to use this remedy because the buyer will not usually know until well after the goods have been delivered, that the seller has no right to sell.

In *Rowland v Divall* (1923) the Court of Appeal held that the buyer had a more extensive remedy. In that case, the defendant honestly bought a stolen car from the thief and sold it to the plaintiff, who was a car dealer, for £334. The plaintiff sold the car for £400. In due course, some four months after the sale by the defendant to the plaintiff, the car was repossessed by the police and returned to its true owner. Clearly on these facts, there was a breach of s 12(1) and the plaintiff could have maintained a damages action, but in such an action it would have been necessary to take account not only of the plaintiff's loss, but also of any benefit he and his sub-buyer had received by having use of the car. The Court of Appeal held, however, that the plaintiff was not restricted to an action for damages, but could sue to recover the whole of the price. This was on the basis that there was a total failure of consideration; that is, that the buyer had received none of the benefit for which he had entered the contract, since the whole object of the transaction was that he should become the owner of the car.

Rowland v Divall was carried a stage further in *Butterworth v Kingsway Motors* (1954). Here X, who was in possession of a car under a hire-purchase agreement, sold it to Y before he had paid all the instalments. Y sold the car to Z, who sold it to the defendant, who sold it to the plaintiff. X meanwhile continued to pay the instalments. Several months later, the plaintiff discovered that the car was subject to a hire-purchase agreement and demanded the return of the price from the defendant. Eight days later, X paid the last instalment and exercised his option under the hire-purchase contract to buy the car. The result of this was that the ownership of the car passed from the finance company to X and so on down the line to the plaintiff. It followed that the plaintiff was no longer at risk of being dispossessed but it was nevertheless held that he could recover the price. Later developments did not expunge the breach of 12(1), since the defendant had not had the right to sell at the time of the sale. It will be seen that the plaintiff, who had suffered no real loss, in effect received a windfall since his use of the car was entirely free.	**4.5** **Scope of *Rowland v Divall***

A statutory exception to *Rowland v Divall*, has been created by s 6(3) of the Torts (Interference with Goods) Act 1977. This deals with the situation where the goods have been improved by an innocent non-owner. If on the facts of *Butterworth v Kingsway Motors*, one of the parties in the chain had replaced the engine, then the plaintiff would have had to give credit for this enhancement of the car's value in his action for the price. It would not matter for this purpose whether the new engine was fitted by the defendant or by one of the previous owners, provided that the engine was fitted by someone who, at the time of fitting, believed that he was the owner.

Section 12(2) provides two subsidiary obligations which cover situations which might not be covered by s 12(1). Section 12(2)(a) deals with the case where the seller owns the goods, but has charged them in a way not disclosed to the buyer. A	**4.6** **Subsidiary obligations**

possible example would be if I were to sell you my watch which, unknown to you, is at the pawnbroker's.

A good example of the operation of the warranty of quiet possession under s 12(2)(b) is *Microbeads v Vinhurst Road Markings* (1975). In this case the buyer found himself subject to a claim by a patentee of a patent affecting the goods. The patent had not in fact existed at the time the goods were sold and there was, accordingly, no breach of s 12(1). The Court of Appeal held, however, that s 12(2) covered the case where the patent was issued after the sale.

Section 12(2) states that the obligations contained in it are warranties and it follows that the buyer's only remedy, in the event of breach, is an action for damages.

4.7   Can the seller exclude his or her liability under s 12?

In its 1893 version, s 12 contained after the words 'in a contract of sale' the words 'unless the circumstances of the contract are such as to show a different intention'. This strongly suggested that the draftsman contemplated the possibility that the contract might contain a clause excluding or qualifying the seller's duties under the section. The Supply of Goods (Implied Terms) Act 1973 (re-enacted as s 6 of the Unfair Contract Terms Act 1977), provides that a seller cannot exclude or limit his obligations under s 12(1) and 12(2).

The seller is permitted to contract on the basis that he only undertakes to transfer whatever title he actually has. In other words the seller may say 'I do not know whether I am owner or not but if I am, I will transfer ownership to you.'

This possibility is governed by s 12(3)–(5) which provides:

'12 (3) This subsection applies to a contract of sale in the case of which there appears from the contract or is to be inferred from its circumstances an intention that the seller should transfer only such title as he or a third person may have.

(4) In a contract to which subsection (3) above applies there is an implied warranty that all charges or encumbrances known to the seller and not known to the buyer have been disclosed to the buyer before the contract is made.

(5) In a contract to which subsection (3) above applies there is also an implied warranty that none of the following will disturb the buyer's quiet possession of the goods, namely –

(a) the seller;

(b) in a case where the parties to the contract intend that the seller should transfer only such title as a third person may have, that person;

(c) anyone claiming through or under the seller or that third person otherwise than under a charge or encumbrance disclosed or known to the buyer before the contract is made.'

It will be seen that s 12(3) envisages the possibility that it may be inferred from the circumstances that the seller is only contracting to sell whatever title he has. This would obviously be unusual but an example which is often given is that of a sale by sheriff after she has executed a judgment debt. If, for instance, the sheriff takes possession of the television set in the judgment debtor's house and sells it, she will usually have no idea whether it belongs to the judgment debtor or is subject to a hire-purchase or rental agreement. It will be seen that s 12(4) and 12(5) contain modified versions of the obligations which are usually implied under s 12(2).

This section deals with the rules of English law which decide when ownership is to pass from seller to buyer. Why is this question important? There are two main reasons. The first is that as a matter of technique, English law makes some other questions turn on the answer to this question. So as a rule, the passing of risk is linked to the passing of property, as is the seller's right to sue for the price, under s 49(1).

4.8   The passing of property

The second reason is that who owns the goods usually becomes important, if either buyer or seller becomes insolvent.

The basic rules as to the passing of property are set out in ss 16 and 17 of the Sale of Goods Act which provide:

'16   Where there is a contract for the sale of unascertained goods no property in the goods is transferred to the buyer unless and until the goods are ascertained.

17 (1) Where there is a contract for the sale of specific or ascertained goods the property in them is transferred to the buyer at such time as the parties to the contract intend it to be transferred.

(2) For the purpose of ascertaining the intention of the parties regard shall be had to the terms of the contract, the conduct of the parties and the circumstances of the case.'

So the first rule is that property cannot pass if the goods are unascertained. This makes the distinction between specific and unascertained goods fundamental. The second rule is that if the goods are specific or ascertained, the parties are free to make whatever agreement they like about when property is to pass.

Where a contract is subject to standard conditions of sale or purchase, one would certainly expect to find a provision expressly dealing with the passing of property. In other cases the transaction will be set against a commercial background, which provides determinative clues to the parties' intentions. So in international sales, the parties will often provide that payment is to be 'cash against documents' and this will usually mean that property is to pass when the buyer takes up the documents and pays against them.

Nevertheless, there will be many cases where the parties do not direct their thoughts to this question. Assistance is then provided by s 18 which provides rules for ascertaining the intention of the parties 'unless a different intention appears'. Rules 1, 2 and 3 deal with sales of specific goods.

'18   Unless a different intention appears, the following are rules for ascertaining the intention of the parties as to the time at which the property in the goods is to pass to the buyer.

Rule 1. – Where there is an unconditional contract for the sale of specific goods in a deliverable state the property in the goods passes to the buyer when the contract is made, and it is immaterial whether the time of payment or the time of delivery, or both, be postponed.

Rule 2. – Where there is a contract for the sale of specific goods and the seller is bound to do something to the goods for the purpose of putting them into a deliverable state, the property does not pass until the thing is done and the buyer has notice that it has been done.

Rule 3. – Where there is a contract for the sale of specific goods, in a deliverable state but the seller is bound to weigh, measure, test, or do some other act or thing with reference to the goods for the purpose of ascertaining the price, the property does not pass until the act or thing is done and the buyer has notice that it has been done.'

Rule 1 contemplates that in the case of specific goods, property may pass at the moment the contract is made. However, this will not in practice be that common, since in *RV Ward v Bignall* (1967) it was said that in modern conditions it would not require much material to support the inference that property was to pass at a later stage.

Rule 1 only applies where the contract is 'unconditional' and the goods in a 'deliverable state'. In the present context unconditional is usually taken to mean that the contract does not contain any term which suspends the passing of property until some later event. The words 'deliverable state' are defined by s 61(5) which provides that 'Goods are in a deliverable state within the meaning of this Act when they are in such a state that the buyer would under the contract be bound to take delivery of them'.

It would seem that if the goods are actually delivered to the buyer, rule 1 would not prevent property passing. So if A sells a car to B and delivers a car containing a latent defect which would have justified rejection if B had known of it, it seems that property probably passes to B on delivery. It is probable that in formulating rule 1, the draftsman had principally in mind the situation covered by rule 2, where the goods are not defective, but need something doing to them before the buyer is required to accept delivery. An example would be when there is a sale of a ton of coffee beans and the seller agrees to bag the beans before delivery.

Rule 4 deals with *sale or return* and provides:

'18.   Rule 4 – When goods are delivered to the buyer on approval or on sale or return or other similar terms the property in goods passes to the buyer:

(a) when he signifies his approval or acceptance to the seller or does any other act adopting the transaction;

(b) if he does not signify his approval or acceptance to the seller but retains the goods without giving notice of rejection, then, if a time has been fixed for the return of the goods, on the expiration of that time, and, if no   time has been fixed, on the expiration of a reasonable time.'

If the transaction is one of sale or return, the buyer loses the right to return the goods if she approves or accepts them or otherwise adopts the transaction. This means that if the buyer does something which an honest person would not do unless she intended to adopt the transaction, she will be treated as having adopted it. So in *Kirkham v Attenborough* (1897) the buyer borrowed money from a pawnbroker on the security of the goods and this was treated as an adoption. Alternatively, property may pass to the buyer under rule 4(b) because she has failed to reject in time.

Rule 5 deals with unascertained goods and provides:

'18.   Rule 5. (1) Where there is a contract for the sale of unascertained or future goods by description, and goods of that description and in a deliverable state are unconditionally appropriated to the contract, either by the seller with the assent of the buyer or by the buyer with the assent of the seller, the property in the goods then passes to the buyer; and the assent may be express or implied, and may be given either before or after the appropriation is made.

(2) Where, in pursuance of the contract, the seller delivers the goods to the buyer or to a carrier or other bailee or custodier (whether named by the buyer or not) for the purpose of transmission to the buyer, and does not reserve the right of disposal, he is to be taken to have unconditionally appropriated the goods to the contract.'

In practice this is the most important of the rules. We have already seen that in the sale of unascertained goods, property cannot pass until the goods are ascertained even if the parties were to try to agree otherwise. This basic principle was recently reaffirmed by the Privy Council in *Re Goldcorp Exchange Ltd* (1994). In this case, a New Zealand company dealt in gold and sold to customers on the basis that the company would store and insure the gold free of charge. They issued certificates to the customers. No specific gold was set aside for any specific customer though there were assurances (which were not kept) that a sufficient supply of gold would be held at all times to meet orders for delivery by customers. In fact, the company became hopelessly insolvent and had inadequate supplies of gold. The Privy Council held that it was elementary that property had not passed from the sellers to the buyers.

This case can be usefully contrasted with *Re Stapylton Fletcher Ltd* (1995). In this case, wine merchants bought and sold wine and also sold it on the basis that they would store it for customers until it was fit to drink. In this case, the wine merchant kept the boxes of wine which they were holding for customers in a separate unit. This unit contained nothing but wine which was being stored for customers and, at all times, the right quantities of vintages were in stock and the total was in strict compliance with the customers' storage records. On the other hand, the wine merchant did not mark individual cases of wine with the customer's name, since, which was usually the case, there was more than one case of a particular vintage, it was convenient to supply customers off the top of the pile which necessarily meant that individual cases were not allocated. The wine merchants became insolvent. In this case, it was held that the wine was sufficiently ascertained for the customers to become tenants in common of the stock in the proportion that their goods bore to the total in store for the time being. This decision is very important because it shows that the ascertainment rule does not prevent two or more owning goods in common where there is an undivided bulk. A further important qualification is made by the Sale of Goods (Amendment) Act 1995. This makes amendments to ss 18 and 20 of the 1979 Act. The principal effect is that if the owner of part of an undivided bulk sells it to a buyer who pays the price, property in an undivided share of the bulk can be passed if the parties so agree. Once the goods are ascertained the property will pass at the time agreed by the parties. Where the parties have reached no express agreement rule 5 propounds a test based on appropriation.

In some cases ascertainment and appropriation may take place at the same time. This was so in *Karlhamns Oljefabriker v Eastport Navigation* (1982). This is quite likely to be the case where the goods are appropriated by delivery to a carrier as happens particularly in international sales (though in such sales there are often express agreements as to the passing of property). So if the seller contracts to sell 1000 tons Western White Wheat cost, insurance and freight (cif) Avonmouth and puts 1000 tons of Western White Wheat aboard a ship bound for Avonmouth this may both ascertain and appropriate the goods. In many such cases, however, the seller will load 2000 tons having sold 1000 tons to A and 1000 tons to B. In such a case the goods will not be ascertained until the first 1000 tons are unloaded at the destination. Even where the seller puts only 1000 tons on board this will not necessarily constitute appropriation because he may not at that stage have committed himself to using *that* 1000 tons to perform *that* contract.

This was clearly decided in *Carlos Federspiel v Twigg* (1957) where the seller had agreed to sell a number of bicycles to the buyer. The seller had packed the bicycles, marked them with the buyer's name and told the buyer the shipping marks. The seller then went insolvent. The buyer argued that the bicycles had been appropriated to its contract and that property had passed to it. This argument was rejected on the grounds that the seller could properly have had a change of mind and appropriated new bicycles to the contract.

It is essential that there is a degree of irrevocability in the appropriation. It is this which makes delivery to the carrier often the effective act of appropriation.

We have seen in the previous section that, subject to the goods being ascertained, the parties may make whatever agreement they like about when property is to pass. So property may pass even though the goods have not been delivered and the price not yet paid. Conversely the parties may agree that the property is not to pass even though the goods have been delivered and paid for. It is very likely that a seller who employs standard conditions of sale and normally gives her customers credit will wish to provide that property does not

4.9   Retention of title clauses

pass simply on delivery but only at some later stage such as when payment is made. This possibility is clearly implicit in ss 17 and 18. It is, however, explicitly stated in s 19:

'19 (1) Where there is a contract for the sale of specific goods or where goods are subsequently appropriated to the contract, the seller may, by the terms of the contract or appropriation, reserve the right of disposal of the goods until certain conditions are fulfilled; and in such a case, notwithstanding the delivery of the goods to the buyer, or to a carrier or other bailee or custodier for the purpose of transmission to the buyer, the property in the goods does not pass to the buyer until the conditions imposed by the seller are fulfilled.

(2) Where goods are shipped, and by the bill of lading the goods are deliverable to the order of the seller or his agent, the seller is *prima facie* to be taken to reserve the right of disposal.

(3) Where the seller of goods draws on the buyer for the price, and transmits the bill of exchange and bill of lading to the buyer together to secure acceptance or payment of the bill of exchange, the buyer is bound to return the bill of lading if he does not honour the bill of exchange, and if he wrongfully retains the bill of lading the property in the goods does not pass to him.

It will be seen that s 19 talks about the seller reserving 'the right of disposal of the goods'. This is effectively another synonym for ownership.

In the context of international sales this has long been well recognised as standard practice. It has also no doubt long been standard practice for sellers supplying goods on credit in domestic sales to have simple clauses saying that the goods are theirs until they are paid. No problem arises with such clauses. This was reaffirmed in *Armour v Thyssen Edelstahlwerke AG* (1990) where the House of Lords overturned decisions of the Scottish courts treating a simple reservation of title as creating a charge. Lord Keith of Kinkel, delivering the principal speech, said:

'I am, however, unable to regard a provision reserving title to the seller until payment of all debts due to him by the buyer as amounting to the creation by the buyer of a right to security in favour of the seller. Such a provision does in a sense give the seller security for the unpaid debts of the buyer. But it does so by way of a legitimate retention of title, not by virtue of any right over his own property conferred by the buyer.'

However, in the last 20 years much more elaborate and complex clauses have begun to be used regularly. The starting point of modern discussion is the decision of the Court of Appeal in *Aluminium Industrie v Romalpa* (1976). The plaintiff was a Dutch company which sold aluminium foil to the defendant, an English company. The plaintiff had elaborate standard conditions of sale which provided, among other things:

(a) that ownership of the foil was to be transferred only when the buyer had met all that was owing to the seller;

(b) required the buyer to store the foil in such a way that it was clearly the property of the seller until it had been paid for;

(c) that articles manufactured from the foil were to become the property of the seller as security for payment and that until such payment had been made the buyer was to keep the articles manufactured as 'fiduciary owner' for the seller and if required to store them separately so that they could be recognised.

The buyer was permitted to sell finished products to third parties on condition that, if requested, they would hand over to the seller any claims which they might have against the said buyers.

It is important to note the width of the basic clause about transfer of ownership. The goods were being supplied regularly on credit terms. In such a situation it is perfectly possible even though the goods are being punctiliously paid for on time that there is always money outstanding to the seller so that property never passes at all. So if the standard credit terms of the trade are to pay 28 days after delivery of the invoice and there are deliveries of goods every 21 days there will nearly always be money owing to the seller, even though the buyer is paying on time. In the *Romalpa* case itself the buyer eventually became insolvent owing the plaintiff over £120,000. The buyer had some £50,000 worth of foil and also had in a separate bank account some £35,000 which represented the proceeds of foil which the plaintiff had supplied to the defendant and which the defendant had then sub-sold. The Court of Appeal held that the plaintiff was entitled both to recover the foil and also the £35,000 which was in the separate account.

This case illustrates in a dramatic way the practical importance of these retention of title clauses. They are basically a device to protect the seller against the buyer's insolvency. If the buyer becomes insolvent, a seller who has a valid retention of title clause will have a significantly improved position.

4.9.1   The *Romalpa* case

Small businesses become insolvent every day and large businesses not infrequently. What usually happens in such cases is that nearly all the assets fall into the hands of the Inland Revenue and Customs and Excise who have preferential claims and into the hands of the bank who will have taken a mortgage over the company's premises and a floating charge over the company's other assets.

Such a step is perfectly effective if all that is done is to use the power of s 19 to delay the passing of ownership from seller to buyer.

However, many sellers, like the one in the *Romalpa* case, have much more elaborate clauses. Since 1976 these clauses have been the subject of a number of litigated cases and in many of them the courts have held that the clause is ineffective. This is partly because these decisions have turned on the particular wording of specific clauses and partly on a perception by the judges that the sellers, in seeking to do too much, have overreached themselves. The general problem which lies behind the cases is that, whatever the abstract legal analysis, the seller's practical objective is to create a form of security interest in the goods. The companies legislation provides a limited number of possibilities for the creation of security interests in the property of companies. (In practice the buyer has always been a company in the litigated cases. If the buyer were not a company, these difficulties would disappear.) In particular, in a number of cases the other creditors of the buyer have successfully argued that the retention of title clause is invalid because it amounts to an unregistered charge over the company's assets. This argument does not succeed if all that the seller has done is to have a straightforward s 19 clause providing that ownership remains with it until it has been paid (*Clough Mills v Martin* (1984)). This is permissible even if the seller retains ownership over goods which have been paid for, because such ownership would be subject to an implied term that the seller could only deal with the goods to the extent needed to discharge the balance of the outstanding debts.

So, retention of title clauses work perfectly satisfactorily if the buyer intends to keep the goods in its hands unaltered. However, buyers often intend either to resell the goods or to incorporate the goods in a larger product, or to use the goods as raw materials for the manufacture of goods. In an attempt to secure rights in cases of this kind sellers have often adopted elaborate clauses of the kind mentioned in the discussion above of the *Romalpa* case.

In some cases the contract has provided that the buyer is to have legal ownership of the goods but that 'equitable and beneficial' ownership is to remain in the seller. Such a clause was considered in *Re Bond Worth* (1979) where the goods supplied were raw materials used by the buyer for the manufacture of carpets. Slade J held that the clause was invalid as being an attempt to create an unregistered charge. It seems, therefore, that in general the seller must attempt to retain legal ownership. However, this will not work where the goods are being incorporated into larger goods unless the goods remain identifiable. An interesting case in this respect is *Hendy Lennox v Grahame Puttick Limited* (1984) where the goods were diesel engines which were being used by the buyer for incorporation into diesel generating sets. The engines remained readily identifiable because all the engines were those provided by the seller and each engine had a serial number. Furthermore, the engines could, with relative ease, have been disconnected and removed from the generating sets. It was held that in such a situation the seller could continue to assert rights of ownership even after the engines had been incorporated into the generators.

In other cases, the goods are incorporated into finished products in a way in which it would be impossible to unscramble. Sellers have sometimes sought to provide in this situation that they retain ownership in the raw materials or that the finished product is to be treated as theirs. This would probably present no problems if the seller had supplied all the ingredients for the finished products but in practice this has never been the facts of a reported case. The cases which have arisen have been those in which one of the ingredients in the finished product has been provided by a seller who employed a retention of title clause and the other ingredients by sellers who did not. In practice, in all of these cases the courts have held that the seller does not in fact retain a valid interest in the finished product. So in *Borden v Scottish Timber Products* (1981) a seller who supplied resin to a buyer who used it to manufacture chipboard obtained no property interest in the chipboard and in *Re Peachdart* (1984) a seller who supplied leather for the making of handbags failed successfully to assert a claim against the handbags. It is not clear whether the seller could improve on these cases by more sophisticated drafting. Suppose a seller on the facts of *Re Peachdart* had provided in the contract that the handbags were to be the joint property of the seller and the manufacturer. It is at least possible that this would create rights which the court would protect. In New Zealand it has been held that a seller of trees could retain ownership rights after the trees have been converted into logs by the buyer.

4.9.2   Sale of goods as raw materials

4.9.3	Resale of goods

The buyer may have bought the goods intending to resell them. Normally the retention of title clause will not be effective to prevent the sub-buyer acquiring a good title. However, a seller may insert a clause in the contract providing that the buyer is to have permission to sub-sell the goods but that the proceeds of such sub-sale are to be put into a separate bank account which is to be held on trust for the seller. If the buyer in fact opens such an account and pays the proceeds into it this would be an effective clause. In practice a buyer who is having financial problems and is approaching insolvency is very likely to find ways of paying the proceeds of sub-sales into an account with which he can deal so that such a clause will not provide complete practical protection for the seller.

4.10 Transfer of title where the seller is not the owner

In this section we consider cases where the seller was not in fact the owner nor the authorised agent of the owner at the time of the sale. This situation may arise in a range of cases running from the situation where the seller has stolen the goods all the way to a case where the seller honestly believes that he is the owner of the goods but has himself been misled by a previous seller. In this type of case there is a conflict of interest between that of the original owner of the goods who is seeking to recover them or their value and the ultimate buyer who has paid good money for goods which he believed the seller was entitled to sell to him. In general it is desirable to protect the interests both of the owners of property and of honest buyers who pay a fair price. In the case of transactions in land the choice comes down unhesitatingly in favour of protecting the interests of owners. This is possible because transferring ownership of land is a highly formal act normally carried out by lawyers. In practice, therefore, it is extremely difficult for an honest buyer who employs a competent lawyer not to discover that the seller is not entitled to sell. In practice it would be extremely difficult to apply this technique to transactions in goods. Some legal systems have therefore decided that the primary interest is to protect the honest buyer who pays a fair price and has no ground for suspecting that his seller is not the owner. English law has not taken this choice, however. Instead it has started from the position that the seller cannot normally transfer any better rights than he himself has. This is often put in the form of the Latin maxim *nemo dat quod non habet* (roughly, no one can transfer what he does not have). Lawyers often talk in shorthand about the *nemo dat* rule. However, although it is clear that this is the basic rule, it is equally clear that it is subject to a substantial number of exceptions. Most of the exceptions are set out in ss 21–26 of the Sale of Goods Act 1979.

Section 21(1) of the Act provides:

> 'Subject to this Act, where goods are sold by a person who is not their owner, and who does not sell them under the authority or with the consent of the owner, the buyer acquires no better title to the goods than the seller had, unless the owner of the goods is by his conduct precluded from denying the seller's authority to sell.'

For present purposes the sting of this section lies in its tail which is an application of the general legal doctrine of estoppel. The operation of the doctrine is to prevent (estop) a party from advancing an argument which she would otherwise be entitled to put forward. So, for instance, a party may be prevented from putting forward an argument because it has been the subject matter of a previous judicial decision on the same facts which is binding on her. An example of the operation of doctrine in the present context is *Eastern Distributors Limited v Goldring* (1957). In this case the owner of a van wished to raise money on it and for this purpose entered into an arrangement with a car dealer which involved the deception of a finance company. The scheme was that the dealer would pretend to have bought the van and to be letting it to the owner on hire-purchase terms. The owner signed, in blank, one of the finance company's hire-purchase agreements, together with a delivery note stating that he had taken delivery of the van. The dealer then completed a further form purporting to offer to sell the van to the finance company. The result was that the finance company paid the dealer. On these facts it could perhaps have been argued that the owner had actually authorised the dealer to sell his van to the finance company. However, the case was decided on the basis that the owner had not authorised the dealer to sell the van to the finance company but that he was estopped from so arguing. This was on the basis that by signing the forms in the way he had, he had made it easy for the dealer to deceive the finance company as to who was the true owner of the van.

It is common in analysing the operation of estoppel in this area to distinguish between estoppel by representation, which arises where it could be said that the true owner has represented that someone else has authority to sell the goods, and estoppel by negligence which arises where the true owner has behaved carelessly in respect of the goods in such a way as to enable the goods to be dealt with in a way which causes loss to a third party. However, in practice, the courts have been very cautious in applying either limb of the doctrine. In particular, it is clear that the owner does not by the mere act of putting his goods into the hands of someone else represent that that person has authority to sell them; nor is it negligent to do so unless it is possible to analyse the transaction in such a way as to support the argument that the true owner owed a duty of care in respect of the goods to the party who has been deceived.

The narrow scope of both estoppel by representation and estoppel by negligence is shown by *Moorgate Mercantile v Twitchings* (1977) in which the majority of the House of Lords rejected the application of both doctrines.

Another restriction of the scope of s 21(1) was revealed by the decision in *Shaw v Commissioner of Police* (1987). In this case the claimant, Mr Natalegawa, a student from Indonesia, owned a red Porsche. He advertised it for sale in a newspaper and received a call from a gentleman calling himself Jonathan London who said he was a car dealer and was interested in buying the car on behalf of a client. The claimant allowed London to take delivery of the car and gave him a letter saying that he had sold the car to London and disclaiming further legal responsibility for it. In return he received a cheque for £17,250 which in due course proved worthless. London agreed to sell the car to the plaintiff for £11,500, £10,000 to be paid by banker's draft. When London presented the draft the bank refused to cash it and London disappeared. In due course the police took possession of the car and both the plaintiff and the claimant sought possession of it. The Court of Appeal held that as far as s 21 was concerned the case would have fallen within its scope if the sale by London to the plaintiff had been completed. It was clear, however, that as far as the contract between the plaintiff and London was concerned, property in the car (if London had had it) was only to pass when London was paid. Since London had never been paid, the transaction was an agreement to sell and not a sale.

4.10.2 Sale in market overt

Section 22(1) of the Sale of Goods Act 1979 provides:

> 'Where goods are sold in market overt, according to the usage of the market, the buyer acquires a good title to the goods, provided he buys them in good faith and without notice of any defect or want of title on the part of the seller.'

As the language suggests this is a very old, indeed the oldest, exception to the general rule. It starts from the perception that a dishonest person is less likely to sell goods that she does not own in an open market than in a private sale. This rule reflects the supervision given to markets in the Middle Ages and may well have been historically true. This rationale has little place in modern business conditions and the exception has been removed by the Sale of Goods (Amendment) Act 1994.

Section 23 of the Sale of Goods Act 1979 provides:

> 'When the seller of goods has a voidable title to them, but his title has not been avoided at the time of the sale, the buyer acquires a good title to the goods, provided he buys them in good faith and without notice of the seller's defect of title.'

4.10.3   Sale under a voidable title

This exception applies where the seller, instead of having no title at all, has a title which is liable to be avoided. The most obvious example would be where the seller had obtained possession of the goods by fraud. Where a contract is induced by one party's fraud the result is not that the contract is void but that it is voidable, that is liable to be set aside by the deceived party. Where an owner of goods has parted with them to a fraudulent buyer, he is entitled to set aside the contract and, if he acts in time, can recover the goods. However, if the fraudulent person has meanwhile sold the goods on to an innocent buyer, that innocent buyer will obtain a title which is better than that of the original owner.

A critical question, therefore, is what does the original owner have to do to set the voidable contract aside? Telling the fraudulent person or taking the goods from her would certainly do but in practice the fraudulent person and the goods have usually disappeared. In *Car and Universal Finance Ltd v Caldwell* (1965) the Court of Appeal held that it was possible to avoid the contract without either telling the fraudulent person or retaking possession of the goods by immediately informing the police and the motoring organisations.

Section 24 of the Sale of Goods Act 1979 provides:

> 'Where a person having sold goods continues or is in possession of the goods, or of the documents of title to the goods, the delivery or transfer by that person, or by a mercantile agent acting for him, of the goods or documents of title under any sale, pledge, or disposition thereof, to any person receiving the same in good faith and without notice of the previous sale, has the same effect as if the person making the delivery or transfer were expressly authorised by the owner of goods to make the same.'

4.10.4   Seller in possession after sale

It is easy to apply this section to the case where the seller simply sells goods to A and then, without ever having delivered them to A, sells the same goods to B.

Difficulties have arisen however because the section talks of the seller who continues or is in possession of the goods. Suppose that a car dealer sells a car to A who pays for it and takes it away and then the following day brings it back for some small defect to be rectified. While the car is at the dealer's premises, the dealer sells it to B. It would be possible to read the section as giving B's rights precedence over those of A but it is quite clear that if A had taken his car to any other dealer who had sold it to B, A's rights would have prevailed over those of B. It would be very odd to make the positions of A and B depend on whether A takes his car for service to the person from whom he has bought it or to someone else. In fact the courts have not read the section in this way but they have given different explanations for not doing so.

In *Staffordshire Motor Guarantee v British Wagon* (1934) a dealer sold a lorry to a finance company who then hired it back to him under a hire-purchase agreement. The dealer then, in breach of the hire-purchase agreement, sold the lorry to another buyer. It was held that the rights of the finance company prevailed over those of the second buyer. The explanation given was that for s 24 to apply the seller must continue in possession 'as a seller'. However, this view was later rejected by the Privy Council on appeal from Australia in *Pacific Motor Auctions v Motor Credits* (1965) and by the Court of Appeal in *Worcester Works Finance v Cooden Engineering* (1972). In these cases it was said that the crucial question was whether the seller's possession was physically continuous. If it was, as in the *Staffordshire Motor Guarantee* case, then s 24 applied.

| 4.10.5 | Buyer in possession after sale |

Section 25 of the Sale of Goods Act 1979 provides:

25 (1) Where a person having bought or agreed to buy goods obtains, with the consent of the seller, possession of the goods or the documents of title to the goods, the delivery or transfer by that person, or by a mercantile agent acting for him, of the goods or documents of title, under any sale, pledge, or other disposition thereof, to any person receiving the same in good faith and without notice of any lien or other right of the original seller in respect of the goods, has the same effect as if the person making the delivery or transfer were a mercantile agent in possession of the goods or documents of title with the consent of the owner.

(2) For the purposes of subsection (1) above –

(a) the buyer under a conditional sale agreement is to be taken not to be a person who has bought or agreed to buy goods, and

(b) conditional sale agreement' means an agreement for the sale of goods which is a consumer credit agreement within the meaning of the Consumer Credit Act 1974 under which the purchase price or any part of it is payable by instalments, and the property in the goods is to remain in the seller (notwithstanding that the buyer is to be in possession of the goods) until such conditions as to the payment of instalments or otherwise as may be specified in the agreement are fulfilled.'

It will be seen that this section is in a sense the reverse of s 24 since it deals with the situation where possession of the goods has passed to the buyer before ownership has passed to him and permits such a buyer to transfer ownership to a sub-buyer. The wording talks of 'a person having bought or agreed to buy goods'. Normally, if the buyer has bought the goods there would be a complete contract of sale and property would have passed to her. In that case of course, she would be in a position to transfer ownership to a sub-buyer without any question of s 25 arising. The section is concerned with the situation where the buyer has obtained possession of the goods (or the documents of title to the goods) with the consent of the seller but without becoming owner.

The section does not apply where someone has obtained goods without having agreed to buy them. So in *Shaw v Commissioner of Police* (1987) a car had been obtained from the owner on the basis that the person obtaining it might have a client who might be willing to buy it. It was held that he was not a buyer within the meaning of s 25 and was not therefore in a position to transfer ownership to a sub-buyer. In the same way a customer under a hire-purchase agreement is not a buyer for the purpose of s 25 because in such a case the customer has only agreed to hire the goods and is given an option to buy the goods which he is not legally obliged to exercise even though commercially it is extremely likely that he will. On the other hand, a customer who has agreed to buy the goods but has been given credit is a buyer within s 25, even though the agreement provides that he is not to become the owner until he has paid for the goods. Section 25(2) contains a statutory modification of this rule in the case where the buyer has taken under a 'conditional sale agreement' as defined in s 25(2)(b), that is where the price is to be paid by instalments and falls within the scope of the Consumer Credit Act 1974. The reason for this exception is to make the law about conditional sale agreements within the Consumer Credit Act the same as for hire-purchase agreements within the Consumer Credit Act.

Section 25 has important effects on the reasoning contained in *Car and Universal Finance v Caldwell* (1965) discussed above.

In some cases of this kind, although the buyer's voidable title would have been avoided he would still be a buyer in possession within s 25. This was shown in *Newtons of Wembley Limited v Williams* (1965) where the plaintiff agreed to sell a car to A on the basis that the property was not to pass until the whole purchase price had been paid or a cheque had been honoured. A issued a cheque and was given possession of the car but in due course his cheque bounced. The plaintiff took immediate steps to avoid the contract as in the *Caldwell* case and after he had done this A sold the car to B in a London street market and B sold the car to the defendant. The Court of Appeal held that although the plaintiff had avoided A's title, A was still a buyer in possession of the car and that B had therefore obtained a good title from A when he bought from him in good faith and had taken possession of the car. It was an important part of the Court of Appeal's reasoning that the sale by A to B had taken place in the ordinary course of business of a mercantile agent (see para 4.5.6).

| 4.10.6 | Agents and mercantile agents |

In practice most sales are made by agents since most sellers are companies and employ agents to carry on their business. This presents no problem where, as would usually be the case, agents make contracts which they are authorised to make. Furthermore, under general contract law, agents bind the principal not only when they do things which they are actually authorised to do, but also when they do things which they appear to be authorised to do. The common law concerning principal and agent is expressly preserved in the Sale of Goods Act by s 62.

However, it is clear that in the law of sale things have been developed by use of a concept of 'mercantile agents' which is wider than that of agency in the general law of contract and this development arose because of a limitation which was imposed on the general law of agency. If I put my car into the hands of a motor dealer to sell on my behalf, I will normally be bound by the contract which she makes even though she goes outside my authority, for instance by accepting a lower price than I have agreed. However, if instead of selling the car, the dealer pledges it as security for a loan, she would not be treated as having apparent authority to do so. This is so, even though from the point of view of someone dealing with the dealer her relationship to the car looks quite the same whether she is selling it or pledging it.

The pledging of goods and documents of title is a very important part of financing commercial transactions in some trades. So people importing large amounts of commodities, such as grain or coffee, may very likely pledge the goods or documents of title to the goods, in order to borrow money against them. It was felt unsatisfactory therefore to have this distinction between the agent who sells and the agent who pledges and this was the subject of statutory amendment by a series of Factors Acts starting in 1823 and culminating in the Factors Act 1889.

The Factors Act 1889 continues in force after the passage of the Sale of Goods Act 1893 and 1979. Section 21(2) of the Sale of Goods Act provides that:

'nothing in this Act affects –

> (a) the provisions of the Factors Acts or any enactment enabling the apparent owner of goods to d i s p o s e of them as if he were their true owner.'

Sections 8 and 9 of the Factors Act provide:

> '(8) Where a person, having sold goods, continues, or is, in possession of the goods or of the documents of title to the goods, the delivery or transfer by that person, or by a mercantile agent acting for him, of the goods or documents of title under any sale, pledge, or other disposition thereof, *or under any agreement for sale, pledge, or other disposition thereof,* to any person receiving the same in good faith and without notice of the previous sale, shall have the same effect as if the person making the delivery or transfer were expressly authorised by the owner of the goods to make the same.

> (9) Where a person, having bought or agreed to buy goods, obtains with the consent of the seller possession of the goods or the documents of title to the goods, the delivery or transfer, by that person or by a mercantile agent acting for him, of the goods or documents of title, under any sale, pledge, or other disposition thereof, *or under any agreement for sale, pledge, or other disposition thereof,* to any person receiving the same in good faith and without notice of any lien or other right of the original seller in respect of the goods, shall have the same effect as if the person making the delivery or transfer were a mercantile agent in possession of the goods or documents of title with the consent of the owner.'

It will be seen that these provisions are very similar to the provisions of ss 24 and 25 of the Sale of Goods Act. The difference is the presence of the words in italics in the text above. A key question is clearly what is meant by a 'mercantile agent'. This is defined by s 1(1) of the Factors Act as meaning 'a mercantile agent having in the customary course of his business as such agent authority either to sell goods, or to consign goods for the purpose of sale, or to buy goods, or to raise money on the security of goods'. The effect of dealings by mercantile agents is set out in s 2 of the Factors Act:

> '(2) (1) Where a mercantile agent is, with the consent of the owner, in possession of goods or of the documents of title to goods, any sale, pledge, or other disposition of the goods, made by him when acting in the ordinary course of business of a mercantile agent, shall, subject to the provisions of this Act, be as valid as if he were expressly authorised by the owner of the goods to make the same; provided that the person taking under the disposition acts in good faith, and has not at the time of the disposition notice that the person making the disposition has not authority to make the same.
>
> (2) Where a mercantile agent has, with the consent of the owner, been in possession of goods or of the documents of title to goods, any sale, pledge, or other disposition, which would have been valid if the consent had continued, shall be valid notwithstanding the determination of the consent: provided that the person taking under the disposition has not at the time thereof notice that the consent has been determined.
>
> (3) Where a mercantile agent has obtained possession of any documents of title to goods by reason of his being or having been, with the consent of the owner, in possession of the goods represented thereby, or of any other documents of title to the goods, his possession of the first-mentioned documents shall, for the purposes of this Act, be deemed to be with the consent of the owner.
>
> (4) For the purposes of this Act the consent of the owner shall be presumed in the absence of evidence to the contrary.'

The most important limitation on the width of the power given by s 2 is that in order for the mercantile agent to be able to pass title it must not only be in possession with the owner's consent, but must be in possession *as a mercantile agent* with the owner's consent. So, for instance, a car dealer which has both a sale room and a service facility is clearly a mercantile agent and has the consent of its service customers to have possession of their cars for service, but if it were to put one of these cars into the sale room and sell it, this would not be a transaction protected by the Factors Acts because it would not have had possession of the car as a mercantile agent, but rather as a repairer.

In *Pearson v Rose and Young* (1951) where the plaintiff delivered his car to a mercantile agent in order to obtain offers but with no authority to sell it. The agent succeeded in obtaining the log book by a trick in circumstances where it was clear that the owner had not consented to the dealer having possession of the log book. Having got both the log book and the car, the dealer then dishonestly sold it. The Court of Appeal held that this was not a transaction protected by the Factors Act. Although the dealer had possession of the car with the owner's consent, he did not have possession of the log book with the owner's consent. He could have sold the car without the log book, but the Court held that this would not have been a sale in the ordinary course of business of a mercantile agent. The sale with the log book, where the log book had been obtained without the owner's consent, was also outside the Act.

In *National Employer's Insurance v Jones* (1990) a car was stolen and sold to A who sold it to B who in turn sold it to a car dealer C, who sold it to another car dealer D, who sold it to the defendant who bought it in good faith. The defendant argued that the transaction fell within the literal scope of s 9 because D had obtained possession of the goods with the consent of the dealer who had sold the goods to him and who was certainly a mercantile agent. It is true that both s 9 and s 25 talk about consent of the *seller* and not consent of the *owner*. The House of Lords held that the word 'seller' in s 9 and s 25 must be given a special meaning and could not cover a seller whose possession could be traced back through however many transactions to the unlawful possession of a thief.

One of the most common forms of dishonesty is for a person to acquire a car on hire-purchase terms and then to dispose of it for cash before he has completed the hire-purchase contract. In practice, he will find it difficult to dispose of the car for cash to an honest dealer because the existence of the hire-purchase transaction would normally be discovered by reference by the dealer to HPI. However, it is very easy for a person who has acquired a car on hire-purchase to sell it for cash on the second-hand market and difficult for someone buying from him to know that the seller is not in fact the owner of the goods. Such transactions are not protected by s 25 because someone acquiring goods on hire-purchase is not a buyer, nor by the Factors Act because the seller is not a mercantile agent.

4.10.7   Hire-purchase Act 1964 Part III

The Hire-purchase Act 1964 created a new exception to the *nemo dat* rule by providing that if a car which was subject to a hire-purchase or credit sale agreement was sold to a private purchaser, that purchaser would acquire a good title if he bought it in good faith and without notice of the hire-purchase or credit sale agreement.

This protection is accorded only to private purchasers and does not apply to dealers. However, the private purchaser does not need to be the person who actually buys and makes the initial purchase of the goods from the person who is dishonestly disposing of goods. So, if X has a car on hire-purchase terms and dishonestly sells it to a dealer B who then sells it to C who buys it in good faith, not knowing of the defects in A's or B's title, then C will obtain a good title, even though he has bought from B the dealer and not from A the original hirer and even though B himself did not obtain a good title.

Private purchasers are those who are not 'trade or finance purchasers', and a trade or finance purchaser is one who at the time of the disposition carried on a business which consisted wholly or partly either:

(a) of purchasing motor vehicles for the purpose of offering or exposing them for sale; or

(b) of providing finance by purchasing motor vehicles for the purpose of letting them under hire-purchase agreements or agreeing to sell them under conditional sale agreements.

It is perfectly possible to carry on either of these activities part time, so that someone who buys and sells cars as a sideline will be a trade purchaser, if he is doing it as a business; that is, with a view to making a profit. On the other hand a company which is not in the motor trade or the financing of motor purchase business will be a private purchaser for the purpose of Part III of the 1964 Act.

Ownership

This chapter reflects the fact that sale is not only a contract but also a conveyance. That is, a transfer of ownership in the goods. It considers three questions which arise in this connection:

- What are the obligations of the seller in relation to transfer or ownership?

- When does property (ownership) pass from seller to buyer? The general rule is at the moment agreed by the parties but this is subject to a prior requirement that property cannot normally pass until the goods are ascertained.

- When can a buyer become owner even though the seller was not the owner?

The seller's duties are set out in s 12 of the Sale of Goods Act. Of the three separate obligations, by far the most important is that set out in s 12(1) under which the seller undertakes that he has the right to sell the goods. It is important to note that the seller is in breach of this obligation, even though he believes that he is entitled to sell the goods and even though the buyer's enjoyment of the goods is never disturbed (*Rowland v Birall* (1923)).

The first rule is that property cannot pass if the goods are unascertained (s 16). This makes the distinction between specific and unascertained goods fundamental. The second rule is that if the goods are specific or ascertained, the parties are free to make whatever agreement they like about when property is to pass (s 17). Where the parties do not specifically direct their thoughts to this question, assistance is provided by s 18 which provides rules for ascertaining the intention of the parties 'unless a different intention appears'. It is important to note the qualifications made by the Sale of Goods (Amendment) Act 1995. The principal affect is that if the owner of part of an undivided bulk sells it to a buyer who pays the price, property in an undivided share of the bulk can be passed if the parties so agree.

Introduction

The seller's duties as to the transfer of ownership

The passing of property

Transfer of title where the seller is not the owner

The general rule is that the seller cannot normally transfer any better rights that he himself has. This is often put in the form of the Latin maxim *nemo dat quod non habet* (no one can transfer what he does not have). Most of the exceptions are set out in ss 21–26 of the Sale of Goods Act 1979 and include the following:

- estoppel (s 21(1));
- sale under a voidable title (s 23);
- seller in possession after sale (s 24);
- buyer in possession after sale (s 25);
- agents and mercantile agents (Factors Act 1889 and s 21(2) Sale of Goods Act);
- Hire-purchase Act 1964 Part III.

Chapter 5

Non-existent Goods, Risk and Frustration

Section 6 of the Sale of Goods Act 1979 provides:

> 'Where there is a contract for the sale of specific goods and the goods without the knowledge of the seller have perished at the time when the contract was made, the contract is void.'

This section is based on the famous pre-Act case of *Couturier v Hastie* (1856). In that case the contract was for the sale of a specific cargo of corn which was on board a named ship sailing from Salonica to London. In fact, at the time the contract was made, the cargo of corn had been sold by the master of the ship in Tunis because it was fermenting owing to storm damage. The seller sued the buyer, claiming that he was entitled to the price even though he had no goods to deliver. The seller's argument was that in a contract of this kind the buyer had agreed to pay against delivery of the shipping documents which would have given him rights against the carriers and against the insurers of the goods. The House of Lords held that the seller's action failed.

Couturier v Hastie has been taken by some as an example of a general principle that if the parties' agreement is based on some shared fundamental mistake, then the contract is void. Other writers have treated it as an example of an overlapping but rather narrower principle that if, unknown to the parties, the subject matter of the contract does not exist or has ceased to exist, then the contract is void. Section 6 of the Sale of Goods Act 1979 does not turn on either of these principles.

In order to apply s 6 one needs to know what is meant by the goods having *perished*. In *Couturier v Hastie* the corn was treated as having perished because as a commercial entity the cargo had ceased to exist. In *Barrow, Lane and Ballard Limited v Philip Phillips & Company Limited* (1929), there was a contract for 700 bags of groundnuts which were believed to be in a warehouse. In fact, unknown to the parties, 109 bags had been stolen before the contract was made. It was held that s 6 applied and the contract was void. It will be seen that only some 15% of the contract parcel had been stolen, but this was treated as sufficient to destroy the parcel as a whole.

Goods will not be treated as having perished merely because they have been damaged. On the other hand there may be damage so extensive as effectively to deprive the goods of the commercial character under which they were sold. So in *Asfar & Company Limited v Blundell* (1891), the contract was for a sale of a cargo of dates. The dates had become contaminated with sewage and had begun to ferment. Although all the dates were still available, the cargo was treated as commercially perished.

It will be seen that s 6 only applies to the sale of specific goods and only applies where the goods have perished 'without the knowledge of the seller'. A difficult question is what the position would be if the seller ought to have known that the goods had perished. The literal wording of s 6 suggests that if the seller does not know that the goods have perished, even though he could easily have discovered it, the contract is void. It does not follow, however, that the buyer would be without a remedy since in some such cases the seller would be liable for having represented negligently that the goods did exist. This is one of the possible explanations of the famous Australian decision of *McRae v Commonwealth Disposals Commission* (1951), although this was actually a case where the goods had never existed rather than one where the goods had once existed and perished.

5.2   The doctrine of risk

The previous section was concerned with problems which arise where the goods have 'perished' before the contract is made. Obviously the goods may be destroyed or damaged after the contract is made. The principal tool used to allocate the loss which arises where the goods are damaged or destroyed after the contract is made is the doctrine of risk. This is a special doctrine developed for the law of sale, unlike the doctrine of frustration which is a general doctrine of the law of contract and which will be discussed in the next section.

5.2.1   What is the effect of the passing of risk?

It is important to emphasise that the doctrine of risk does not operate to bring the contract of sale to an end. It may, however, release one party from their obligations under the contract. So, for instance, if the goods are at the seller's risk and they are damaged or destroyed, this would in effect release the buyer from their obligation to accept the goods, but it would not release the seller from the obligation to deliver them. Conversely, if the goods are at the buyer's risk and are damaged or destroyed she may still be liable to pay the price even though the seller is no longer liable for not delivering the goods. In some cases where the goods are damaged this would be the fault of a third party and that third party may be liable to be sued.

5.2.2   When does risk pass?

The basic rule as to when risk passes is set out in s 20 of the Sale of Goods Act 1979 which provides:

'(1) Unless otherwise agreed, the goods remain at the seller's risk until the property in them is transferred to the buyer, but when the property in them is transferred to the buyer the goods are at the buyer's risk whether delivery has been made or not.

(2) But where delivery has been delayed through the fault of either buyer or seller the goods are at the risk of the party at fault as regards any loss which might not have occurred but for such fault.

(3) Nothing in this section affects the duties or liabilities of either seller or buyer as a bailee or custodier of the goods of the other party.'

It will be seen that English law has adopted the basic rule that risk is to pass at the same time as property.

The parties can and frequently do separate the passing of risk and property. So in standard conditions of sale the seller will often provide that risk is to pass on delivery but that property is not to pass until the goods have been paid for. This is because the seller does not wish to be bothered with insuring the goods once he or she has delivered them, but is anxious to retain ownership of the goods as security against not being paid in full.

There seems, however, to be at least two kinds of case where risk may pass at a different time from property even though there is no expressed or implied agreement. The first arises in the case of sales of unascertained goods. As we have seen property cannot pass in such a case until the goods are ascertained. However, there may be cases where property is not ascertained because the goods form part of an unascertained bulk, but nevertheless fairness requires that risk should pass. The classic example is *Sterns v Vickers* (1923), where the sellers had some 200,000 gallons of white spirit in a tank belonging to a storage company. They sold to the buyers some 120,000 gallons of the spirit and gave the buyers a delivery warrant. The effect of the delivery warrant was that the storage company undertook to deliver the white spirit to the buyers or as the buyers might order. In fact the buyers sub-sold, but the sub-purchaser did not wish to take possession of the spirit at once and arranged with the storage company to store it on his behalf, paying rent for the storage. Clearly, although there had been a sale and a sub-sale, ownership was still in the hands of the original sellers since the goods were still unascertained. While the bulk was unseparated, the spirit deteriorated. The Court of Appeal held that although there was no agreement between the parties, the risk had passed as between the original seller and buyer to the buyer. The reason for this was that as soon as the buyers had the delivery warrant, they were immediately able to obtain delivery of the spirit and therefore risk should pass to them even though they chose not to take immediate possession of the goods.

The second situation is illustrated by the pre-Act case of *Head v Tattersall* (1870), which it is generally assumed would be decided in the same way after the Act. In this case the plaintiff bought a horse from the defendant who warranted that it had been hunted with the Bicester hounds. The contract provided that the horse might be returned by a certain day if it appeared that it had not in fact been hunted with the Bicester hounds. The horse had in fact not been hunted with the hounds and the plaintiff chose to return it before the agreed date. On the face of it the plaintiff was clearly entitled to do this, but before the horse had been returned it had been injured while in the plaintiff's possession, although without any fault on his part. The court held that the plaintiff was entitled to return the horse.

The general rule stated in s 20(1) of the Sale of Goods Act 1979 is subject to the qualifications contained in sub-sections (2) and (3). Sub-section (2) means that if the seller is late in making the delivery or the buyer is late in accepting delivery, this may mean that the incidence of risk is different from what it would otherwise have been. This would be so, however, only if the loss is one which might not have occurred if delivery had not been delayed. However, the onus will be on the party who is in delay to show that the loss would have happened in any event. Sub-section (3) is really no more than a specific example of the general principle that the passing of risk is to do with the allocation of the risk of damage which is not the fault of either party. The most important example of this is where the risk is on one party, but the other party is in possession of the goods and fails to take good care of them.

We should also note s 33 of the Sale of Goods Act 1979 which provides:

> 'Where the seller of goods agrees to deliver them at his own risk at a place other than that where they are when sold, the buyer must nevertheless (unless otherwise agreed) take any risk of deterioration in the goods necessarily incident to the course of transit.'

Practical examples of the application of this section are very hard to find.

5.3   The doctrine of frustration

The doctrine of frustration is part of the general law of contract. In principle there can be no doubt that this doctrine applies to contracts for the sale of goods like any other contract.

Section 7 of the Act contains a provision which deals expressly with frustration. This provides:

> 'Where there is an agreement to sell specific goods and subsequently the goods, without any fault on the part of the seller or buyer, perish before the risk passes to the buyer, the agreement is avoided.'

This section is clearly a very incomplete statement of the doctrine of frustration as applied to contracts of sale. It deals only with specific goods and it deals only with goods which perish, whereas frustration may involve many other events than the destruction of the goods. For instance, where goods are sold internationally, there is often a requirement to obtain an export or import licence. Failure to obtain such a licence would not normally be a frustrating event because the parties would know at the time of the contract that the licence was required and the contract would often expressly or impliedly require one of the parties to obtain (or at least to use their best endeavours to obtain) the licence. However, it might be that after the contract was made a government introduced a wholly new export or import licensing system which was unforeseen. There might be plausible arguments in such a case that the contract was frustrated.

It is also possible to argue that a contract for the sale of unascertained goods is frustrated, but of course such goods cannot usually perish (except for the special case of sale of part of a bulk as discussed below). In practice the courts, although admitting the possibility that sales of unascertained goods can be frustrated, have been very slow in fact to hold them frustrated. (See *Blackburn Bobbin Limited v T W Allen Limited* (1918), *and Tsakiroglou & Company Limited v Noblee and Thorl* (1962).)

In *Howell v Coupland* (1876), a farmer sold in March for delivery upon harvesting the following autumn, 200 tons of potatoes to come from his farm. In fact only 80 tons were harvested. The buyer accepted delivery of the 80 tons and brought an action for damages for non-delivery of the balance of 120 tons. It was held that the unforeseen potato blight which had affected the crop released the seller from his obligation to deliver any more than had in fact been grown. It should be noted that in fact the buyer was perfectly happy to accept and pay for the 80 tons; it was certainly arguable that if the potato blight released the seller, it also released the buyer from any obligation to take the potatoes at all. Obviously there could be commercial situations in which if the buyer could not obtain the full 200 tons from one source, it was perfectly reasonable of him to refuse to accept any delivery at all. The case does not decide that a buyer could not elect to do this.

5.3.1   When does the doctrine of frustration apply?

In *HR & S Sainsbury Limited v Street* (1972), the farmer contracted to sell to a corn merchant 275 tons of barley to be grown on his farm. In this case there was a generally poor harvest and only 140 tons were harvested on the defendant's farm. The defendant argued that the contract was frustrated and sold the 140 tons to another merchant. (The reason no doubt being that because of the generally poor harvest, barley prices were higher than expected and the defendant was then able to get a better price from another merchant.) McKenna J held that the farmer was in breach of contract by not delivering the 140 tons which had actually been harvested, although the bad harvest did relieve him of any obligation to deliver the balance of 135 tons. Again it should be noted that in this case the buyer was willing and indeed anxious to take the 140 tons and the case does not therefore decide that the buyer in such a case was bound to take the 140 tons, although the doctrine of frustration where it operates, does normally operate to release both parties from future performance of the contract.

5.3.2   The effect of frustration

If a frustrating event takes place, its effect is to bring the contract to an end at once and relieve both parties from any further obligation to perform the contract. This is so even though the frustrating event usually only makes it impossible for one party to perform. So the fact that the seller is unable to deliver the goods does not mean that the buyer is unable to pay the price, but the seller's inability to deliver the goods relieves the buyer of the obligation to pay the price. This rule is easy to apply where the contract is frustrated before either party has done anything to perform it, but the contract is often frustrated after some acts of performance have taken place.

At common law it was eventually held in the leading case of *Fibrosa v Fairbairn* (1943), that if a buyer had paid in advance for the goods, he could recover the advance payment in full if no goods at all had been delivered before the contract was frustrated. However, that decision is based on a finding that there had been a 'total failure of consideration'; that is that the buyer had received no part of what it expected to receive under the contract. If there was a partial failure of consideration, that is, if the buyer had received some of the goods, then it would not have been able to recover an advance payment of the price even though the advance payment was significantly greater than the value of the goods which it had received. This obviously appears unfair on the buyer. The decision in the *Fibrosa* case was also potentially unfair on the seller. Even though the seller has not delivered any goods before the contract is frustrated, it may well have incurred expenditure where the goods have to be manufactured for the buyer's requirements and some or perhaps even all of this expenditure may be wasted if the goods cannot easily be resold because the buyer's requirements are special. These defects in the law were largely remedied by the Law Reform (Frustrated Contracts) Act 1943 which gave the court a wide discretion to order repayment of prices which had been paid in advance or to award compensation to a seller who had incurred wasted expenditure before the contract was frustrated.

Section 2(5)(c) of the 1943 Act provides that the Act shall not apply to:

'Any contract to which section 7 of the Sale of Goods Act, ... applies or ... any other contract for the sale, or for the sale and delivery, of specific goods, where the contract is frustrated by reason of the fact that the goods have perished.'

So the 1943 Act does not apply to cases where the contract is frustrated either under s 7 of the Sale of Goods Act or in other cases where it is frustrated by the goods perishing. On the other hand, the 1943 Act does apply where the contract is frustrated by any event other than the perishing of the goods.

Non-existent Goods, Risk and Frustration

This chapter discusses three separate doctrines which may affect the contract.

Introduction

The first is the rules which apply when the goods did not exist when the contract was made, particularly the special example of the case where the goods did once exist but have perished.

The second is the doctrine of risk which decides whether seller or buyer bears the loss if the goods are damaged or destroyed after the contract is made.

The third concerns the application of the doctrine of frustration to contracts of sale.

Section 6 of the Sale of Goods Act provides that where there is a contract for the sale of specific goods, and the goods without the knowledge of the seller have perished at the time when the contract was made, the contract is void. *Couturier v Hastia* (1956) has been taken by some as an example of the general principle that if the parties' agreement is based on some shared fundamental mistake, then the contract is void.

Non-existent goods

Goods may be destroyed or damaged after the contract is made. The principal tool used to allocate the loss which arises when the goods are damaged or destroyed after the contract is made is the doctrine of risk. Section 20 adopts the basic rule that risk is to pass at the same time as property. There seems, however, to be at least two kinds of case where risk may pass at a different time from property even though there is no expressed or implied agreement:

The doctrine of risk

- in the case of sales of unascertained goods (*Sterns v Vickers* (1923));

- in the case of sales of some specific goods (*Head v Tattersall* (1870)).

Section 7 of the Sale of Goods Act deals expressly with frustration, but it is a very incomplete statement of the doctrine of frustration as applied to contracts of sale. It deals only with specific goods and it deals only with goods which perish, whereas frustration may involve many other events than the destruction of goods.

The doctrine of frustration

Chapter 6

Defective Goods

Liability for defective goods may be either contractual, tortious or criminal. The main part of this chapter will be devoted to considering the situations in which the buyer has a contractual remedy against the seller on the grounds that the goods are not as the seller contracted. However, liability for defective goods may also be based on the law of tort. Since 1932 it has been clear that in most cases there will be liability in tort where someone suffers personal injury or damage to his property arising from the defendant having negligently put goods into circulation. A major development in tort liability has taken place since the adoption in 1985 by the European Community of a directive on product liability, enacted into English law by Part I of the Consumer Protection Act 1987. This Act is aimed at imposing liability for defective products on producers of products but sellers may be producers either where their distribution is vertically integrated so that the same company is manufacturing, marketing and distributing the goods retail, or, where although they are not manufacturing the goods, they sell them as if they were theirs (as in the case of major stores which sell 'own brand' goods).

A seller may also come under criminal liability. A typical, and all too common example, is the second-hand car dealer who turns back the odometer so as to make it appear that the second-hand car has covered less miles than is in fact the case. This is a criminal offence under the Trade Descriptions Act.

It might be thought to be a relatively simple task to decide whether or not a seller has made express undertakings about the goods. In fact, this is not the case and English law has managed to make this a much more difficult question than it would appear at first sight.

The theoretical test is usually formulated by asking what the parties intended. If the parties had said what they intended, this test would be easy to apply but more often than not, the parties do not say what they intend. In practice, if the parties express no intention, the court is in effect substituting its own view of what the parties, as reasonable people, probably intended. This is necessarily a vague and flexible test. Over the years a number of factors have been taken into account. One argument would be that the statement was of a

6.1 Introduction

6.2 Liability in contract: express terms

trivial commendatory nature such that no one should be expected to treat it as meant to be contractually binding.

Another factor would be whether there was a significant time lag between the making of the statement and the completion of the contract. Contrast *Routledge v McKay* (1954), and *Schawel v Reade* (1913).

The parties may render the contract into writing. Obviously if they incorporate everything that is said in negotiations into the written contract, it will be clear that they intend it to be legally binding. But suppose an important statement is made in negotiations and is left out of the written contract. At one time it was believed that the so-called parol evidence rule meant that such statements did not form part of the contract.

In practice, courts are quite willing to entertain arguments that what looks like a complete written contract is not in fact a complete contract at all, but simply a partial statement of the contract. In fact the courts have recognised two different analyses here, though their practical effect is often the same. One analysis is to say that there is a contract partly in writing and partly oral; the other analysis is to say that there are two contracts, one in writing and one oral. The practical effect in both cases is to permit evidence to be given of oral statements which qualify, add to, or even contradict what is contained in the written contract. An excellent example of this is the case of *Evans v Andrea Merzario* (1976).

6.3   Liability for misrepresentation

Where the seller has made statements about the goods but the court has held that these statements are not terms of the contract, such statements may give rise to liability in misrepresentation.

6.3.1   What is a misrepresentation?

Basically a misrepresentation is a statement of a fact made by one party to the contract to the other party before the contract is made which induces that other party to enter into the contract but is not characterised as being a term of the contract.

It should be noted, however, that not all of the terms of a contract are concerned with making statements of fact. Many terms contain promises as to future conduct, for example, that we will deliver the goods next week. In principle a promise to deliver goods next week is not capable of being a misrepresentation because it is not a statement of fact. For such a promise to give rise to liability it must be a term of the contract. This principle is well established but it is subject to one very important qualification. Hidden within many statements which look like statements of intention or opinion or undertakings as to the future there may be a statement of fact. This is because, as was said by Bowen LJ in *Edgington v Fitzmaurice* (1885) 'the state of a man's mind is as much a fact as the state of his digestion'.

In order to create liability it is necessary to show not only that there has been a misrepresentation but that the other party to the contract entered into the contract because of the misrepresentation. Even where one party knows there is misrepresentation he may not have entered into the contract because of it but may have relied on his own judgment or indeed known that the statement was untrue. On the other hand it is not necessary to show that the misrepresentation was the only reason for entering into the contract. It would be sufficient to show that the misrepresentation was a significant reason for entering into the contract. People often enter into contracts for a combination of reasons and provided that one of the reasons is the misrepresentation this will be quite sufficient.

Originally misrepresentation created liability only where it was fraudulent; that is, where the person making the statement did not honestly believe that it was true. The narrow common law definition was applied by the House of Lords in the famous case of *Derry v Peek* (1889). To establish liability in fraud it had to be shown that the person making the statement knew that it was untrue or at least did not care whether it was true or false.

6.3.2   Types of misrepresentation

The decision of the House of Lords in 1963 in *Hedley Byrne v Heller* (1964) established that it was possible for a careless statement made by one person and relied on by another, causing that other to suffer financial loss, to give rise to liability. The precise limits of the decision in *Hedley Byrne* are still being worked out by the courts and it is clear that the statement has to be not only careless but made in circumstances in which the defendant owed a duty of care to the plaintiff. This involves consideration of such factors as whether the defendant should have contemplated that the plaintiff would have relied on them; and whether the plaintiff did in fact rely on the defendant, and whether in normal circumstances it was reasonable for them to have done so. What is clear is that there may be such a duty of care between one contracting party and another where, in the run-up to the contract, it is reasonable for that party to rely on advice which is given by the other (see *Esso Petroleum v Mardon* (1976)).

Section 2(1) of the Misrepresentation Act 1967 provides that:

'Where a person has entered into a contract after a misrepresentation has been made to him by another party thereto and as a result thereof he has suffered loss, then, if the person making the misrepresentation would be liable to damages in respect thereof had the misrepresentation been made fraudulently, that person shall be so liable notwithstanding that the misrepresentation is not made fraudulently, unless he proves that he had reasonable ground to believe and did believe up to the time the contract was made that the facts represented were true.'

The rule enacted by this sub-section significantly overlaps with the common law rule laid down in *Hedley Byrne v Heller* but it is not the same rule. The *Hedley Byrne* rule is wider in that it applies whether or not there is a contract between plaintiff and defendant. Indeed many of the cases under *Hedley Byrne* are of this kind. On the other hand the Misrepresentation Act only applies where the result of the misrepresentation is that a contract is entered into between the person making the representation and the person to whom it is made. However, where the Act applies it is more favourable to the plaintiff because in effect it provides for recovery of damages for negligent misrepresentation and puts on the person making the misrepresentation the burden of proving that it was not negligent. Furthermore, the statutory provision establishes liability for negligent misrepresentation in relation to all contracts, whereas the rule in *Hedley Byrne* would only apply to those contracts where one contracting party owes the other a duty of care in relation to statements made during negotiations, as in *Esso v Mardon*.

6.3.3   Remedies for misrepresentation

A plaintiff who has entered into a contract as a result of a misrepresentation by the defendant can recover damages either by showing that the defendant was fraudulent as in *Derry v Peek*, or by showing that the defendant owed a duty of care and was in breach of that duty as in *Esso v Mardon* or if the defendant is unable to show that it was not negligent in making the misrepresentation. A plaintiff, if she wishes, can rely on all three of these theories. In practice prudent plaintiffs do not usually make allegations of fraud unless they have a very strong case since English courts traditionally are reluctant to stigmatise defendants as fraudulent.

The possibility of recovering damages for negligent as well as fraudulent misrepresentation substantially reduces the importance of deciding whether the statement of fact is a contractual term or a misrepresentation although it does not totally remove the significance of this distinction. It should be noted, however, that it does not follow that the same amount of damages can be recovered in a contract action as in an action for misrepresentation.

Alternatively, the plaintiff may seek to rescind the contract on the grounds of the defendant's misrepresentation. During the course of the 19th century it became established in the Court of Chancery that rescission was available as a general remedy to parties who had entered into contracts as a result of misrepresentation, even if the misrepresentation was entirely innocent. This is still the case. However, although rescission is a remedy easily granted where the contract has been made but not performed it can have dramatic results where the contract has been carried out. Section 2(2) of the Misrepresentation Act 1967 has therefore conferred on the court a general power to award damages instead of allowing rescission. The right to rescission may also be lost by the operation of what are often called the bars to rescission. This again is a reflection of the fact that rescission is a potentially drastic remedy and so plaintiffs have a choice whether to rescind or not and if they choose not to rescind then they are said to affirm the contract and thereby to lose the right. There is some theoretical discussion as to whether one could lose this right simply by doing nothing. The practical answer is that plaintiffs who know they have the right to rescind are very ill-advised not to make a prompt decision. Rescission is also impossible where the plaintiff cannot restore in substance what he has received under the contract as the subject matter of the contract has been consumed or used. Courts sometimes take a broad view on this question, particularly where the defendant is fraudulent. So if the defendant sells a business to the plaintiff on the basis of fraudulent representations as to the value of the business, the defendant may well not be able to resist rescission by arguing that the business being offered back is not the one that he or she sold. To require exact restoration in such cases would obviously be impractical. The principle that the contract is capable of being affirmed and is not rescinded until the plaintiff chooses to do so is often expressed by saying that the contract is voidable. This means that the contract is capable of having legal effects up to the moment that it is avoided. A very important consequence of this is that rights may be conferred on third parties and that the recognition of those rights prevent rescission. Classic examples are in the case of fraudulent buyers. Suppose a buyer obtains goods from a seller by a fraudulent representation, for instance that his cheque is of value, and then sells the goods onto a third party before the seller discovers the fraud. This can undoubtedly create rights in the third party which cannot be defeated by rescission.

6.4	**Implied terms**	The implied terms laid down for contracts of Sale of Goods are contained in ss 13, 14 and 15 of the Sale of Goods Act 1979. These provisions are undoubtedly of central importance and they are amongst the most commonly quoted and relied on provisions in the whole Act. Similar provisions have been laid down by statute for contracts of hire-purchase starting with the Hire Purchase Act 1938. Much more recently general provisions applying to all contracts under which property in goods is transferred other than contracts of sale and hire-purchase have been laid down by the Supply of Goods and Services Act 1982. This Act also lays down very similar provisions in relation to contracts of hire. So we may now say that in any contract under which property or possession in goods is transferred there will be a core of basic obligations, subject only to the ability of the seller to qualify or exclude his liability.

6.4.1   Obligations of the seller
as to description

Section 13 of the Sale of Goods Act 1979 provides:

'(a) Where there is a contract for the sale of goods by description, there is an implied condition that the goods will correspond with the description.

(b) If the sale is by sample as well as by description it is not sufficient that the bulk of the goods corresponds with the sample if the goods do not also correspond with the description.

(c) A sale of goods is not prevented from being a sale by description by reason only that, being exposed for sale or hire, they are selected by the buyer.'

The first thing to note about s 13 is that, unlike s 14, it applies to contracts for the sale of goods of all kinds and is not limited to the case of the seller who sells goods in the course of a business. So even a private seller is bound by this section. Secondly we should note that the section involves a paradox. If one contracts to sell a horse and delivers a cow, one might say that the cow does not fit the description of the horse contained in the contract and s 13 applies. But one might also say that the failure to deliver a horse is a breach of an express term of the contract. This was recognised in *Andrews Brothers v Singer* (1934). In this case the seller contracted to deliver a new Singer car under a standard printed form in which the seller sought to exclude liability for implied terms. The Court of Appeal said that the exclusion of implied terms was ineffective to exclude the seller's obligation to deliver a 'new Singer car' because that was an express term of the contract. The section obviously assumes that there will be cases in which a description is attached to the goods which is not an express term but becomes an implied condition by virtue of s 13(1). This raises two central questions: what is a sale by description? and what words are to be treated as forming part of the description?

What is a sale by description? The Act contains no definition of one. In the 19th century it was often assumed that sales by description were to be contrasted with sales of specific goods. However, this distinction has not been maintained in the post Act law. So in *Varley v Whipp* (1900) it was held that a contract to buy a specific second-hand reaping machine which was said to have been 'new the previous year' and very little used was a sale by description. In that case, though the goods were specific, they were not present before the parties at the time that the contract was made; however in *Grant v Australian Knitting Mills* (1936) the Privy Council treated the woollen undergarments which were the subject of the action as having been sold by description, even though they were before the parties at the time of the contract. The effect of this development is that virtually all contracts of sale are contracts for sale by description except for the very limited group of cases where the contract is not only for the sale of specific goods but no words of description are attached to the goods.

This makes the second question, what is the description?, very important. It might be the law that if the contract is one of sale by description and words of description are used then they inevitably form part of the description.

However, it is clear that not all words which could be regarded as words of description will be treated as part of the description of the goods for the purpose of s 13. An important case is *Ashington Piggeries v Christopher Hill* (1972). In this case the plaintiff was in the business of compounding animal feedstuffs according to formulae provided by its customers. It was invited by the defendant to compound a vitamin fortified mink food in accordance with a formula produced by the defendant. The plaintiff made it clear that it was not expert in feeding mink but suggested substitution of herring meal for one of the ingredients in the defendant's formula. Business continued on this footing for about 12 months and the plaintiff then began to use herring meal which it bought from a supplier under a contract which stated that it was 'fair average quality of the season' and was to be taken 'with all faults and defects ... at a valuation'. In fact, unknown to any of the parties, this meal contained a chemical produced by chemical reaction which was potentially harmful to all animals and particularly to mink. These facts raised the questions of whether the plaintiff was liable to the defendant and whether the supplier was liable to the plaintiff. The House of Lords held that as between the plaintiff and defendant it was not part of the description that the goods should be suitable for feeding mink. As between the plaintiff and its supplier, the House of Lords held that the goods did comply with the description 'Norwegian herring meal' which was part of the description but it was not part of the description that the goods should be 'fair average quality of the season'. The goods could not have been correctly described as 'meal' if there was no animal to which they could be safely fed. Why were the words 'fair average quality of the season' not part of the contractual description? The answer given by the House of Lords was that these words were not needed to identify the goods.

In *Harlingdon and Leinster Enterprises v Christopher Hull Fine Art* (1989) both the defendant and the plaintiff were art dealers. In 1984 the defendant was asked to sell two oil paintings which had been described in a 1980 auction catalogue as being by Gabriele Münter, an artist of the German expressionist school. The defendant contacted the plaintiff amongst others and an employee of the plaintiff had visited the defendant's gallery. Mr Hull made it clear that he was not an expert in German expressionist paintings. The plaintiffs bought one of the paintings for £6000 without making any more detailed enquiries about it. The invoice described the painting as being by Münter. In due course it was discovered to be a forgery. The majority of the Court of Appeal held that it was not part of the description of the painting that it was by Münter. The principal test relied on by the Court of Appeal was that of reliance. It was pointed out that paintings are often sold accompanied by views as to their provenance. These statements may run the whole gamut of possibilities from a binding undertaking that the painting is by a particular artist to statements that the painting is in a particular style. Successful artists are of course often copied by contemporaries, associates and pupils. It would be odd if the legal effect of every statement about the identity of the artist was treated in the same way. This is certainly not how business is done since much higher prices are paid where the seller is guaranteeing the attribution and the Court of Appeal therefore argued that it makes much better sense to ask whether the buyer has relied on the seller's statement before deciding to treat the statement as a part of the description. On any view this case is very close to the line. It appears plausibly arguable that the majority did not give enough weight to the wording of the invoice or to the fact that the buyers appear to have paid a 'warranted Münter' price. It should be noted that the buyers did not argue, as they might have done, that it was an express term of the contract that the painting was by Münter.

In this last case, the Court of Appeal held that as the attribution to Münter was the only piece of potentially descriptive labelling attached to the painting it was not a sale by description. In other cases, such as the *Ashington Piggeries* case, it would be clear that some of the words attached are words of description but it may be held that other words are not. Whether one is asking the question is there a sale by description or the question what is a description, the question whether the words are used to identify the goods and are relied on by the buyer will be highly relevant factors.

Where there has been a sale by description, the court then has to decide whether or not the goods correspond with the description. In a number of cases, courts have taken very strict views on this question. An extreme example is *Re Moore and Landauer* (1921). That was a contract for the purchase of Australian canned fruit. It was stated that the cans were in cases containing 30 tins each. The seller delivered the right number of cans but in cases which contained only 24 tins. It was not suggested that there was anything wrong with the fruit or that it made any significant difference whether the fruit was in cases of 30 or 24 cans. Nevertheless, it was held that the goods delivered did not correspond with the contract description. Similarly, in *Arcos v Ronaasen* (1933) the contract was for a quantity of staves half an inch thick. In fact, only some 5% of the staves delivered were half an inch thick, though nearly all were less than 9/16th of an inch thick. The evidence was that the staves were perfectly satisfactory for the purpose for which the buyer had bought them, that is the making of cement barrels

but the House of Lords held that the goods did not correspond with the description. In *Reardon Smith v Hansen-Tangen* (1976), Lord Wilberforce said that these decisions were excessively technical.

Section 14 of the Sale of Goods Act 1979 provides:

'(1) Except as provided by this section and section 15 below and subject to any other enactment, there is no implied condition or warranty about the quality of fitness for any particular purpose of goods supplied under a contract of sale.

(2) Where the seller sells goods in the course of a business, there is an implied condition that the goods supplied under the contract are of merchantable quality, except that there is no such condition –

(a) as regards defects specifically drawn to the buyer's attention before the contract is made; or

(b) if the buyer examines the goods before the contract is made, as regards defects which that examination ought to reveal.

(6) Goods of any kind are of merchantable quality within the meaning of subsection (2) above if they are as fit for the purpose or purposes for which goods of that kind are commonly bought as it is reasonable to expect having regard to any description applied to them, the price (if relevant) and all the other relevant circumstances.'

The obligations stated in these sub-sections, as in the parallel obligation as to fitness for purpose set out in s 14(3), apply only to a seller who sells goods in the course of a business. The Act does not say that the seller must be in the business of selling goods of that kind and indeed members of professions or central or local government will not normally be in the business of selling goods of a particular kind but may be within the scope of s 14.

It will be noted that the obligation that the goods shall be of merchantable quality applies to 'goods supplied under the contract' and not to the goods which are sold. Obviously the goods which are sold would usually be the goods which are supplied under the contract but this will not always be the case. A good example is *Wilson v Rickett Cockerell* (1954) where there was a contract for the sale of Coalite. A consignment of Coalite was delivered but included a piece of explosive which had been accidentally mixed with the Coalite and which exploded when put on the fire. This case was decided under the 1893 version of the Act which did not expressly have the reference to 'goods supplied under the contract' but the Court of Appeal held that the obligation that the goods should be of merchantable quality applied to all the goods which were supplied under the contract and of course it followed that the delivery was defective. The amendment of the wording in the present version of the Act clearly confirms the correctness of this decision.

The expression 'merchantable quality' is not one which is in modern popular usage even amongst merchants. What does it mean? The 1893 Act did not contain any definition of the expression. The present version of the Act contains the definition contained in s 14(6). In *Rogers v Parish* (1987) the Court of Appeal said that there was no need to go back to cases before 1973 when the definition was first introduced. This is no doubt correct as far as presentation of cases in court is concerned but the cases between 1893 and 1973 are useful as illustrating the sort of problems which arise. It is thought that the definition in s 14(6) is intended to encapsulate the reasoning in most of the previous cases and to resolve some unclear points rather than to reverse any major earlier decision.

A reasonable translation of the words 'merchantable quality' would mean 'commercially saleable', that is that the goods are in a condition in which a commercial seller could sell them and find a buyer. Since the goods are in fact the subject of a contract of sale in order for there to be a dispute, it is clear that the seller will have sold them and that they are, in a sense, saleable. Obviously, this cannot be the point however. The critical question is whether the goods would be saleable if the buyer knew of the qualities which they in fact possessed. Clearly this raises a series of questions depending upon what is 'wrong' with the goods. No doubt there are some goods which are so defective that nobody would buy them whatever the price. In many cases, however, goods could be sold if the price reflected what was wrong with them or could be sold to some buyers who wanted them for other purposes. In some cases, whether a buyer would buy goods knowing their condition depends upon the price. So in *BS Brown v Craiks* (1970) the buyer ordered a quantity of cloth which was to be used for making dresses. The cloth delivered was unsuitable for making dresses though it would have been suitable for industrial purposes. The buyer had not told the seller for what purpose the cloth was required. The contract price was 36.25d per yard which was higher, but not much higher, than the going rate for industrial cloth. The House of Lords held that the goods were of merchantable quality. The buyer had paid a high price in the industrial range but had not paid a 'dress price'. If the facts had been exactly the same except that the price had been 50d per yard the result would presumably have been different, since in such a case there would have been an irresistible argument that the seller was charging a dress price and therefore had to supply goods of dress quality.

In other cases it will be very important under what description the goods are sold. In *Kendall v Lillico* (1969) the plaintiffs bought animal feeding stuff for pheasants which was contaminated with a substance which was contained in Brazilian groundnut extraction which was one of the ingredients which made up the feeding stuff. The defendant settled the claim of the plaintiffs and claimed over against the suppliers. Although the suppliers had supplied Brazilian groundnut extraction which was contaminated, they were not supplying goods of unmerchantable quality because the Brazilian groundnut extraction was perfectly suitable as a basis for feeding stuff for poultry. The purpose for which the goods bought are to be used is of critical importance in relation to s 14(3) as shall be seen below. It is also important, however, as to s 14(2). If the extraction had been sold as poultry feed, it would not have been merchantable because feed which is poisonous to poultry cannot be sold as poultry feed. If sold as animal food, it would be a completely different matter since the extraction was perfectly suitable for feeding to many, though not to all, animals. This illustrates a very important general proposition, which is that if the goods have a number of potential purposes, they will usually be of merchantable quality if they can be used for one of the purposes for which such goods are commonly used, unless they are sold under a contract description which points to a single purpose for which they cannot effectively be used. The difference in this respect between *BS Brown v Craiks* and *Kendall v Lillico* is that in *Brown* there were two purposes, one of which commanded a higher price than the other, whereas in *Kendall* the various purposes appear to have commanded much the same price.

It would appear that the decisions discussed above would be the same under the 1979 statutory definition. In *Aswan Engineering v Lupdine* (1987) the Court of Appeal rejected an argument that the wording of s 14(6) meant that the goods were not of merchantable quality unless they were fit for all the purposes for which goods of that kind were commonly bought.

There has been considerable discussion about the relationship between the requirement of merchantable quality and the realities of buying new cars. It is extremely probable that a new car will have some defects. Normally the buyer will in fact expect to get these defects put right under the manufacturer's warranty. Does this affect the seller's obligation to deliver a car of merchantable quality? It appears not. In *Bernstein v Pamson Motors* the plaintiff bought a new car and some three weeks later when it had done only 140 miles, it broke down because the engine completely seized up. It was held that this made the car unmerchantable. Similarly in *Rogers v Parish* a new Range Rover had, during its first six months of life, a whole series of defects as to the engine, gear box, body and oil seals. The defects did not make the car unsafe or unroadworthy and each of them was put right but the Court of Appeal held that there was a breach of the requirement of merchantable quality. The Court of Appeal thought that the manufacturer's obligations under the guarantee were irrelevant to the legal position of buyer and seller. Any argument that the buyer must expect some defects in a new car could hardly apply on the facts of either of these cases because no buyer would expect a car to seize up after 140 miles or to require a replacement engine or gear box in the first six months of its life. These principles are equally applicable in principle to second-hand cars (or indeed other second-hand goods), though obviously the reasonable expectations of a buyer of second-hand goods will not be identical with the reasonable expectations of the buyer of new goods.

In *Shine v General Guarantee Corporation* (1988) the subject of the sale was a 1981 Fiat X1-9 sports car which was offered for sale second-hand in August 1982 at £4595. The evidence was that this was the going rate for such a car in good condition. In fact, for some 24 hours in January 1982, the car had been totally submerged in water and had been written off by the insurance company. The Court of Appeal held that the car was not of merchantable quality since no-one would have bought the car knowing of its condition without at least a substantial reduction of the price. It will be seen that this reason in effect, in a case of this kind, requires the seller either to lower the price or to draw the buyer's attention to the relevant defect.

It will be noted that the obligation in s 14(2) of the Sale of Goods Act 1979 is excluded either as regards a defect which is specifically drawn to the buyer's attention before the contract is made or, where the buyer examines the goods before the contract is made, to defects which that examination ought to have revealed. The latter proviso requires a further word of comment. Of course, examination does not exclude liability for defects which would not have been revealed by careful examination. Many of the defects discussed in this chapter are of this kind. Furthermore, this section does not require the buyer to examine the goods so he or she is not prevented from complaining when he or she does not examine at all the defects which a reasonable examination would have revealed. The practical effect of this is that the buyer ought either to carry out a careful examination or no examination at all. To carry out a cursory examination is likely to produce the worst of both worlds.

The Sale and Supply of Goods Act 1994 substitutes a new s 14(2) for the existing s 14(2) of the Act. The 1979 and 1994 versions of s 14(2) are set out below.

Sale of Goods Act 1979

14 Implied terms about quality or fitness

(2)   Where the seller sells goods in the course of a business, there is an implied condition that the goods supplied under the contract are of merchantable quality, except that there is no such condition –

> (a) as regards defects specifically drawn to the buyer's attention before the contract is made; or

> (b) if the buyer examines the goods before the contract is made, as regards defects which that examination ought to reveal.

Sale and Supply of Goods Act 1994

14 Implied terms about quality or fitness

(2)   Where the seller sells goods in the course of a business, there is an implied term that the goods supplied under the contract are of satisfactory quality.

(A) For the purposes of this Act, goods are of satisfactory quality if they meet the standard that a reasonable person would regard as satisfactory, taking account of any description of the goods, the price (if relevant) and all the other relevant circumstances.

(B) For the purposes of this Act, the quality of goods includes their state and condition and the following (among others) are in appropriate cases aspects of the quality of goods.

> (a) fitness for all the purposes for which goods of the kind in question are commonly supplied.

> (b) appearance and finish.

> (c) freedom from minor defects.

> (d) safety, and

> (e) durability.

(C) The term implied by subsection (2) above does not extend to any matter making the quality of goods unsatisfactory -

> (a) which is specifically drawn to the buyer's attention before the contract is made.

> (b) where the buyer examines the goods before the contract is made, which that examination ought to reveal, or

> (c) in the case of a contract for sale by sample, which would have been apparent on a reasonable examination of the sample.'

The new version makes a number of changes. Perhaps the most obvious is the replacement of the words 'merchantable quality' by the words 'satisfactory quality'. The thinking behind this change was that the expression 'merchantable quality' is not used anywhere, either in English law or in colloquial English, except in the context of the Sale of Goods Act. It is, therefore, an expression which is understood only by lawyers specialising in sale of goods law. It was thought that buyers and sellers who were told that the goods must be of merchantable quality would not get much guidance from this statement. This may be agreed, but the problem was to find an appropriate substitute. The Act is based on a Law Commission Report of 1987 in which it had been suggested that 'merchantable quality' should become 'acceptable quality'. It may perhaps be thought to be of relatively little importance which of these words is used. Although 'acceptable' and 'satisfactory' are both words which are used every day and which most people will understand, they do not by themselves help buyers and sellers to know at all clearly where the line is to be drawn between acceptable and unacceptable and satisfactory and unsatisfactory goods. So, this change by itself is really almost entirely cosmetic.

Some of the textual changes in the 1994 version are simply rearrangements of provisions which appear in the 1979 version. So, the exceptions from a liability to deliver goods of a satisfactory quality where the defect is specifically drawn to the buyer's attention or the buyer has examined the goods and that examination ought to have revealed the actual defects which are contained in s 14(2)(a) and (b) are now to be found in s 14(2)(C)(a) and (b). The substantial changes relate to the definition of 'satisfactory quality'.

Part of the definition in s 14(6) of the 1979 Act now appears in s 14(2)(A), that is the reference to 'taking account of any description of the goods, the price (if relevant) and all the other relevant circumstances'. One change relates to the wording of that part of s 14(6) which refers to goods being 'as fit for the purpose or purposes for which goods of that kind are commonly bought as it is reasonable to expect'. The decision in *Aswan Engineering v Lupdine* (1987) that goods were of merchantable quality within this definition if they were fit for any one of the purposes for which they were commonly bought has in effect been reversed by the present provision contained in s 14(2)(B)(a) which means that goods will not be of satisfactory quality unless they are fit for all the purposes for which such goods are commonly supplied. This might appear a rather technical change but, in fact, it is of considerable practical importance. It substantially reduces the need to rely on s 14(3) and shows that the seller knows the buyer's purpose in buying the goods. Where goods are bought for one of a number of common purposes, the buyer will be able to rely on s 14(2) if they are not fit for all those purposes even, it would appear, if they are fit for the purpose for which the buyer requires them. If they are fit for the purpose for which the buyer actually requires them, the buyer will usually suffer no loss but it is likely that, sooner or later, a case will occur where the buyer tries to get out of the contract because of some movement in the market and uses this as an excuse. Suppose, for instance, that the buyer is a dairy farmer who buys the goods for the purposes of feeding to cows and that the same material is commonly fed to pigs but that the particular batch, though perfectly suitable for feeding cows, will not do for pigs. It would appear that if the buyer realises this at the time of delivery, he could probably reject under the present wording.

The other changes which are made are contained in s 14(2)(B)(c), (d) and (e). These add further detail to the definition of merchantable/satisfactory quality. There were very few reported cases which involved consideration of whether these issues fell within the statutory definition as to quality. It was said that there are a large number of small cases coming before county courts or the arbitration process in small claims courts where different judges were taking different views as to where to draw the line. This is obviously a matter of particular importance to consumers. Is a consumer who buys a new washing machine and finds it has a major scratch across the paint work bound to accept it; is a consumer whose washing machine stops and is irreparable after 13 months' use entitled to complain that he expected to get three to five years' repairable use out of the washing machine? Is a combination of minor defects on your new motor car sufficient to make it unsatisfactory? The wording of the new section must make an affirmative answer to these questions much more likely.

6.4.3   Fitness for purpose

Section 14(3) of the Sale of Goods Act 1979 provides:

'Where the seller sells goods in the course of a business and the buyer, expressly or by implication, makes known –

(a) to the seller, or

(b) where the purchase price or part of it is payable by instalments and the goods were previously sold by a credit-broker to the seller, to that credit-broker, any particular purpose for which the goods are being bought, there is an implied condition that the goods supplied under the contract are reasonably fit for that purpose, whether or not that is a purpose for which such goods are commonly supplied, except where the circumstances show that the buyer does not rely, or that it is unreasonable for him to rely, on the skill or judgment of the seller or credit-broker.'

In the 1893 version of the Act the implied term about fitness for purpose was s 14(1) and the implied term about merchantable quality was s 14(2). This change in the order may reflect a change in view as to which of the obligations is primary and which is secondary. In practice, buyers who complain of the goods being defective very commonly rely on both merchantable quality and fitness for purpose arguments and there is a significant degree of overlap. The two major differences between s 14(2) and s 14(3) are that where goods are sold for a number of purposes, the buyer may have a better chance of succeeding under s 14(3) if she has disclosed the particular purpose for which she requires the goods to the seller; on the other hand, to establish liability under s 14(3) the buyer has to show that she has relied on the skill and judgment of the seller. In many cases this may easily be inferred but there is no such requirement at all in relation to the obligation of merchantable quality under s 14(2). A layman reading s 14(3) for the first time might be forgiven for thinking that in order to be able to rely on it the buyer must do something to draw to the seller's attention the purpose for which she requires the goods. However, this is not the way in which the section has been construed. Where goods are produced for a single purpose, the court will easily infer that the goods are being bought for that purpose even though all that the buyer does is to ask for goods of that kind. So it has been held that to buy beer or milk makes it clear that one is buying it for drinking; that to buy tinned salmon makes it clear that it has been bought for the purpose of being eaten; that to buy a hot water bottle makes it clear that it has been bought for the purpose of being filled with very hot water and put in a bed; and to buy a catapult makes it clear that it has been bought for the purpose of catapulting stones. In other words, if there is a single purpose, it is easy to infer that goods must be fit for that purpose and if the seller is a seller of goods of that kind it is easy to infer that the buyer is relying on the seller's skill and judgment.

It should be emphasised that liability under this sub-section, as indeed under s 14(2), turns on the goods not being of merchantable quality or fitness for purpose respectively. It is no defence for the seller to show that he or she did all that could possibly have been done to ensure that the goods were fit for the purpose or of merchantable quality if he has failed to do so.

The position is different where goods have more than one purpose. We may distinguish at least two variants on this possibility. One is where goods are used for a purpose which is a specialised and more demanding version of the standard purpose. Suppose that a buyer is buying pig food to feed to a herd of pigs which have super-sensitive stomachs. Suppose further that the buyer orders a pig food from a supplier who supplies pig food which would be entirely suitable for pigs with normally robust digestions. In that case if that is all that has happened the supplier will not be in breach of contract since although what has happened has revealed the ordinary purpose for which the goods were required, it does not reveal the extraordinary requirements of the buyer. In order to be able to complain that the pig food was not suitable for the pigs, the buyer would need to make it clear to the supplier precisely what the requirements were.

Alternatively the goods may be capable of being used for a range of purposes which are different. For instance as in *Kendall v Lillico* (1969) where the goods were suitable for feeding cattle but not suitable for feeding poultry. A buyer could recover on these facts if, but only if, he made it clear to the seller that the purpose was to buy food for feeding poultry. In fact, in that case, it was held that the seller did have a sufficient knowledge of the buyer's purpose to make him liable and this case is therefore a good example of goods which were merchantable because they were commercially saleable as cattle feed but which were not fit for the buyer's purpose. Similarly in *Ashington Piggeries v Christopher Hill* the goods did comply with the contract description so that there was no liability under s 13 but it was held that the buyer had adequately disclosed to the seller his intention to feed the compound to mink and therefore found liability on s 14(3).

6.4.4	Sales by sample

Section 15 of the Sale of Goods Act 1979 provides:

'(1) A contract of sale is a contract for sale by sample where there is an express or implied term to that effect in the contract.

(2) In the case of a contract for sale by sample there is an implied condition –

(a) that the bulk will correspond with the sample in quality;

(b) that the buyer will have a reasonable opportunity of comparing the bulk with the sample;

(c) that the goods will be free from any defect, rendering them unmerchantable, which would not be apparent on reasonable examination of the sample.

(3) In subsection (2)(c) above "unmerchantable" is to be construed in accordance with section 14(6) above.'

Sales by sample are common in the sale of bulk commodities because a seller can display to the buyer a sample of what he has and the buyer can agree that she will take so many pounds or tons. The sample here in effect largely replaces the need for any description by words of the goods and it is therefore natural to imply, as in s 15(2)(a), a term that the bulk will correspond with the sample in quality.

The terms set out in ss 13, 14 and 15 of the Sale of Goods Act 1979 are the basic implied terms. In principle, there seems to be no reason why the general principles about implication of terms in the general law of contract should not apply. So, if a contract of sale is made against a background of a particular trade or local custom, it will be open for one party to seek to show that the custom exists, is reasonable and contracts of sale made in this particular context are regarded by those in the trade or living in the locality as subject to this implied term.

6.4.5   Other implied terms

Similarly, there is no reason why a party should not seek to show that in a particular contract a term is to be implied in order to give business efficacy to the contract. Perhaps the best example of an implied term which is not explicitly set out in the Act but which has been recognised is shown in *Mash & Murrell v Joseph I Emmanuel* (1961). In this case there was a contract for the sale of Cyprus potatoes cif Liverpool. On arrival in Liverpool the potatoes were found to be uneatable but the evidence was that they were eatable on loading in Limassol. Diplock J said that liability turned on the reason why the potatoes were uneatable. There were various possible reasons such as bad stowage or inadequate ventilation during the voyage. These would not have been the seller's fault and the risk of these possibilities would pass to the buyer on shipment, leaving the buyer to an action against the carrier. However, one possibility was that the potatoes, although eatable when shipped, were not in a fit state to withstand a normal voyage from Cyprus to Liverpool. Diplock J said that it was an implied term of the contract in the circumstances that the goods would be fit to withstand an ordinary journey. The Court of Appeal differed with the conclusion that Diplock J reached but not with his analysis of this point.

6.4.6   Rights and remedies

The Law Commission produced a consultative document in 1983 and a full report in 1987. The report shows that there is a tension between the definition of the seller's obligations which we have just discussed and the buyer's remedies for breach of those obligations which is discussed in Chapter 10. Under the existing framework of the Sale of Goods Act, each of the implied obligations in ss 13, 14 and 15 is said to be a condition and, as will be explained in Chapter 10, this is taken to mean that if there is any breach of the obligation the buyer is entitled to reject the goods. Court have sometimes thought that although the goods were defective, the defects were not of a kind which ought to have entitled the buyer to reject the goods. The leading example of this is *Cehave v Bremer* (1976). That was a contract for the sale of citrus pulp pellets which were intended by the buyer to be used for animal feed. There was damage to the goods and the buyer purported to reject them. There was then a forced sale by the Admiralty Court in Holland at which the buyer rebought the goods at a much lower price and used them for feeding cattle. In these circumstances, the Court of Appeal was looking for a good reason to find that the buyer was not entitled to reject. What it did was to hold that the defect in the goods did not make them unmerchantable though it clearly reduced their value somewhat. The problem with this approach is that although it may be perfectly reasonable to restrict the buyer's right to reject the goods, it does not usually follow from this that the buyer should be left without any remedy at all. Often the buyer ought to have a remedy at least in money terms to reflect the difference in value between what he contracted for and what he has received. There is also an important difference as far as rejection is concerned between consumers and those who buy goods commercially, particularly those who buy goods for resale. It is often perfectly reasonable to say to such buyers that they ought to put up with the goods and be satisfied with a reduction in price; it is much less commonly reasonable to say this to a consumer. This perception underlies further changes made by the Sale and Supply of Goods Act 1994 which are discussed in Chapter 10.

6.5   Liability in tort

This book is primarily concerned with liability in contract between buyer and seller but completeness requires some mention of claims which the buyer may have against other people, especially the manufacturer. In some circumstances the buyer may have a contract claim against the manufacturer. Sometimes indeed the manufacturer and seller are the same person and in that case, of course, no problem arises. In other cases, although the manufacturer and seller are not the same person, the manufacturer may have entered into a separate contract with the buyer. The most obvious way in which such a contract might come about is by the operation of the manufacturer's guarantee. Most consumer durables are now issued accompanied by a guarantee in which the manufacturer typically promises to repair or replace the goods if they do not work within a period, generally a year.

Curiously enough, there is surprisingly little authority in English law as to whether manufacturers' guarantees give rise to a contract between manufacturer and customer. The leading case is the classic one of *Carlill v Carbolic Smokeball Company* (1893). In this case the plaintiff, Mrs Carlill, bought a smokeball manufactured by the defendant from a retail chemist, relying on elaborate advertising by the defendant in which it offered to pay £100 to anyone who used the smokeball according to the directions and then caught flu. Typically modern manufacturers' advertising tends to be couched in much less contractual language. The technical problem with giving contractual force to the manufacturer's guarantee is that often customers will not know of the guarantee until after they have bought the goods and further they will often not have done anything in exchange for the guarantee. So there may be difficulty in satisfying the technical requirement of the English law of contract that promises are only binding if they are supported by consideration.

Of course the manufacturer will often be liable in contract to the person to whom it has supplied the goods and the buyer may therefore be able to start off a chain of actions in which the buyer sues the retailer, the retailer sues the wholesaler and the wholesaler sues the manufacturer. By this means, if the fault in the goods is due to the manufacturer, liability can often be shunted back to it by a series of actions. However, this would not always be possible. The manufacturer may in fact be outside the country and difficult to sue; someone may have successfully sold the goods subject to an exclusion or limitation clause which prevents liability being passed up the chain or it may be that the chain breaks down in some other way.

The question arises whether the buyer can sue the manufacturer direct in tort. Before 1932 it was widely believed that the answer to this question was 'No' and that the only actions in respect of defective goods were contractual actions. This was clearly revealed to be wrong by the majority decision of the House of Lords in *Donoghue v Stevenson* (1932).

Although it is common to talk of liability in terms of manufacturers, liability in fact rests upon any person who produces or handles goods in circumstances where it is reasonably foreseeable that carelessness in the handling of the goods will cause physical injury or property damage and there is in fact carelessness. So in appropriate cases liability can attach to wholesalers, repairers, those who service goods and indeed on sellers. So for instance a seller of a motor car would normally do a detailed check on the car before delivering it in order to discover defects. The seller who failed to do this would be liable in tort not only to the buyer (who has in any case an action in contract) but to anyone else foreseeably injured, for example a member of the buyer's family (who would of course have no contract action). The defendant will not be liable in such an action unless she can be shown to have been negligent. This is a fundamental difference between tort actions and contract actions which do not require any proof of negligence.

There is another major limit on liability in tort. As the law is currently understood, it seems that plaintiffs can only recover where they have suffered either physical injury or property damage. So if a manufacturer of a motor car negligently installs a braking system and the plaintiff has an accident and is injured, the plaintiff should be able to recover but if the plaintiff discovers that the braking system is defective and stops driving the car before having an accident, he will not be able to recover in tort against the manufacturer for the loss of value of the car because it is not as good a car as it was thought to be. To put it another way, actions for shoddy goods lie in contract and not in tort.

The difficulty of proving negligence in certain types of defective product have led to calls for the adoption of a regime in which the liability of the manufacturer should be strict, that is should depend solely on the establishment that the goods were defective and not on a requirement to prove that the manufacturer was at fault. Both the Law Commission (in 1977) and the Royal Commission on Civil Liberty and Compensation for Death or Personal Injury, usually called the Pearson Commission (in March 1978) recommended statutory change to introduce such a regime. In July 1985 the European Community adopted a product liability directive and Parliament enacted Part I of the Consumer Protection Act 1987 which from 1 March 1988 introduced a product liability regime into English law. This Act does not remove any of the existing remedies which somebody damaged by defective goods may have. What it does do is to introduce an additional set of remedies. In practice, it is likely that plaintiffs injured by defective goods after 1 March 1988 will seek to argue for liability both in contract or tort under the old law and under the Consumer Protection Act. Although where the Act applies plaintiffs would usually be better off suing under the Act than in an action in tort, they would often still be better off pursuing a contract action, if they have one.

Many of the changes which have taken place in the law discussed in this chapter in recent years have been driven by consumerism, that is the development of consumers as an organised group able to lobby for laws which protect their interests. One of the major problems with protecting the consumer is that changes in the substantive law of contract and tort do not help very much if the sums at issue are small and the cost of using lawyers is large. One way of dealing with this has been to provide special systems for trying small consumer cases in county courts from which lawyers are excluded. Another important development has been the building up of criminal law in the field of consumer protection. The great advantage of this from the consumer's point of view is that it has no cost since the operation of the criminal law is a service provided by the state. The disadvantage is that usually one does not receive financial compensation for one's own particular loss though in certain cases the courts have been given power in the course of criminal proceedings to make compensation orders for those who have been injured by criminal trading behaviour. Nevertheless, at the prevention level, it is clear that the criminal law is of fundamental importance. Dishonest second-hand car dealers are much more likely to refrain from turning back the mileometers of cars they sell because of the fear that they may be caught and prosecuted than because of the fear that a customer to whom they sell a car will sue.

The notion that criminal law had a role to play in the fair regulation of the market is very old since it goes back to rules designed to produce fair weights and measures which have existed since medieval times. Again it is not possible here to do more than pick out a few salient points.

The most important Act in practice is the Trade Descriptions Act 1968 which gives rise to over 30,000 prosecutions a year. This makes it a criminal offence to apply a false trade description to goods in the course of a trade or business or to offer to supply any goods to which a false trade description is applied. The concept of trade description is very wide and has been treated as embracing eulogistic statements such as describing a car as a beautiful car or in 'immaculate condition' which would probably be regarded as not giving rise to liability in contract at all. Section 11 contains elaborate provisions about false or misleading indications as to the price of goods which have been replaced by Part III of the Consumer Protection Act 1987. Section 20(1) of that Act introduces a general offence of giving misleading price information and establishes a code of practice.

6.6 Criminal liability

Defective Goods

This chapter, which is perhaps the most important in this section, considers the remedies which may arise where the goods supplied are defective.

There are numerous possibilities:

1   Liability in contract
    (a) express terms;
    (b) misrepresentation;
    (c) implied terms.

2   Liability in tort
    (a) negligence
    (b) strict liability under the Consumer Protection Act 1987.

3   Criminal liability, for instance under the Trade Description Acts.

Note that 1(c) above is particularly important for courses on sale of goods because it is the one ground of liability which rests exclusively on the Sale of Goods Act.

The main part of Chapter 6 is devoted to considering the situations in which the buyer has a contractual remedy against the seller on the grounds that the goods are not as the seller contracted.

•   Express terms

    The theoretical test is usually formulated by asking what the parties intended. If the parties had expressed what they intended, the test would be easy to apply. If the parties express no intention, the court, in effect, substitutes its own view of what the parties, as reasonable people, probably intended.

•   Misrepresentation

    A misrepresentation is a statement of fact made by one party to the contract to the other party before the contract is made which induces that other party to enter into the contract but is not characterised as being a term of the contract.

- Implied terms

  The implied terms laid down for contracts of sale of goods are contained in ss 13, 14 and 15 of the Sale of Goods Act 1979, as amended by the Sale and Supply of Goods Act 1994.

Liability in tort

Liability in tort rests upon any person who produces or handles goods in circumstances where it is reasonably foreseeable that carelessness in the handling of the goods will cause physical injury or property damage and there is in fact carelessness (*Donoghue v Stevenson* (1932)). So, in appropriate cases, liability can attach to wholesalers, repairers, those who service goods and indeed on sellers. However, it seems that plaintiffs can only recover where they have suffered either physical injury or property damage.

Criminal liability

The most important Act in practice is the Trade Descriptions Act 1968. This makes it a criminal offence to apply a false trade description to goods in the course of a trade or business or to offer to supply any goods to which a false trade description is applied.

Chapter 7

Exemption and Limitation Clauses

During the last 150 years English law has come, principally by means of developing the implied terms discussed in Chapter 6, to impose substantial obligations on the seller particularly as to the quality of the goods. A natural response of sellers is to seek to qualify these obligations by inserting into the contract terms which seek to exclude, reduce or limit liability. Over the last 50 years English law has come to impose very considerable restrictions on the ability of the seller to do this even where the seller can persuade the buyer to agree to a contract which contains such a clause or clauses. This chapter will be concerned with explaining the devices which have been developed for this purpose.

It is important, however, to start by emphasising that such clauses are remarkably heterogeneous in form. It would be a mistake to assume that the underlying policy questions in relation to all types of clause are identical. Most clauses operate so as to qualify the results of the seller breaking the contract. This may be done in a wide variety of ways.

(a) The contract may provide that none of the implied terms set out in Chapter 6 shall be implied.

(b) The contract may provide that if the seller breaks the contract his liability should be limited to a particular sum, say £100.

(c) The contract may provide that if the seller breaks the contract he should only be liable to replace or repair the goods.

(d) The contract may provide that the seller shall not be liable for particular kinds of loss. So, for instance, contracts often provide that the seller is not liable for consequential loss so that if he fails to deliver the goods he will not be liable for loss of profit which the buyer suffers through not having the goods.

(e) The contract may provide that if the buyer wishes to complain he must do so within, say, 14 days.

(f) The contract may provide that if the buyer wishes to complain he must do so by means of arbitration.

(g) The contract may provide that if the goods are defective the buyer is not to be entitled to reject them but only to have the price reduced, and so on.

On the other hand a clause may operate to define what it is that the seller is agreeing to do. Suppose an auctioneer of horses says that one of the horses which is up for sale is 'warranted sound except for hunting'. This could be regarded as excluding liability if the horse would not hunt but it is more properly regarded as making it clear that the seller is not assuming any liability for the soundness of the horse as a hunter though it is warranting that the horse is sound in other respects. This distinction is fundamental since there is a great difference between saying from the outset that one does not assume an obligation and accepting an obligation and then seeking to qualify the consequences of it. This distinction was recognised in a different context in *Renton v Palmyra* (1957).

Common law and statute have developed rules which control the ability of the parties to exclude or qualify liability. Although as regards contracts of sale the statutory regime is much more extensive and important it is convenient to consider the common law position first.

| 7.2 | **The position at common law** | The position at common law is such that where there exists a contractual document which has been signed by the parties, the basic rule is that the parties can be taken to have agreed to what the contract means even though they have never read it and would not understand it if they had. |

7.2 The position at common law

The position at common law is such that where there exists a contractual document which has been signed by the parties, the basic rule is that the parties can be taken to have agreed to what the contract means even though they have never read it and would not understand it if they had.

7.2.1 Is the excluding clause part of the contract?

More difficult questions arise where there is no signed contract but it is argued that excluding terms have been incorporated into the contract by notices or the delivery of non-contractual documents like tickets. There is no doubt that in certain circumstances one can incorporate terms into a contract by displaying a notice at the point at which the contract is made or, as on the railway, by handing over a ticket which contains references to the contractual conditions. These conditions need not be set out in the ticket provided they are sufficiently identified. So almost ever since the railways began tickets have borne on the front the words 'For conditions see back' and on the back a reference to the company's timetable. In principle this is perfectly acceptable. Similarly, there is no reason why one of the parties should not say by notice or ticket that all the contracts it makes are subject to the rules of a particular trade association. The critical test was that laid down in *Parker v South Eastern Railway* (1877), that is, whether or not in the circumstances the delivery of the ticket is sufficient notice of the terms referred to on it. In principle, it appears that the standard of reasonable notice is variable, so that the more surprising the term, the greater the notice required. So in

Thornton v Shoe Lane Parking (1971) the plaintiff wished to park his car in the defendant's multi-storey car park. Outside the park was a notice stating 'All cars parked at owner's risk'. The ticket she received contained references to terms displayed inside. Inside the car park there were notices which purported to exclude not only liability for damage to cars but also liability for damage to drivers. The Court of Appeal held that in the circumstances the plaintiff was not bound by it because he had not been given adequate notice so that he could make a real choice whether to park his car in that car park or somewhere else. It was obviously an important part of this reasoning that whereas car parks very commonly carry notices excluding liability for damaged cars, it is much less usual for them to carry notices excluding liability for damage to drivers. In the later case of *Interfoto Picture Library v Stiletto Visual Programs* (1988) the Court of Appeal stated, as a general proposition, that where contracts were made by processes which involved the delivery by one side to the other of standard printed terms, the author of the terms was under a general duty to draw to the attention of the other side any terms which were unusual. Of course it follows that in a contested case it may be necessary to produce evidence of what terms are usual in a particular profession, trade or industry.

The principal tool used by common law to control exemption clauses has been the process of construction, that is the process by which the court construes (decides the meaning of) the contract. Courts have traditionally approached this process of construction by making a number of assumptions. These assumptions may often overlap but are probably analytically distinct. So it is assumed that it is unlikely for one party to agree that the other party shall not be liable even where she is negligent; similarly it is thought that the more serious a breach of contract has been committed by one party, the less likely it is that the other party will have agreed in advance that such a serious breach does not matter. The thrust of both of these assumptions is that if one party wishes to exclude its liability for negligence or a serious breach of the contract it needs to say so in clear terms. A third assumption which overlaps with these two but may have separate application is the *contra proferentem* principle which says that if one party has drafted or is responsible for the drafting of a document and the document is ambiguous then any ambiguities should be resolved in favour of the other party.

It has also been said that where one party has only entered into the contract because she has been misled by the other about the effect of the exclusion clauses then the exclusion

7.2.2   Limitations imposed by the common law on the effectiveness of exemption clauses

clauses are without effect. This principle would obviously apply where the misrepresentation was fraudulent but it seems to apply even if the misrepresentation was entirely innocent (see *Curtis v Chemical Cleaning and Dyeing Company* (1951)).

It is not clear whether the principle that surprising clauses should be specifically drawn to the attention of the other party applies where the document is signed. The cases in which it has arisen have not been cases of signed documents but the underlying rationale would seem to be equally applicable in such a case.

7.3	**Statutory control of exemption and limitation clauses**

There is a history of statutory control of exemption clauses going back to the middle of the 19th century when there were controls over the terms on which carriers of goods could seek to exclude liability. It is only much more recently, however, that general statutory regulation of such clauses has become accepted as an appropriate technique. A major step was the Supply of Goods (Implied Terms) Act 1973 which made major changes in the possibility of excluding clauses in the fields of sale and hire-purchase. These changes were re-enacted but with major additions in the Unfair Contract Terms Act 1977. This Act has provisions dealing specifically with contracts for the supply of goods and also provisions of general application which may affect contracts for the supply of goods.

7.3.1	Unfair Contract Terms Act ss 6 and 7

Both ss 6 and 7 of the Unfair Contract Terms Act deal with clauses which seek to exclude liability for failure to transfer ownership, and this has already been discussed in Chapter 4. The main thrust of the sections is in relation to the implied terms as to the quality of the goods. Section 6 lays down the same rule for contracts of hire-purchase as for contracts of sale. Section 7 lays down the same rules for other contracts under which ownership or possession is to pass. For simplicity of exposition the rest of this account talks of contracts of sale but there is a uniform regime for all of these contracts.

Section 6 divides contracts into two groups; those where the buyer is dealing as a consumer and those where it is not. Where the buyer is dealing as a consumer ss 13, 14 and 15 cannot be excluded. If the buyer is not dealing as a consumer ss 13, 14 and 15 can be excluded if the term satisfies the requirement of reasonableness. In effect, therefore, the implied terms become mandatory in consumer sales and even in commercial sales the seller will only be able to exclude them if he is able to satisfy a court that the term excluding or limiting liability was in all the circumstances, reasonable. The operation of this scheme obviously involves two questions:

(a) who is a consumer, and

(b) what is reasonable in this context?

The answer to the first question is to be found in s 12 which provides:

'(1) A party to a contract "deals as consumer" in relation to another party if –

(a) he neither makes the contract in the course of a business nor holds himself out as doing so; and

(b) the other party does make the contract in the course of a business; and

(c) in the case of a contract governed by the Law of Sale of Goods or Hire Purchase, or by section 7 of this Act, the goods passing under or in pursuance of the contract are of a type ordinarily supplied for private use or consumption.

(2) But on a sale by auction or by competitive tender the buyer is not in any circumstances to be regarded as dealing as consumer.'

Setting aside then the special cases of auction and competitive tender which can never be consumer sales, it can be seen that a consumer sale requires three elements: a consumer buyer, a non-consumer seller and consumer goods. So a sale by one consumer to another is not for this purpose a consumer sale. In any case, of course, a consumer seller does not attract liability under s 14 of the Sale of Goods Act. It is thought, however, that a consumer seller who seeks to exclude liability under s 13 of the Sale of Goods Act would be subject to the test of reasonableness. There is no definition of consumer goods and there are obvious marginal cases – for example, someone who buys a van intending to use it as a means of family transport. It is thought that courts will take a broad view of consumer goods for this purpose. The most difficult question is whether the buyer is making the contract in the course of a business or holding himself out as doing so. There are many cases where a buyer buys goods partly for business and partly for non-business use. A typical example is the purchase of a car by a self-employed person. It is very likely that such a person would use the car substantially for family and social purposes but it is also very likely that for tax reasons it would be bought through the business. Many commentators had assumed that this would have made the transaction a non-consumer transaction but the contrary view was taken by the Court of Appeal in *R & B Customs Brokers v United Dominions Trust* (1988). In this case the plaintiff was a limited company, owned and controlled by Mr and Mrs Bell. The company conducted the business of shipping brokers and freight forwarding agents. It decided to acquire a Colt Shogun four wheel drive vehicle which turned out to be defective. The question was whether the transaction was a consumer transaction, in which case the exclusion clauses in the defendant's standard printed form would be totally ineffective. The defendant argued that the transaction must be a business transaction because companies only exist for the purpose of doing business. (This is obviously a stronger case on this point than if the plaintiffs had not incorporated themselves but had simply done business as a partnership having no separate legal personality.) The Court of Appeal held, however, that the company was a consumer and not a business for the purpose of s 12. The principal reason for this decision was that the company was not in the business of buying cars.

The second question is what is reasonable? Section 11(1) says that whether the term is reasonable depends on:

'Having regard to the circumstances which were, or ought reasonably to have been, known to or in the contemplation of the parties when the contract was made.'

Section 11(4) provides:

'Where by reference to a contract term or notice a person seeks to restrict liability to a specified sum of money, and the question arises (under this or any other Act) whether the term or notice satisfies the requirement of reasonableness, regard shall be had in particular (but without prejudice to subsection (2) above in the case of contract terms) to:

(a) the resources which he could expect to be available to him for the purpose of meeting the liability should it arise; and

(b) how far it was open to him to cover himself by insurance.'

This provision gives statutory force to the general notion that a clause limiting liability has a better chance of being treated as reasonable than a clause which seeks to exclude liability altogether. But this is only the case under s 11(4) if the seller can show that the limit of liability is reasonably related to the resources which he has available. In other words, a small business can more readily defend a low limit of liability than a large one. However, many liabilities are of course insured and it is therefore relevant to consider whether the seller can cover itself by insurance. In general it is difficult for sellers effectively to insure against the cost of replacing the goods but they can insure against the possibility of having to pay damages for loss caused by defective goods. However, such insurance is commonly written with a premium which is calculated in relation to the maximum which the insurer will cover. It would seem that it is probably open to a seller to show that it was not economically possible for her to insure for liability for more than, say, £100,000 for any one claim. This would be relevant to the decision as to whether limitation of liability was reasonable under s 11(4).

The court is also required to have regard to five guidelines which are set out in the second schedule to the Act. These are:

'(a) the strength of the bargaining positions of the parties relative to each other, taking into account (among other things) alternative means by which the customer's requirements could have been met;

(b) whether the customer received an inducement to agree to the term or in accepting it had an opportunity of entering into a similar contract with other persons, but without having to accept a similar term;

(c) whether the customer knew or ought reasonably to have known of the existence and extent of the term (having regard, among other things, to any custom of the trade and any previous course of dealing between the parties);

(d) where the term excludes or restricts any relevant liability if some condition is not complied with, whether it was reasonable at the time of the contract to expect that compliance with that condition could be practicable;

(e) whether the goods were manufactured, processed or adapted to the special order of the customer.'

As far as (a) is concerned the more equal the bargaining position of the parties the more likely it is that the court could be persuaded that the clause is reasonable. Similarly, if one party is in a monopoly position it is likely to have considerable difficulty in persuading the court that the terms are reasonable, whereas if there is a wide range of possible suppliers this is likely to point in the other direction and particularly if some of them offer more favourable terms. There is an overlap here with (b), so that if a buyer has a choice of paying a higher price and getting a contract without exclusion clauses, whether that is from the same seller or different sellers the buyer who chooses the lower price may find that the clause is regarded as reasonable.

Guideline (c) calls for some comment. If the term is incorporated in the contract it must in some sense be the case that the buyer knows or has the opportunity of knowing it. It seems clear that more is required for the guideline to apply. It is thought that what is envisaged here is the case of an experienced buyer who knows the terms common in a particular trade and is not taken by surprise by them. (The reasoning in the *Stiletto* case above is obviously relevant here.) An example of the application of guideline (d) would be where the contract requires the buyer to complain of defects in the goods within a short period. Such a requirement might well be held reasonable in regard to defects which are obvious on delivery, particularly if the goods are to be delivered by a third party carrier, since notice may enable the seller to claim against the carrier. On the other hand such a clause would usually not be reasonable if the defect was not immediately obvious.

The guidelines do not exhaust the factors which may be taken into account in deciding on what is reasonable. The leading decision is *George Mitchell (Chester Hall) Limited v Finney Lock Seeds Limited* (1983). In this case the defendant was a firm of seed merchants which agreed to supply the plaintiff, a farming concern, with 30 pounds of Dutch winter cabbage seed for £192. The contract was treated as subject to an invoice which contained a clause purporting to limit liability if the seed were defective to a replacement of the seed or refund of the price and to exclude

> 'All liability for any loss or damage arising from the use of any seeds or plants supplied by us and for any consequential loss or damage arising out of such use ... or for any other loss or damage whatsoever.'

In fact the seed delivered was not winter cabbage seed and was also defective. The plaintiff's crop was therefore a total failure. The plaintiff claimed that the cash value of the crop would have been some £63,000. The defendant claimed to be liable only to repay £192. If one looks at the guidelines in such a case, guidelines (b), (d) and (e) have little or no impact; there is probably not much to choose in the bargaining strength of the parties and clauses of this kind are well known in the seed trade so that it is unlikely that the reasonable farmer would be taken by surprise. On the other hand it might be difficult to find a seed merchant who would supply a seed on substantially different terms.

The House of Lords held that the clause was unreasonable. The principal factor relied on by the House of Lords was that the defendant had led evidence that in practice in such cases it commonly made *ex gratia* payments. The purpose of leading this evidence was to show that the defendant was reasonable. Instead the House of Lords took it as evidence that even the defendant did not regard its own clause as reasonable. These rather special circumstances are perhaps unlikely to arise again because in future sellers will not be so incautious as to lead such evidence. Other factors to which significant weight was attached included the fact that the breach by the sellers was a particularly clear and substantial one and that there was evidence that it was easier for sellers to insure against losses of this kind than for buyers. Undoubtedly, which parties can most economically and efficiently insure is often a critical factor in deciding whether a clause is reasonable. So if a seller could show that a particular loss was of a kind against which buyers commonly insure this would significantly increase his or her chances of persuading a court that the clause was reasonable. Similarly, if the task being undertaken is relatively simple and its consequences fall within a modest compass it will be less easily shown to be reasonable to seek to exclude liability.

Another interesting case which is worth mentioning is *Walker v Boyle* (1982) where Dillon J held that neither the fact that the contract (for the sale of land) was on standard nationally used terms nor the fact that both parties were represented by solicitors throughout prevented the clause being unreasonable. This was because the clause in question sought to shift from seller to buyer the risk of the seller giving an inaccurate answer to questions, the answers to which were entirely within the seller's control.

Section 2 provides:

'(1) A person cannot by reference to any contract term or to a notice given to persons generally or to particular persons exclude or restrict his liability for death or personal injury resulting from negligence.

(2) In the case of other loss or damage, a person cannot so exclude or restrict his liability for negligence except in so far as the term or notice satisfies the requirement of reasonableness.

(3) Where a contract term or notice purports to exclude or restrict liability for negligence a person's agreement to or awareness of it is not of itself to be taken as indicating his voluntary acceptance of any risk.'

7.3.2   Unfair Contract Terms Act s 2

Although this section is aimed at liability in negligence it is capable of applying to sellers and other suppliers of goods because in some cases the buyer may be able to formulate a claim against them as based on negligence. For instance, where the seller has negligently given pre-contract advice or, has carried out a negligent pre-delivery inspection of a motor car. It will be seen that s 2 forbids contracting out of liability when negligence causes death or personal injury and subjects contracting out for negligence which causes other forms of loss to the test of reasonableness. What is said above about reasonableness will apply here also.

7.3.3   Unfair Contract Terms Act s 3

Section 3 provides:

'(1) This section applies as between contracting parties where one of them deals as consumer or on the other's written standard terms of business.

(2) As against that party, the other cannot be reference to any contract term:

(a) when himself in breach of contract, exclude or restrict any liability of his in respect of the breach; or

(b) claim to be entitled:

(i) to render a contractual performance substantially different from that which was reasonably expected of him, or

(ii) in respect of the whole or any part of his contractual obligation, to render no performance at all except in so far as (in any of the cases mentioned above in this subsection) the contract term satisfies the requirement of reasonableness.'

This provision is of very general scope. It will be seen that it applies either where one of the contracting parties is a consumer or where the contract is on one party's written standard terms of business. Obviously there will be very many contracts of sale where the buyer is a consumer and many both commercial and consumer contracts where the contract is on the seller's standard written terms of business. So many contracts of sale will be subject so s 3. This section is therefore very important in relation to obligations under contracts of sale other than those covered by the implied terms in ss 13, 14 and 15. It would apply, for instance, to the questions of when the seller is to deliver the goods. Many sellers state in their written standard terms of business that the dates of delivery are estimates only and so on. It would certainly be open to a court to enquire whether such a provision was reasonable. In practice it is very difficult to see that it can be reasonable simply to have a blanket excuse for being late in delivery. It would be a different matter if the seller inserted a clause excusing failure to deliver on time for specified events which were outside the seller's control. Such clauses are of course very common and in principle they would appear reasonable.

It should be noted that the scope of s 3 is potentially very wide because it covers not only attempts to exclude liability for breach of contract but also attempts to provide in the contract to be able to deliver a contractual performance substantially different from that which was reasonably expected or to render no performance at all. A careful draftsman might seek to formulate the contract so as to give the seller the right to offer an alternative performance or in certain circumstances not to perform at all without these acts being breaches but it seems that such clauses would still be subject to the test of reasonableness. If one applied this literally it would mean that a clause providing that the seller need not deliver the goods until the buyer had paid for them in advance was subject to the test of reasonableness. In practice it is unlikely that a court would be at all anxious to construe the words in this sense and in any case it would usually hold that such a clause was reasonable.

The Directive on Unfair Terms in Consumer Contracts was adopted by the Council of Ministers on 5 April 1993. Member States were required to implement its provisions by 31 December 1994. The Directive was not mandatory as to its precise terms; it laid down a minimum standard which Member States must reach for protection of consumers against unfair terms in consumer contracts. Most Member States of the European Union already had legislation in place which deals with this area. In the case of the United Kingdom, the relevant legislation is the Unfair Contract Terms Act 1977. The Act is both wider and narrower than the Directive. It would have been possible for the government to identify those areas at which the Directive is aimed, which the Act has not reached and to legislate to expand consumer protection to these areas. The government decided not to do this and instead to introduce secondary legislation under s 2(2) of the European Communities Act 1972.	**7.4** **European statutory control**

The Unfair Terms in Consumer Contracts Regulations were laid before Parliament on 14 December 1994 and come into force on 1 July 1995.

The Regulations apply only to consumer contracts, to standard forms of contract, and to contracts for the supply of goods and services. Let us consider each of these limitations in turn.	7.4.1 To what contracts do the regulations apply?

Although the concept of consumer contracts is used in the Act, it is clear that the Act is much wider in scope. It should be noted also that the Regulations define a consumer as 'a natural person who in making a contract to which these Regulations apply, is acting for purposes which are outside his business'.

The Regulations do not apply to contracts which have been individually negotiated. They are limited to contracts which have been 'drafted in advance'. Of course, it is extremely common in consumer contracts, if there is a written document, for the document to have been drafted in advance by the businesses' advisers. Nevertheless, even in such contracts there may be some negotiation, particularly about the price. The Regulations say that 'the fact that a specific term or certain aspects of it have been individually negotiated does not exclude the application of the Regulations if an overall assessment of the contract indicates that it is nevertheless a pre-formulated standard contract'.

The Regulations apply only to contracts for the supply of goods and services. The limitation to consumer contracts would exclude most international sales.

7.4.2	**The effect of the regulations**	Under the Regulations, terms classified as unfair are struck out and in principle the rest of the contract would be left in being unless the effect of striking out the offending term is to leave a contract which makes no sense. There are two important differences between the Act and the Regulations here. The first is that, despite its name, the Act is not concerned with unfair terms. Whether a term is unfair is never a test of its validity under the Act. Some terms are simply struck out. Other terms are valid if reasonable. Invalidity does not depend on fairness or unfairness.

The second difference is that, subject to arguments about the precise scope of s 3, the Act only applies to clauses which seek to exclude or limit liability. In principle, the Regulations can be used to attack any term which can be argued to be unfair.

7.4.3	**Unfairness under the regulations**	Clause 5(1) of the Regulations provides that 'an unfair term in a contract concluded with a consumer by a seller or supplier shall not be binding on the consumer' and 5(2) 'the contract shall continue to bind the parties if it is capable of continuing in existence without the unfair term'. Unfairness is defined by Clause 4(1) of the Regulations which provides '"Unfair term" means any term which, contrary to the requirement of good faith, causes a significant imbalance in the parties' rights and obligations arising under the contract to the detriment of the consumer.' So the possible scope of arguments about unfairness is very wide. However, there is one very important limitation which is contained in Clause 3(2) which provides 'In so far as it is in plain intelligible language no assessment shall be made of the fairness of any term which (a) defines the main subject matter of the contract or (b) concerns the adequacy of the price or remuneration as against the goods or services sold or supplied.' This means that it will not be open to a consumer to argue that a contract is unfair because she has been charged too much. This provision represents a vital decision as to a central part of the application of the unfairness concept. It is

perfectly easy to understand why it was thought not expedient to leave judges with the task of deciding whether the price was fair. This would be the sort of question which could often not be answered without hearing complex economic evidence of a kind which many lawyers and judges are not trained to evaluate. On the other hand, questions of price must often be an important ingredient in questions of fairness and unfairness. Supposing I sell you a car which has been badly damaged in an accident, requires extensive repair work and is totally unroadworthy as it stands. If I sell you the car at a price which reflects all these defects, it is hard to say that the contract is unfair. If I sell you the car at a price which would be appropriate for the same car in perfect second-hand condition but seek to conceal the defects and to exclude liability by the words in the small print, it is much more plausible to regard the contract as unfair.

The Regulations give quite a lot of guidance as to what is good or bad faith. The second schedule requires that particular regard should be had to 'the strength of the bargaining positions of the parties; whether the consumer has an inducement to agree to the terms; whether the goods or services were sold or supplied to the special order of the consumer; and the extent to which the seller or supplier has dealt fairly and equitably with the consumer'. It will be seen that the first three of these conditions are also relevant to reasonableness under the Act.

Section 6 of the Regulations provides 'A seller or supplier shall ensure that any written term of a contract is expressed in plain intelligible language.' Where 'there is doubt about the meaning of a term, the interpretation most favourable to the consumer shall prevail'. The second sentence is simply a statement in statutory form of a rule which the English courts have always applied and which indeed is to be found in virtually all legal systems. The wording of the first sentence of s 6 is however of great practical importance. Many businesses operate at the moment by making glowing statements in their marketing and trying to weasel out of them in the small print by obscure and complex jargon. Section 6 will make this ineffective and certainly therefore requires consumer contracts to be carefully re-read and in many cases extensively re-written.

Finally, it should be noted that s 4(4) provides that s 3 contains 'an indicative and non-exhaustive list of the terms which may be regarded as unfair'. There is no corresponding list in the Act but such lists are a common feature of continental legislation. It should be noted that the list is not a black list in that the Regulations do not say that the use of terms included on the list means that the clause is unfair. It is rather a grey list in the sense that inclusion on the list raises a strong inference that in most circumstances a clause of this kind should be treated as unfair.

7.4.4   Terms referred to in s 4(4)

1 Terms which have the object or effect of:

(a) excluding or limiting the legal liability of a seller or supplier in the event of the death of a consumer or personal injury to the latter resulting from an act or omission of that seller or supplier;

(b) inappropriately excluding or limiting the legal rights of the consumer *vis-à-vis* the seller or supplier or another party in the event of total or partial non-performance or inadequate performance by the seller or supplier of any of the contractual obligations, including the option of offsetting a debt owed to the seller or supplier against any claim which the consumer may have against him;

(c) making an agreement binding on the consumer whereas provision of services by the seller or supplier is subject to a condition whose realisation depends on his own will alone;

(d) permitting the seller or supplier to retain sums paid by the consumer where the latter decides not to conclude or perform the contract, without providing for the consumer to receive compensation of an equivalent amount from the seller or supplier where the latter is the party cancelling the contract;

(e) requiring any consumer who fails to fulfil his obligation to pay a disproportionately high sum in compensation;

(f) authorising the seller or supplier to dissolve the contract on a discretionary basis where the same facility is not granted to the consumer, or permitting the seller or supplier to retain the sums paid for services not yet supplied by him where it is the seller or supplier himself who dissolves the contract;

(g) enabling the seller or supplier to terminate a contract of indeterminate duration without reasonable notice except where there are serious grounds for doing so;

(h) automatically extending a contract of fixed duration where the consumer does not indicate otherwise, when the deadline fixed for the consumer to express this desire not to extend the contract is unreasonably early;

(i) irrevocably binding the consumer to terms with which he had no real opportunity of becoming acquainted before the conclusion of the contract;

(j) enabling the seller or supplier to alter the terms of the contract unilaterally without a valid reason which is specified in the contract;

(k) enabling the seller or supplier to alter unilaterally without a valid reason any characteristics of the product or service to be provided;

(l) providing for the price of goods to be determined at the time of delivery or allowing a seller of goods or supplier of services to increase their price without in both cases giving the consumer the corresponding right to cancel the contract if the final price is too high in relation to the price agreed when the contract was concluded;

(m) giving the seller or supplier the right to determine whether the goods or services supplied are in conformity with the contract, or giving him the exclusive right to interpret any term of the contract;

(n) limiting the seller's or supplier's obligation to respect commitments undertaken by his agents or making his commitments subject to compliance with a particular formality;

(o) obliging the consumer to fulfil all his obligations where the seller or supplier does not perform his;

(p) giving the seller or supplier the possibility of transferring his rights and obligations under the contract, where this may serve to reduce the guarantees for the consumer, without the latter's agreement;

(q) excluding or hindering the consumer's right to take legal action or exercise any other legal remedy, particularly by requiring the consumer to take disputes exclusively to arbitration not covered by legal provisions, unduly restricting the evidence available to him or imposing on him a burden of proof which, according to the applicable law, should lie with another party to the contract.

2 Scope of sub-paragraphs (g), (j) and (l)

(a) Sub-paragraph (g) is without hindrance to terms by which a supplier of financial services reserves the right to terminate unilaterally a contract of indeterminate duration without notice where there is a valid reason, provided that the supplier is required to inform the other contracting party or parties thereof immediately.

(b) Sub-paragraph (j) is without hindrance to terms under which a supplier of financial services reserves the right to alter the rate of interest payable by the consumer or due to the latter, or the amount of other charges for financial services without notice where there is a valid reason, provided that the supplier is required to inform the other contracting party or parties thereof at the earliest opportunity and that the latter are free to dissolve the contract immediately.

(c) Sub-paragraphs (g), (j) and (l) do not apply to:

- transactions in transferable securities, financial instruments and other products or services where the price is linked to fluctuations in a stock exchange quotation or index or a financial market rate that the seller or supplier does not control;

- contracts for the purchase or sale of foreign currency, travellers' cheques or international money orders denominated in foreign currency;

(d) Sub-paragraph (l) is without hindrance to price indexation clauses, where lawful, provided that the method by which prices vary is explicitly described.

Exemption and Limitation Clauses

This chapter considers the effect of clauses which attempt to exclude or limit liability. It considers:

1 the various types of clause;

2 common law treatment of such clauses. This is mainly covered by –

   (a) rules about incorporation;

   (b) rules of construction;

3 statutory controls, in particular the Unfair Contracts Terms Act 1977 and the Unfair Terms in Consumer Contracts Regulations 1994. Note that both the Act and the Regulations have provisions which deal directly with sale of goods.

Where there exists a signed contractual document, the basic rule is that the parties can be taken to have agreed to what the contract means even though they have never read it and would not understand it if they had. Where there is no signed contract, but it is argued that excluding terms have been incorporated into the contract, there is no doubt that in certain circumstances one can incorporate terms into a contract by displaying a notice at the point at which the contract is made (*Thornton v Shoe Lane Parking* (1971)) or, as on the railway, by handing over a ticket which contains references to the contractual obligations (*Parker v South Eastern Railway* (1877)).

The principal tool used by common law to control exemption clauses has been the process of construction, ie the process by which the court construes the contract. Courts will often apply the *contra proferentem* principle which says that if one party has drafted or is responsible for the drafting of a document and the document is ambiguous then any ambiguities should be resolved in favour of the other party.

There are two principal enactments which deal specifically with contracts for the supply of goods and also provisions of general application which may affect contracts for the supply of goods:

• Unfair Contract Terms Act 1977;

• Unfair Terms in Consumer Contracts Regulations 1994.

Chapter 8

Remedies

This chapter is intended to discuss what remedies may be available to either the buyer or the seller if the other party breaks the contract. The positions of buyer and seller in a contract of sale are not of course symmetrical; the seller's obligation is to deliver the goods and the buyer's obligation is to pay the price. The failure of the seller to deliver the goods or to deliver goods of the right quality and so on will have different results from the failure of the buyer to pay the price, and may call for some difference in remedies. Nevertheless, the remedies available to the parties do derive very largely from the general law of contract and it seems more convenient therefore to approach the problem first by considering the general principles and then by considering how the position of the buyer and seller may differ.

8.1 General principles

There will be a number of cases in which the injured party has no effective remedy for the other party's breach. This is because the most usual remedy is damages to compensate for the financial loss flowing from the breach and it will quite often be the case that little or no financial loss has flowed.

What are the possible remedies? One party may be entitled to withhold performance until the other has performed. In certain circumstances, one party will be entitled not only to withhold performance but to bring the contract to an end – to terminate it. A particular and very important example of this is the buyer's right to reject the goods, though the right to reject the goods is not exactly the same as the right to terminate and is not subject to exactly the same rules.

In certain circumstances, one party may be entitled to get the contract specifically enforced. In other circumstances the seller may bring an action for the price and although this action is historically different from the buyer's action for specific performance it produces, from the seller's point of view, many of the same consequences.

In practice, the most common remedy for breach of a contract of sale of goods will be an action for damages. If the contract has been broken by one party, the other party will always have an action for damages though, as pointed out above, the damages may only be nominal in amount. The critical question is how much can be recovered by a buyer or seller in an action for damages.

The remedies we have discussed so far are what we may call the standard remedies provided by the general law. However, the law permits the parties to make further provisions about remedies. We have already seen in Chapter 7 the rules which have developed where the contract seeks to limit the remedies which would normally be available. It is possible on the other hand to seek to extend the range of remedies. So the contract may provide that if the seller is late in delivering he shall pay so much a day by way of liquidated damages for each day of delay. Conversely, the contract may provide that the buyer is to pay a deposit or that he is to pay part of the price in advance. Some of these possibilities are so common that substantial bodies of rules have been developed about them. These will be discussed more fully later under 'Party provided remedies' (see para 8.5). 'Sellers' remedies against the goods' (see para 8.6) discusses certain special remedies which the seller has against the goods where the buyer is insolvent. In practice, the seller's most effective remedy is to have retained ownership.

8.2   **Withholding performance, termination and the buyer's right to reject**

Withholding performance and termination are analytically separate but in practice there is a major degree of overlap. This is because the factual situations which lead one party to wish to withhold performance or to terminate are very similar. In practice, the threat by one party to withhold performance will either lead the other party to attend to her performance, in which case the contract will go on, or not, in which the case the innocent party would usually have to decide a little later whether to terminate or not.

8.2.1   Withholding performance

A critical question in deciding whether one party is entitled to withhold performance is to consider what the contract says or implies about the order of performance. So, for example, s 28 of the 1979 Act says:

> 'Unless otherwise agreed, delivery of the goods and payment of the price are concurrent conditions, that is to say, the seller must be ready and willing to give possession of the goods to the buyer in exchange for the price and the buyer must be ready and willing to pay the price in exchange for possession of the goods.'

The seller may have agreed to give the buyer credit. Suppose an oil company agrees to supply a filling station with all its requirements of oil for three years, payment to be made seven days after delivery. It is not open to the oil company unilaterally to change the terms and insist on payment in cash, even if the buyer has broken the contract by not always paying within the seven day limit (*Total Oil (Great Britain) Ltd v Thompson Garages (Biggin Hill) Ltd* (1972)).

If we turn to consider the circumstances in which one party may terminate the contract, general contract law uses two principal approaches. One, which has been heavily used in relation to the sale of goods, is to proceed in terms of classifying the term of the contract which has been broken. This approach postulates that there are certain terms of the contract, commonly called conditions, which are so important that any breach of them should entitle the other party to terminate the contract. It is for this reason that a buyer can reject goods for breach of description even though the breach appears in commercial terms to be quite trivial, as in *Arcos v Ronaasen* (1933) and *Re Moore and Landaeur* (1921), discussed above in Chapter 6. Many of the obligations which we have discussed in the preceding chapters are expressed as being conditions and so attract the operation of this rule. In addition, there seems to be no reason why the parties may not agree that other express terms of the contract are to be treated as conditions.

A second way of approaching the problem of termination is to ask how serious is the breach of contract which has been committed by the defendant. Basically, there are two principal possibilities. One is that one party has behaved in such a way as to make it clear that it is repudiating its obligations under the contract. A party can do this either by explicitly repudiating or by doing something which is inconsistent with any continuing intention to perform the contract.

Deciding whether a particular course of conduct amounts to an implicit repudiation of a party's obligations may raise difficult questions of judgment. This is particularly the case where a party does something which turns out to be a breach of the contract but which it claims it was contractually entitled to do. The difficulties can be seen by contrasting two decisions of the House of Lords in *Federal Commerce and Navigation v Molena Alpha* (1979) and *Woodar Investment Development v Wimpey Construction* (1980).

A second class of case in which one party is entitled to terminate is where the other party has performed in such a defective way as effectively not to have performed at all. Of course, some defective performances may be treated as evidence of an intention to repudiate. The thrust of this argument however is that one party, although she is doing her best, is doing it so badly that the other party is entitled to treat the contract as at an end. Such a breach is often called a fundamental breach.

Whether one is talking in terms of breach of condition or in terms of repudiatory or fundamental breach, it is clear that the

8.2.2   Termination for breach of contract

8.2.3   Termination for fundamental breach

contract does not come to an end simply because one of these events takes place. In each case, the innocent party has a choice. It can treat the breach of condition, the repudiatory breach or the fundamental breach, as bringing the contract to an end or it can continue to call for performance of the contract. In practice it will often become clear that the contract breaker cannot or will not perform and persistence in this course will inevitably lead the innocent party, in the end, to bring the contract to an end but, as a matter of legal theory, the contract comes to an end as a result of the innocent party's decision to terminate, not as a result of the guilty party's breach. The most obvious practical importance of this is that the innocent party's decision not to terminate will often give the other party a second chance to perform his side of the contract properly. Where the innocent party does elect to terminate the contract, the contract is not treated as never having existed but as terminated from that moment so that existing contractual rights and duties are not expunged. It follows that the innocent party can terminate and also claim damages for breach of contract if damages have been suffered.

| 8.2.4 | Termination for late performance |

There are special rules about late performance. Although the rules are similar to those in relation to other forms of breach in that they distinguish between important late performance and cases where late performance, although in breach of contract, is relatively unimportant, they have developed in a slightly different way because this was an area where equity intervened so as, in certain circumstances, to grant specific performance of the contract to one party even though he was late in performing.

The modern position may be stated as follows. A late performance is always a breach of contract and will give rise to an action for damages for any loss which actually follows from the late performance. However, whether the contract can be terminated for late performance depends on whether 'time is of the essence of the contract'. Time may be of the essence of the contract either because the contract expressly says so or because the contract is of a kind in which the courts treat timely performance as being essential. In general, courts have treated timely performance of the obligation to deliver the goods by the seller as of the essence of the contract, at least in a commercial context, unless the contract expressly says that time is not of the essence. On the other hand, the buyer's obligation to pay the price is not treated as an obligation where time is of the essence unless the contract expressly says so.

Where time is not of the essence but one party is late in performing, the other party is said to be able to 'make time of the essence'. What this means is that the innocent party may say to the late performer that if performance is not completed within a reasonable time, he will bring the contract to an end. It is of the essence of this possibility that the further time given for the performance is reasonable in all the circumstances.

It was seen above that the parties may agree in the contract that a particular obligation is to be treated as a condition. Alternatively, the parties may provide in the contract that one party is to be entitled to terminate. Such provisions are in fact very common. Sometimes, the event which gives rise to the right to terminate may be a breach of contract which would not have entitled the party to terminate were it not for this provision. So, in many contracts which depend on one party paying periodically, it is common to provide that failure to pay promptly entitles the other party to terminate, although a court would not usually hold that a single failure to pay promptly was either a repudiatory breach or a fundamental breach. In some cases a party may contract for the right to terminate without there being any breach of contract by the other side. So if the government places an order for a new fighter aeroplane, it may provide in the contract that the whole project can be cancelled if at a later stage defence policy changes. This would be a perfectly rational contractual arrangement to make. One would expect such a contract to contain provisions that the supplier was to be paid for the work which had actually been done up to the time of cancellation but the contract might well exclude the profit which the supplier would have made if the contract had been carried forward to completion. Clauses of this kind require careful negotiation and drafting.

Where the contract contains provisions for termination for events which are not in fact breaches of contract justifying termination on general principles, it may be important whether the contract makes the obligation essential or simply gives rise to a right to terminate. This is illustrated by the important case of *Lombard North Central v Butterworth* (1987).

8.2.5   Termination clauses

The buyer's right to reject the goods is in a sense simply an example of the right to withhold performance or to terminate. It may be only the withholding of performance because in a few cases the seller will be able to make a second tender of the goods. This would usually only be where she can make a second tender within the contractually permitted time for delivery. Suppose the contract calls for delivery in January and the seller makes a defective tender on the 1 January; she may well be able to make an effective tender later in the month.

8.2.6   Buyer's right to reject for breach of condition

Where, as will often be the case, the contract calls for delivery on a particular day and time is of the essence, this possibility will in practice not exist and then rejection of the goods will effectively terminate the contract. Since many of the seller's obligations are expressed to be conditions, the buyer will have the right to reject the goods for breach of condition in a wide variety of circumstances. These include:

(a) a delivery of less or more than the contract quantity or of other goods mixed with the contract goods, as discussed in Chapter 3;

(b) failure by the seller to perform his obligations as to title as discussed in Chapter 4; or

(c) failure by the seller to carry out his obligations as to the quality of the goods as discussed in Chapter 6.

8.2.7 Losing the right to reject

The buyer will also often be able to reject the goods because delivery is late, as discussed above. There is a major difference, however, between the rules governing the buyer's right to reject goods for breach of condition and the general law about termination. Usually an innocent party cannot lose the right to terminate the contract until it has discovered that it has got it. However, it is clear that in some circumstances the buyer may lose the right to reject for breach of condition through acceptance even though it does not know that it has the right to reject because it has not yet discovered the defect which gives rise to this right. This is because the buyer loses the right to reject the goods by acceptance and it is possible for acceptance to take place before the buyer discovers the defect in the goods. This is because under s 35(1) one of the ways in which the buyer can accept the goods is to retain them after the lapse of a reasonable time and a reasonable time is held to run from delivery and not from discovering that the goods are defective. This is discussed more fully above at para 3.4. The right of rejection is modified by two provisions which are incorporated by virtue of s 4 of the Sale and Supply of Goods Act 1994. The first of these is a new s 15A which provides:

'(1) Where in the case of a contract of sale –

(a) the buyer would, apart from this subsection, have the right to reject goods by reason of a breach on the part of the seller of a term implied by section 13, 14 or 15 above, but

(b) the breach is so slight that it would be unreasonable for him to reject them,

then, if the buyer does not deal as consumer, the breach is

not to be treated as a breach of condition but may be treated as a breach of warranty.

(2) This section applies unless a contrary intention appears in, or is to be implied from, the contract.

(3) It is for the seller to show that a breach fell within subsection (1)(b) above.

(4) This section does not apply to Scotland.'

It is assumed that, for a consumer buyer, the right of rejection is of particular importance. The great attraction of rejection, from the consumer point of view, is that it avoids any need to resort to litigation and forces the seller to decide whether it is worthwhile litigating. It can be assumed that, in respect of all goods except cars, consumers will be extremely reluctant to litigate, whatever the defects. The right of rejection is therefore particularly important. It is assumed, on the other hand, that, in the case of commercial sales, a reduction in price will more often than not satisfy the buyer's legitimate demands, unless the defect is a serious one. It is open to a commercial buyer to bargain for s 15A to be excluded. It must be noted that it will require some cases to be sure what exactly will count as a slight breach and when it will be unreasonable to reject the goods because of such a breach. There is a two-fold test here. The seller must show both that the breach is slight and that it is unreasonable to reject. It is not to be assumed that simply because the breach is slight it will be unreasonable to reject.

Finally, the buyer is given slightly greater rights of rejection by a new s 35A which provides:

'(1) If the buyer –

(a) has the right to reject the goods by reason of a breach on the part of the seller that affects some or all of them, but

(b) accepts some of the goods, including, where there are any goods unaffected by the breach, all such goods,

he does not by accepting them lose his right to reject the rest.

(2) In the case of a buyer having the right to reject an instalment of goods, subsection (1) above applies as if references to the goods were references to the goods comprised in the instalment.

(3) For the purposes of subsection (1) above, goods are affected by a breach if by reason of the breach they are not in conformity with the contract.

(4) This section applies unless a contrary intention appears in, or is to be implied from the contract.'

By virtue of this new section, the buyer does not lose the right to reject some goods as part of a parcel of goods which are defective because he has accepted other goods in the parcel which are not defective. Under the previous law, the buyer who had 1,000 tonnes of wheat delivered to him, of which 400 tonnes were defective and 600 tonnes alright, had the choices of either rejecting the whole 1,000 tonnes or accepting the whole 1,000 tonnes (in either case, he might claim damages). Under s 35A he will now have the option, if he wishes, to reject 400 tonnes and keep the 600 tonnes which are of good quality. This seems an entirely sensible change.

8.3 Specific enforcement

Section 52 of the Sale of Goods Act provides:

'(1) In any action for breach of contract to deliver specific or ascertained goods the court may, if it thinks fit, on the plaintiff's application, by its judgment or decree direct that the contract shall be performed specifically, without giving the defendant the option of retaining the goods on payment of damages.

(2) The plaintiff's application may be made at any time before judgment or decree.

(3) The judgment or decree may be unconditional, or on such terms and conditions as to damages, payment of the price and otherwise as seem just to the court.'

It will be seen that this section talks only of specific or ascertained goods and the question of whether specific performance can be given for unascertained goods is considered below. As far as specific or ascertained goods are concerned, the section is in very broad terms. However, in practice the courts have been very slow to exercise the broad powers given by the section. The reason for this is that they have usually taken the view that in a contract for sale of goods damages will be an adequate remedy since usually the buyer can go out and buy substitute goods and be adequately compensated by a money payment. See *Cohen v Roche* (1927). A leading case in which specific performance was granted was *Behnke v Bede Shipping* (1927) in which the subject matter of the contract was a ship. It cannot be assumed, however, that specific performance would routinely be given, even for contracts for the sale of a ship. So in *CN Marine v Stena Line* (1982) specific performance was refused of such a contract. A court would want to enquire, in any decision whether to grant specific performance, into all the circumstances, in particular on any hardship which would be caused to one party or the other by giving or refusing specific performance or the conduct of the parties leading up to the contract. This reflects a combination of two policies: the general feeling that specific performance is usually not necessary in the case of goods and the general equitable principle that specific performance is not to be granted mechanically and that all the circumstances are to be considered.

As we said above, s 52 only talks in terms of 'specific or ascertained goods'. This leaves in the air the question whether specific performance can ever be granted of unascertained goods. One view is that the Sale of Goods Act contains an exhaustive code of the remedies available. This view was expressed in relation to specific performance in *Re Wait* (1972). However, in the leading modern case where the question arose, the judge did in fact grant specific performance of a contract for unascertained goods though he did not refer to s 52 or consider the theoretical question of whether he had jurisdiction. This was in *Sky Petroleum v VIP Petroleum* (1974).

Section 52 talks of plaintiffs and defendants and not of buyers and sellers. So it may be that in theory a seller can sue for specific performance. However, this is not likely to be a practical question except in the most extraordinary circumstances since a seller will nearly always be able to sell the goods elsewhere and recover compensation by way of damages for any loss that he suffers. There will be cases, however, where the seller would wish, if possible, to sue for the price rather than to sue for damages. This is principally because in the English system, actions for defined sums of money are much easier, quicker and therefore cheaper than actions for damages. Section 49 of the 1979 Act provides:

'(1) Where, under a contract of sale, the property in the goods has passed to the buyer and he wrongfully neglects or refuses to pay for the goods according to the terms of the contract, the seller may maintain an action against him for the price of the goods.

(2) Where, under a contract of sale, the price is payable on a day certain irrespective of delivery and the buyer wrongfully neglects or refuses to pay such price, the seller may maintain an action for the price, although the property in the goods has not passed and the goods have not been appropriated to the contract.'

Although the action for the price is in a sense the seller's equivalent of the buyer's action for specific performance, the two remedies should be kept clearly distinct. This is for historical reasons. The action for specific performance arises historically from the jurisdiction of the Court of Chancery to grant specific performance which was always said to be discretionary and to turn on taking into account all the relevant circumstances. The action for the price was not an equitable action but basically a common law action for debt.

This means that where sellers are entitled to sue for the price they do not have to show that they have suffered any loss; they do not have to take steps to mitigate the loss as they do in a damages action and the action is not subject to any general discretion in the court. On the other hand, the seller does not have an action for the price simply because the buyer's obligation to pay the price has crystallised and the buyer has failed to pay. The seller has to bring the case within one or other of the two limbs of s 49.

It will be seen that s 49(1) links the right to sue for the price to the passing of property.

Section 49(2) provides an alternative basis for an action for the price where the price is payable 'on a day certain irrespective of delivery'. This clearly covers the simple case where the contract says that the price is payable on 1 January. It certainly does not cover the rather common case where the price is payable on delivery, even where the contractual date for delivery is agreed, because it can then be held that that is not a day certain irrespective of delivery (see *Stein Forbes v County Tailoring* (1916)). What about the cases which fall in between these two extremes? It certainly seems that it will do if the parties agree a date even though at the time of the agreement neither of them knows when it is, such as on Derby Day 1996. *Workman Clark v Lloyd Brazileno* (1908) involved a ship building contract under which it was agreed that the price was to be paid in instalments which were linked to the completion of various stages of the ship. A ship building contract may well provide for instance that 20% of the price is to be paid on the laying of the keel. Obviously, at the time of the contract, no-one will know exactly when the keel will in fact be laid, even if the contract contains provisions as to when it should be laid. Nevertheless, in the *Workman Clark* case it was held that such provisions were for payment on a day certain because when the duty to pay arose, the day on which it fell due was certain.

8.4 Actions for damages

The 1979 Act contains three sections which deal with damages. These are:

'50. (1) Where the buyer wrongfully neglects or refuses to accept and pay for the goods, the seller may maintain an action against him for damages for non-acceptance.

(2) The measure of damages is the estimated loss directly and naturally resulting, in the ordinary course of events, from the buyer's breach of contract.

(3) Where there is an available market for the goods in question the measure of damages is *prima facie* to be ascertained by the difference between the contract

price and the market or current price at the time or times when the goods ought to have been accepted or (if no time was fixed for acceptance) at the time of the refusal to accept.

51. (1) Where the seller wrongfully neglects or refuses to deliver the goods to the buyer, the buyer may maintain an action against the seller for damages for non-delivery.

(2) The measure of damages is the estimated loss directly and naturally resulting, in the ordinary course of events, from the seller's breach of contract.

(3) Where there is an available market for the goods in question the measure of damages is *prima facie* to be ascertained by the difference between the contract price and the market or current price of the goods at the time or times when they ought to have been delivered or (if no time was fixed) at the time of the refusal to deliver.

53. (1) Where there is a breach of warranty by the seller, or where the buyer elects (or is compelled) to treat any breach of a condition on the part of the seller as a breach of warranty, the buyer is not by reason only of such breach of warranty entitled to reject the goods; but he may –

(a) set up against the seller the breach of warranty in diminution or extinction of the price, or

(b) maintain an action against the seller for damages for the breach of warranty.

(2) The measure of damages for breach of warranty is the estimated loss directly and naturally resulting, in the ordinary course of events, from the breach of warranty.

(3) In the case of breach of warranty of quality such loss is *prima facie* the difference between the value of the goods at the time of delivery to the buyer and the value they would have had if they had fulfilled the warranty.

(4) The fact that the buyer has set up the breach of warranty in diminution or extinction of the price does not prevent him from maintaining an action for the same breach of warranty if he has suffered further damage.'

In practice these provisions do not add a great deal to the general law of contract and many cases are decided without reference to them.

8.4.1	Mitigation of damages

It is often said that the plaintiff must mitigate his damages. This is strictly speaking an inaccurate way of putting the point. The plaintiff can do what he likes but would only be able to recover damages which result from reasonable behaviour after the contract is broken. This is really an application of the general principle that the plaintiff can only recover what arises in the ordinary course of events and in the ordinary course of events those who suffer breaches of contract respond in a reasonable way (or at least the law treats them as if they will). This principle can be an important limitation on the amount that the plaintiff recovers. This is illustrated by the case of *Payzu v Saunders* (1919), where the defendant had agreed to sell to the plaintiffs a quantity of silk, payment to be made a month after delivery. The defendant, in breach of contract, refused to make further deliveries except for cash and the plaintiffs treated this as being a repudiation and elected to terminate the contract. This they were certainly entitled to do. They then sued for damages on the basis that the market price of silk had risen and that they could claim the difference between the contract price and the market price at the date of the buyers' repudiation. This argument was rejected on the grounds that, the market having risen, it would have been cheaper for the buyers to accept the seller's offer to deliver against cash at the contract price. It will often be difficult for the plaintiff to know immediately after the contract what is the best course. In principle, if the plaintiff acts reasonably, it should be able to recover its financial loss even though, with the wisdom of hindsight, it appears that the plaintiff could have minimised the loss by doing something different (*Gebruder Metelmann v NBR (London)* (1984)).

8.4.2	The market rate

How do we apply these general principles to the specific case of contract for the sale of goods? One answer is given by ss 50(3) and 51(3) which, it will be seen, are in very similar terms. This states the market rule. English litigation in the field of sale of goods has been dominated by commodity contracts where there is a national or international market and it is possible to say with precision what the market price is during the hours when the market was open. In such a situation it is assumed that if the seller refuses to deliver, the buyer will buy against the seller in the market or that if the buyer refuses to accept, the seller will sell against the buyer in the market and that the starting point for enquiry is the difference between the contract price and the market price. This is basically a very simple rule to apply and it is a useful example of the application of the general principle. The fact that it is the only specific case actually discussed in the Act perhaps, however, gives it more prominence than it really deserves. It should be emphasised that the rule does not apply where there is no 'available market' and even where there is an available market, the rule will not necessarily apply.

Whether the market rule is the right rule to apply will depend, among other things, on the nature of the loss suffered by the plaintiff. This is shown by the case of *Thompson v Robinson* (1955). In that case, the plaintiff was a car dealer which contracted to sell a Standard Vanguard car to the defendant who wrongfully refused to take delivery. At this time, there was effective resale price maintenance for new cars so that there was no difference between the contract price and the market price and the buyer argued that the plaintiff had suffered no loss. However, the plaintiff showed that in fact there was a surplus of Standard Vanguard cars and that it had therefore lost its profit on the deal which could not be replaced by selling the car to someone else since it had more cars than it could sell. In this case, the plaintiff's loss was the loss of the retail mark up, that is the difference between the price at which the car was bought from the manufacturer and the price at which it could be sold. If the dealer could sell as many cars as it could obtain, then it would not effectively have lost this sum, as was held in the later case of *Charter v Sullivan* (1957).

From the buyer's point of view a most important question arises where it wishes to argue that what has been lost is a particularly valuable sub-sale. Suppose A has contracted to sell to B for £100 and B has contracted to sell to C for £150. Suppose further that A fails to deliver in circumstances where B cannot buy substitute goods in time to perform his contract with C and loses his profit on the transaction. Can he recover the profit? If we were applying the standard rules, this would appear to turn either on whether this was a loss in the usual course of things, which it might well be if the buyer was a dealer since the sub-sale would then appear to be entirely usual, or where the buyer had told the seller of the sub-sale. In practice, the courts have been reluctant to go so far. The leading case is *Re Hall and Pims Arbitration* (1928). In this case, the contract was for the sale of a specific cargo of corn in a specific ship. The contract price was 51s 9d per quarter and the buyer resold at 56s 9d per quarter. The seller failed to deliver and, at the date when the delivery should have taken place, the market price was 53s 9d per quarter. Clearly the buyer was entitled at least to the difference between 51s 9d and 53s 9d per quarter but claimed that to be entitled to the difference between 51s 9d and 56s 9d, the price at which it had agreed to re-sell. It was held by the House of Lords that this was right.

8.4.3   Loss of a sub-sale

However, this was a very strong case for two reasons. The first was that both the sale and the sub-sale were of the specific cargo so that there would be no question of the buyer going into the market to buy substitute goods. The second was that the contract of sale between plaintiff and defendant expressly provided for re-sale by the buyer.

Section 50 is concerned with the case where the buyer refuses to accept the goods and s 51 with the case of the seller who fails to deliver. Of course the seller can break the contract not only by failing to deliver but also by delivering late or making a defective delivery. This is dealt with by s 53 which was set out above. It will be seen that again this sets out reliance on the market rule. It is clear, however, that there are many other forms of loss which may arise in the usual course of things. So defective goods may cause damage to persons or property before their defects are discovered. Late delivery may cause loss of profit where the goods were to be used to make profits.

| 8.4.4 | Notional loss |

A major problem with all of these rules about damages is the extent to which the plaintiff is seeking to recover her actual loss or what one might call her notional loss. In general, for instance, when one is applying the market rule it does not seem to matter whether the buyer has gone into the market and bought substitute goods or not. The buyer can recover the difference between the contract price and the market price even though she does not buy against the seller; conversely, the buyer cannot recover more than this where she has stayed out of the market until later and then had to buy back at a higher price. However, it seems sometimes courts will look to see what actually happens. An important and difficult case is *Wertheim v Chicoutimi* (1911), where the seller delivered late. At the time when the goods ought to have been delivered, the market price was 70s a ton but by the time the goods were actually delivered, the market price was 42s 6d a ton. On the principles set out above, it would seem to follow that the buyer should have been able to recover the difference between 70s and 42s 6d for every ton he had contracted to buy. In fact, the buyer had managed to re-sell the goods at the remarkably good price, in the circumstances, of 65s a ton. It was held that he could only recover the difference between 70s and 65s for each ton bought. At first sight this looks reasonable since it might be said that this was the only loss which the buyer had actually suffered. On the other hand, the reasoning deprives the buyer of the profit to which his commercial astuteness at selling well over the market price would normally have entitled him. It is not surprising, therefore, that the correctness of this decision has been much debated.

It seems, within broad limits, that parties have freedom to add on additional remedies by contract. So we have already seen earlier that the right to terminate may be extended by contract. Two other important additional remedies which should be mentioned are liquidated damages and deposits.

Many contracts of sale provide that, in the event of certain breaches, typically late delivery by the seller, he shall pay damages at a rate laid down in the contract, for instance £X for every day by which delivery is delayed. Such provisions have important practical advantages because, as noted above, it is very much easier to bring actions for defined sums of money. However, the parties do not have complete freedom as to what may be agreed in this area. Since the 17th century, the courts have distinguished between liquidated damages which are enforceable and penalties which are not. The distinction turns on whether the sum agreed is a reasonable pre-estimate as at the time of the contract of the amount of loss which is liable to flow from the contract being broken in the way contemplated. If the sum agreed is a reasonable pre-estimate, then it is classified as liquidated damages and is recoverable. If it is more than the reasonable pre-estimate then it is classified as a penalty and is not recoverable, leaving the plaintiff to recover such unliquidated damages as he can in fact establish. It is important to emphasise that the test is not the plaintiff's actual loss but the plaintiff's contemplated loss as at the time of the contract. So liquidated damages can be recovered even though there is no actual loss or less actual loss than the agreed sum, provided the pre-estimate was reasonable.

A contract may provide for the payment in advance by the buyer of sums of money. Here, the law has drawn a distinction between deposits and advance payments. In certain types of contract it is common for the payment to be made in stages, tied to the achievement of particular stages of work. So, as we saw above, in a ship building contract it would be common for there to be a payment of part of the price when the keel is laid. The purpose of these schemes is to help the seller with cash flow. It typically occurs in major capital contracts when the seller or supplier has to spend considerable sums of money on acquiring components and on fitting them together. Suppliers typically are unwilling to finance the whole of the cost of this and stipulate for payment in instalments tied, as we have said, to particular stages of completion.

8.5   Party provided remedies

8.5.1   Liquidated damages

8.5.2   Deposits and advance payments

On the other hand, the buyer may have paid a deposit so as to give the seller a guarantee that the buyer will in fact go through with the contract. So the buyer may have gone into the seller's shop and picked some goods and said that he would like to buy them and come back tomorrow to collect them. In certain trades it would be very common for the seller to take a deposit because sellers know from experience that many buyers do not return and they may lose the opportunity of selling the goods elsewhere.

The importance of the distinction is this. If, having paid money in advance, the buyer then breaks the contract, she will of course be liable to damages and if the damages exceed what has been paid in advance then it will simply be a question of the seller recovering the balance. But the seller's damages may be less than the deposit or advance payment. In this situation, the courts have said that the seller can keep the deposit even if the deposit is greater than the seller's actual loss whereas if there has been an advance payment which is greater than the seller's actual loss, the seller can only keep the actual loss and must return the balance.

The amount of the deposit may be not only greater than the seller's actual loss but than any loss to the seller greater than was reasonably foreseeable at the time of the contract. In such a case it might plausibly be argued that the deposit is in fact a penalty. In practice, however, courts have tended to keep the rules about penalties and deposits in watertight compartments. A marked change of attitude was revealed in the recent case of *Workers Trust and Merchant Bank Ltd v Dojap Investments Ltd* (1993) where the Privy Council was prepared to treat a deposit in a contract for the sale of land as penal where it exceeded the going rate of 10% (even a deposit of 10% might exceed any likely loss but it was effectively held that it was too late to question the taking of deposits at the going rate).

8.6   Sellers' remedies against the goods

The seller's principal concern is to ensure that he is paid for the goods. The most effective and common way of doing this is for the seller to retain ownership of the goods as long as possible. We have already discussed this in Chapter 4. The Act does however give the unpaid seller further rights in relation to the goods as well as his right to sue the buyer for the price or damages. The provisions which are contained in ss 38 to 48 of the Act are complex but do not appear to be of much practical importance in modern situations. The central provision is s 39 which says:

'(1) Subject to this and any other Act, notwithstanding that the property in the goods may have passed to the buyer, the unpaid seller of goods, as such, has by implication of law –

(a) a lien on the goods or right to retain them for the price while he is in possession of them;

(b) in case of the insolvency of the buyer, a right of stopping the goods in transit after he has parted with the possession of them;

(c) a right of re-sale as limited by this Act.

(2) Where the property in goods has not passed to the buyer, the unpaid seller has (in addition to his other remedies) a right of withholding delivery similar to and co-extensive with his rights of lien or retention and stoppage in transit where the property has passed to the buyer.'

It will be seen that, subject to the conditions set out in the other relevant sections, the seller has the possibility of exercising a lien on the goods, that is of retaining possession of them until he is paid, of reselling them or of stopping them in transit, that is by giving notice to the carrier not to deliver to an insolvent buyer.

Remedies

Introduction

This chapter considers the remedies open to the buyer and seller if the other party fails to perform or performs defectively. Note that to a considerable extent these rules are applications of general contract law.

Remedies include:

- withholding performance and termination;
- specific performance;
- the seller's action for the price;
- damages;
- liquidation damages.

Withholding performance and termination

The threat by one party to withhold performance will either lead the other party to attend to her performance, in which case the contract will go on, or not, in which case the innocent party would usually have to decide a little later whether to terminate or not.

Not all breaches of contracts will entitle the innocent party to terminate the contract. General contract law uses two principal approaches. One, which has been heavily used in relation to the sale of goods, is to proceed in terms of clarifying the terms of the contract which has been broken. This approach postulates that certain terms, commonly called conditions, are so important that any breach of them should entitle the other party to terminate the contract. A second way of approaching the problem of termination is to ask how serious is the breach of contract which has been committed by the defendant.

Where the breach is one of condition, in terms of repudiatory or fundamental breach, it is clear that the contract does not come to an end simply because one of these events takes place. In each case the innocent party has a choice. It can treat the breach as bringing the contract to an end or it can continue to call for performance of the contract. If damages have been suffered, the innocent party may also claim damages for breach of contract.

Specific performance

Section 52 provides that in the case of specific or ascertained goods, the court may, if it thinks fit, grant specific performance. However in practice the courts have been very slow to exercise the broad powers given by the section on the basis that in a contract for sale of goods damages will be an adequate remedy since usually the buyer can go out and buy substitute goods and be adequately compensated by a money payment (*Cohen v Roche* (1927)).

Seller's action for the price

Section 49(1) links the seller's right to sue for price to the passing of property. Where sellers are entitled to sue for the price they do not have to show that they have suffered any loss; nor do they have to take steps to mitigate the loss as they would do in a damages action. On the other hand, the seller does not have an action for the price simply because the buyer's obligation to pay has crystallised and the buyer has failed to pay.

Damages

The 1979 Act contains three sections which deal with damages: ss 50, 51 and 53. In practice these provisions do not add a great deal to the general law of contract and many cases are decided without reference to them.

Liquidated damages

The courts have distinguished between liquidated damages which are enforceable and penalties which are not. The distinction turns on whether the sum agreed is a reasonable pre-estimate as at the time of the contracts of the amount of loss which is liable to flow from the contract being broken in the way contemplated.

PART II

LAW OF AGENCY

Chapter 9

Introduction to Law of Agency

A large proportion of contracts are made, at least on one side, through agents, since in most contracts at least one of the parties is a company, and companies have to act through human beings who act on their behalf. This part of the book is concerned with the law relating to the use of agents who make contracts in this way. Three parties are involved, the principal (P), the agent (A), and the third party (T) with whom the agent negotiates so as to bring his principal and the third party into a contractual relationship. In the rest of this part these three parties will be referred to as P, A and T respectively.

There are two major problems which need to be discussed. These may be called the external and internal relationships. The external relationship is concerned with the ways in which A brings P into contractual relations with T. The internal relationship is concerned with dealings between P and A and the obligations which they owe to each other. These two aspects reflect the fact that agency is both a way of bringing contracts about and also a contract in its own right.

Chapter 10 will deal with the external relationship and Chapter 11 with the internal relationship. Some important preliminary points are:

- The word 'agent' is used by lawyers in a more restricted sense than by businesspeople. If you walk down your nearest High Street you will very likely find a shop which describes itself as a Grundig or Sony Agent. It is unlikely that such a shop is in fact an agent in the legal sense. Almost certainly it is buying products from Grundig or Sony, as the case may be, and selling them on on its own behalf to customers. In legal terms it is a distributor, rather than an agent.

- Although agencies are usually created by contracts, a contract is not essential. Within families and between friends a gratuitous agency, in which somebody does something for someone else without expecting to be rewarded, is very common.

- Classically the agent has power to make a contract on behalf of his principal, which will bind the principal. However, it is by no means unusual to have agents whose job it is to negotiate but who do not have power to enter

9.1 Defining an agency

into binding contracts on behalf of the principal. So an estate agent is hired to find someone willing to buy the client's house. He will not normally have authority to enter into a binding contract on the client's behalf.

- An agent may be an agent for some purposes of a particular transaction and a principal for other purposes. For instance, if a client instructs a stockbroker to buy or sell shares on his behalf on the stock exchange, the relationship between the client and the stockbroker is basically that of principal and agent. But when the broker goes on to the exchange to carry out the instructions, he acts as a principal, because the rule of the stock exchange is that all its members deal as principals and not as agents. There are very good commercial reasons for this, since the members of the exchange have no time to investigate clients and necessarily, therefore, do business on the basis that they can trust the other members of the exchange (trust here is concerned at least as much with solvency as with dishonesty). An agent who acts in this way is often called a commission agent.

- Something like the reverse occurs with a *del credere* agent, who in effect guarantees that T will meet his obligations to P. Such an arrangement would not be unlikely where A has much better chances of assessing T's creditworthiness than P does. Of course a del credere agent would expect to command a rather better commission.

- Sometimes it is clear that an intermediary is an agent but unclear whether he acts for one side or the other. So in a contract of insurance is the intermediary acting for the insurer or the insured? In many cases the intermediary will be paid a commission by the insurer and this would seem to make him an agent of the insurer, since it is normally improper for an agent to take payment from the other side. Similarly some intermediaries, particularly in motor insurance fields, are equipped with cover notes. These would be binding when issued to the client if the intermediary is acting on behalf of the insurer. In general, the fact that the insurer has equipped the intermediary with cover notes would be a very good indication that the intermediary is acting for the insurer. On the other hand, the insured quite often tells the intermediary things which would affect the risk and which the intermediary 'forgets' to pass on to the insured. When this happens the insurer will certainly argue that the intermediary is the agent of the insured. The truth is that the situation is confused and it is difficult to analyse the practice of the insurance industry in a way which fits in with basic principles of agency law.

Whether we are talking about the external or internal relationship, we have to decide whether the principal and agent have come into an agency relationship.

As said above, a contract is not needed to create an agency. Normally the agency will come into existence because the parties have agreed that one will be the principal and the other the agent.

In *Garnac Grain v H M Faure & Fairclough* (1967) Lord Pearson said:

> 'The relationship of principal and agent can only be established by the consent of the principal and the agent. They will be held to have consented if they have agreed to what amounts in law to such a relationship, even if they do not recognise it themselves and even if they have professed to disclaim it, as in *Re Megevand, ex p Delhasse*. The consent must, however, have been given by each of them, either expressly or by implication from their words and conduct. Primarily one looks to what they said and did at the time of the alleged creation of the agency. Earlier words and conduct may afford evidence of a course of dealing in existence at that time and may be taken into account more generally as historical background. Later words and conduct may have some bearing, though likely to be less important. As to the content of the relationship, the question to be asked is "what is it that the supposed agent is alleged to have done on behalf of the supposed principal"?'

Clearly they need not use the word agency; indeed, there is no need for them to understand the law of agency, as long as they envisage a relationship which falls within its ambit. In many cases P simply engages A to do something for him, to manage his business, his hotel, to act as his solicitor for the conveyancing of his house.

Usually there are no special formal requirements, but see Powers of Attorney Act 1971.

There are special problems where P is under an incapacity, for example because P is insane or an infant. The general rule is that P cannot do anything through an agent which he could not do directly himself.

9.2   Creation of agency

In *Bolton Partners v Lambert* (1889), T made an offer to A the managing director of the company. A accepted it on the company's behalf, although he had no authority to do so. T gave notice that he was withdrawing his offer but after this the company P purported to ratify A's unauthorised acceptance. The Court of Appeal held that P could, by ratification, repair A's lack of authority and so render the contract binding, even

9.3   Ratification

though T had purported to withdraw before the ratification. This decision was controversial at the time and was strongly criticised by Lord Justice Fry in a famous appendix to his book on Specific Performance. Although it has never been overruled, there are limitations on its scope.

9.3.1	Existence of the principal

Ratification is not possible if P did not exist at the time of the original contract. This has been important in relation to contracts purportedly made on behalf of companies in the course of being formed. In *Kelner v Baxter* (1866) the plaintiffs offered to sell goods to the defendants and this offer was accepted by the defendants in a document, which after their signatures had the words 'on behalf of the proposed Gravesend Royal Alexandra Hotel Company Limited'. At the time of the transaction the hotel company did not exist. It was held that there was a contract binding on the defendants personally. Erle CJ said:

> 'As there was no company in existence at the time, the agreement would be wholly inoperative unless it were held to be binding on the defendants personally. The cases referred to in the course of the argument fully bear out the proposition that, where a contract is signed by one who professes to be signing it "as agent" but who has no principal existing at the time, and the contract would be altogether inoperative unless binding upon the person who signed it, he is bound thereby and a stranger cannot by subsequent ratification relieve him from that responsibility.'

In *Newborne v Sensolid (Gt Brit) Ltd* (1955) the plaintiff, Leopold Newborne, was in the process of forming a company Leopold Newborne (London) Ltd. Before the company was properly formed and registered he entered into a transaction with the defendants to sell them goods and the contract note was signed 'Yours faithfully, Leopold Newborne (London) Ltd' with a hieroglyphic attached which was interpreted as Leopold Newborne. The buyers refused to accept delivery and an action was started in the name of the company. The plaintiff's solicitor then discovered that the company was not registered and therefore took steps to substitute Leopold Newborne as the plaintiff. The defendants argued that they had no contract with Leopold Newborne and that they intended to contract only with the company. That argument was upheld by the Court of Appeal. The Court of Appeal took the view that Mr Newborne had not signed as agent for the company but purported to be giving the company's signature. Lord Goddard CJ said:

> 'This contract purports to be made by the company, not by Mr Newborne. He purports to be selling, not his goods,

but the company's goods. The only person who has any contract here is the company and Mr Newborne's signature is merely confirming the company's signature.'

It is clear from these two cases that there can be no contract with the company if it did not exist at the time of the contract and that later purported ratification makes no difference. The difference between the two cases is whether the human beings involved were liable. In *Kelner v Baxter* it was held that they were, because they had purported to contract as agents for a company which did not exist. In *Newborne v Sensolid*, Mr Newborne was not holding himself out as an agent. He intended to sign as the company and not as agent for the company.

The provision is now governed by the change made by s 9(2) of the European Communities Act 1972 (now Companies Act 1985 s 361(4)), which provides:

'Where a contract purports to be made by a company or by a person as agent for a company, at a time when the company has not been formed, then subject to any agreement to the contrary, the contract shall have effect as a contract entered into by the person purporting to act for the company or as agent for it, and he should be personally liable on the contract accordingly.'

This provision makes no change in the position of the company. It is still not a party to the contract and cannot ratify it. The critical question is what is necessary to show that the general rule that the person acting on behalf of the company is personally liable is ousted by 'any agreement to the contrary'. In *Phonogram Limited v Lane* (1982) the Court of Appeal refused to hold that any agreement to the contrary could be inferred, merely from the fact that the agent had signed 'for and on behalf of' (the unformed company). Granted that the policy of the section to increase the number of cases where there is someone who is personally liable on the contract, it will probably require very strong facts to persuade the court that there is an agreement that no-one is to be liable on the transaction.

A may of course act expressly subject to P's ratification. In this case there will be no contract until P ratifies. It follows that if T revokes before P's ratification there will be no contract (see *Watson v Davies* (1931)).

9.3.2   A states that he is acting subject to P's ratification

The doctrine of ratification cannot be added together with the doctrine of undisclosed principal (see below, para 2.2). If A was not only acting without authority, but apparently on his own behalf, the contract is not binding.

9.3.3   Doctrine of undisclosed principal

In *Keighley, Maxted & Co v Durant* (1901) A was authorised by P to buy wheat at 44s 3d a quarter on a joint account for A and P. Wheat was unobtainable at this price and therefore A agreed to buy from T at 44s 6d a quarter. Though he intended to buy it on behalf of himself and P, A contracted in his own name and did not disclose the agency to T. The next day P ratified the purchase at the unauthorised price but in due course P and A failed to take delivery. It was held by the House of Lords that P was not bound by any contract with T.

It is unclear what the position would be if A said he was acting as an agent but did not disclose his principal.

9.3.4   Ratification within reasonable time

Ratification must take place within a reasonable time. In *Metropolitan Asylums Board v Kingham* (1890) the corporation advertised for tenders for the supply of eggs for six months from 30 September. K put in a tender. On 22 September the board of the corporation resolved to accept and so notified K (it was assumed that a binding acceptance required the corporation seal to be affixed). On 24 September K wrote to say that he had made a mistake in drawing up the tender and had reached the wrong price. On 6 October the corporation purported to ratify its acceptance by fixing its seal to it. It was held that the ratification was ineffective because it came after the date on which performance of the contract was to start. Presumably ratification would have been effective on 29 September.

In *Dibbins v Dibbins* (1896) O and P were partners and agreed that on the death of either of them the survivor should be entitled to purchase the shares of the deceased partner upon giving notice to his executors within three months of the death. O died. Within three months of the death A, acting on P's behalf but without P's authority, gave notice to O's executors of P's intention to exercise the option. P purported to ratify more than three months after the death. It was held that this ratification was ineffective.

9.3.5   Transaction capable of ratification

In *Re Tiedemann & Ledermann Frères* (1899) A sold wheat to X on P's behalf and then re-purchased it himself. He then purported to sell it to Q, R and S on P's behalf, knowing that Q, R and S would not deal with him personally. His real intention was to carry through the transaction on his own behalf. Q, R and S purported to repudiate. It was held that P might ratify. Channell J said:

'The contracts were contracts which could be made on Tiedemann's behalf and were in respect of wheat which he had shipped to Hamburg and could divert to Rotterdam.

They were, therefore, contracts which he had the means to carry out.'

There is a very limited number of cases where the law has created an agency relationship even though the parties did not agree. At one time this was the position for deserted wives who could pledge their husband's credit for necessaries but this has been abolished by the Matrimonial Proceedings and Property Act 1970 s 41(1). Where two or more people live together, it may well be that one of them has actual or apparent authority to contract on behalf of the other. This would be subject to the ordinary rules which are discussed in the next chapter.

The important example is the master of the ship who may jettison cargo, sell or hypothecate the ship in order to raise money for repairs. For such a transaction to be binding it must be impossible for A to communicate with P; A must act in P's interest; A's conduct must be reasonable and there must be some necessity for the agent to act as he did (see *The Winson* (1982)).

Ship masters are not the only example of agents of necessity; it is simply that ships naturally produce fact situations which call for urgent decisions without the easy possibility of contacting P.

Whether the agency has come to an end may be important both for the internal and for the external relationship. If P has terminated A's authority, A will not be able to create a contract between P and T, even though the termination was wrongful as between P and A. In some cases the question will be whether A's apparent authority has been terminated (see the discussion in the next chapter).

As between P and A when the relationship comes to an end, it is primarily a matter of construing the agreement that sets up the relationship. In many cases A will be appointed for a specific purpose and the relationship comes to an end automatically when that purpose is carried out. In other cases, A will be appointed for a fixed term or for an indefinite term which is subject to termination by a stated period of notice on either side. In other cases, A will be appointed for an indefinite term which is subject to an implied term that it can be terminated by reasonable notice on either side.

The most controversial cases are likely to be those in which A is working on a commission basis and made assumptions about how long the relationship will last, which are cut across by what A regards as a premature termination. In *Rhodes v*

9.4   Agency by operation of law

9.5   Terminating the agency

Forwood (1876), P appointed A as sole agent for the sale of coal from P's colliery in Liverpool for a period of seven years. After four years P sold the colliery. It was held that there was no breach of contract. Note that in this case, it was assumed that P was not obliged to sell any coal in Liverpool; he was only obliged to sell any coal sold in Liverpool through A. So if P decided to sell all his coal in Newcastle instead, this would not have been a breach. Obviously if this is correct it would not be a breach for P to stop selling coal altogether by disposing of the colliery. This underlines the importance of construing each contract carefully.

The solution to problems of this kind will often now be different because of the Commercial Agents Regulations 1993. This gives effect to the European Directive on Commercial Agents and introduce a whole new notion into English law, which is that where the agent has participated in the building up of the business, the agent has a quasi property interest in the business which should be protected. It follows that in the area covered by the Directive, broadly situations where A has power to buy and sell on P's behalf, A is entitled to be compensated for invasions of this quasi property interest. The interest is protected even against express terms in the agency contract. The details are complex but the regulations represent a major change in English agency law. They are largely based on Continental systems, particularly German law.

Introduction to Law of Agency

This chapter deals with some preliminary matters:

1   The creation of agency;
2   The doctrine of ratification;
3   Agency by operation of law;
4   Termination of agency.

Although agencies are usually created by contracts, a contract is not essential. Normally, the agency will come into existence because the parties have agreed that one will be the principal and the other the agent (*Garnac Grain v HM Faure and Fairclough* (1967)).

The creation of agency

Where an agent enters into a contract where he had no authority from his principal to do so, the doctrine allows the principal, by ratification, to repair the agent's lack of authority and so render the contract binding (*Botton Partners v Lambert* (1889)). There are, however, limitations on its scope.

The doctrine of ratification

There is a very limited number of cases where the law has created an agency relationship even though the parties did not agree.

Agency by operation of law

As between the principal and agent, when the relationship comes to an end is primarily a matter of construing the agreement that set up the relationship. In many cases, the agent will be appointed for a specific purpose and the relationship comes to an end automatically when that purpose is carried out. In other cases, the agent will be appointed for a fixed term or for an indefinite term which is subject to termination by a stated period of notice on either side. If there is no stated period of notice, the courts will imply a term that the agency can be terminated by reasonable notice on either side.

Termination of agency

The creation of agency

The nature of agent's obligation

Agency by operation of law

Termination of agency

Chapter 10

The External Relationship

The general principle is that A will bind P when he acts within the scope of his authority. However, in order to work out what this means it is necessary to distinguish between different kinds of authority.

In order for T to be liable to P, it is necessary to show that A acted within the scope of his actual authority. Such actual authority may be either express or implied. The authority is express where P has given A express instructions. In many cases little or nothing would have been said by way of express instructions and what will be important is what is to be implied. It may be argued that authority is to be implied because what has been done is necessarily incidental to what was expressly instructed; or that A has been appointed to the position which in the natural course of things carries with it implied authority. Such a position may be managerial, that is, A has been appointed to run B's pub or it may be professional, A has been engaged to act as P's solicitor for the sale of P's house. In the case of commonly repeated transactions the courts have often worked out through the cases what is to be implied. So in the case of selling a house, it is established that solicitors engaged in the conveyancing have implied authority to take a deposit but that estate agents do not (*Sorrell v Finch* (1976)).

For this purpose it does not really make any difference whether the parties know what the cases have decided. P can of course give A wider or narrower authority but if he does not make such a grant A will have the usual implied authority.

Although T is only liable to P if A has acted within the scope of his actual authority, the reverse is not true. T will have a claim against P, not only where A acts within the scope of his actual authority but also where A acts within the scope of his apparent or ostensible authority. This is a fundamental principle of agency law. In practice, in the vast majority of cases T will have no idea what A's actual authority is and will rely on the authority which A appears to have. The arguments as to A's apparent authority are likely to be based on two different lines of thought, though they may well overlap in some cases. One argument will be that A has the authority which people in his position usually have. So if solicitors conducting conveyancing usually have authority to take

10.1 Authority

10.1.1 Actual authority

deposits on behalf of the seller, a particular solicitor acting for a particular seller will appear to have this authority even though in fact the seller has told him not to accept a deposit. The position would be different if T knew that A's implied authority had been revoked but in the nature of things this will very often not be the case.

10.1.2   Apparent authority

A second line of reasoning is that P has held A out as having authority to conduct particular kinds of business. So if Wickfield allows Uriah Heep to take over the day-to-day running of his practice, he cannot complain that people assume that Heep is authorised so to do. These were the exact facts of *Lloyd v Grace Smith & Co* (1912), where the sole partner in a firm of solicitors allowed the conveyancing manager complete autonomy in the running of the conveyancing department and the conveyancing manager practised a fraud on an elderly lady client who had gone to the firm for advice. The acts carried out were clearly within the apparent authority of the conveyancing manager; they did not stop being so because he put the proceeds in his own pocket.

A classic authority is *Freeman & Lockyer v Buckhurst Park Properties (Mangal) Ltd* (1964). In that case the plaintiffs did work for the defendant company on the instructions of one Kapoor who was a director of the company and who in fact was acting as if he was managing director, though he had never been appointed as managing director. It was held that the company had held Kapoor out to the plaintiffs as its managing director and that making the contract was within the usual authority of a managing director, so that the company was bound. Diplock LJ said that there were four requirements:

(a) that a representation that the agent had authority to enter on behalf of the company into a contract of the kind sought to be enforced was made to the contractor;

(b) that such representation was made by a person or persons who had 'actual' authority to manage the business of the company either generally or in respect of those matters to which the contract relates;

(c) that he (the contractor) was induced by such representation to enter into the contract, that is that he in fact relied upon it; and

(d) that under its memorandum or articles of association the company was not deprived of the capacity either to enter into a contract of the kind sought to be enforced or to delegate authority to enter into a contract of that kind to the agent.

Were P is an individual it will be a question of whether P has held A out as having authority.

Where P is a company there will be important and possibly difficult questions as to who in the company was in a position to hold out A as having authority to act. In *British Bank of the Middle East v Sun Life Assurance Co of Canada (UK) Ltd* (1993) a letter was written on behalf of the bank to the insurance company seeking confirmation that an employee of the insurance company had actual authority to execute the relevant document. This document was addressed to the general manager of Sun Life (UK) at the City branch of the company. It was in fact answered by a branch manager. The House of Lords held that the branch manager did not have actual authority to confirm the authority of A and that the mere fact that he had replied to the letter, which clearly called for a reply from someone considerably more senior did not give him that authority.

It follows from this that A cannot himself do something which holds him out as having authority.

In *Armagas v Mundogas* (1986) Mundogas had an option to buy an LPG carrying ship, the *Ocean Frost*, for $5,200,000. The option was exercisable, at the latest, by 6 June 1980. Early in 1980 Mundogas decided that it might be possible to re-sell the ship for more than the option price. The appellants indicated that they might be willing to buy the ship but only if the ship was immediately chartered back to Mundogas for three years at an appropriate hire. Magelssen the vice-president and chartering manager at Mundogas, had actual and apparent authority to sell the ship. He did not have either actual or apparent authority to enter into a three-year charter and he knew that he would not be able to obtain actual authority from his superiors. He and the relevant executive of the ship brokers entered a corrupt deal to deceive both Armagas and Mundogas. This involved representing to Armagas that Magelssen had actual authority to enter into a three-year charter. Mundogas exercised the option and sold the ship to Armagas for $5,750,000. A document for a three-year charter at £350,000 a month was produced and signed by Magelssen, purportedly on behalf of Mundogas. The conspirators' plan was to sub-charter the ship on an annual basis and to use the sub-charter payments to pay the charter. If the charter hire rate stayed at the level at the date of the sale, this scheme might well have worked. Unfortunately for the crooks the charter hire market collapsed and the transaction unravelled. It was held by the House of Lords that the three-year charter was not binding on Mundogas because Magelssen had neither actual nor apparent authority to enter into it and his assertions that he had been granted special authority to enter into this particular transaction did not give him apparent authority. Lord Keith said:

> 'No representation by Mr Magelssen can help Armagas. It must be in a position to found on some relevant representation by the responsible management of Mundogas as to Mr Magelssen's authority.'

There is no reason why P should not communicate with possible Ts to tell them that A does not have the authority which he would otherwise appear to have. So in *Overbrooke Estates v Glencombe Properties* (1974) an auctioneer's standard conditions made it clear that the auctioneer did not have any authority to make statements on behalf of the vendor of a property. This was treated not as being a clause seeking to exclude liability but as a clause defining the actual and apparent authority of the auctioneer and, therefore, effective.

In practice, in many cases there will be arguments both about the implied actual authority and apparent authority of A. So in *Hely-Hutchinson v Brayhead* (1968) the chairman of a company acted as its *de facto* managing director. This was treated by Roskill J as a case of apparent authority but by the Court of Appeal as a case on implied authority.

An instructive case is *Waugh v Clifford* (1982). In this case, the solicitors acting for two parties in litigation reached a compromise. The compromise was in fact contrary to the express instructions of one of the parties, which had been mislaid in the offices of his solicitors. The Court of Appeal held that the compromise was binding because solicitors have implied authority to reach a settlement and therefore apparent authority to do so. However, although apparent usual authority is clearly linked to implied authority the Court of Appeal was careful to stress that it should not be assumed that the boundaries of the two are the same.

The application of the apparent authority doctrine may present particular difficulties in a public law setting because of the notion that employers of the Crown are all servants of the Crown and do not employ each other. In *Attorney General for Ceylon v Silva* (1953), it was said that:

> 'No public officer, unless he possesses some special power, can hold out on behalf of the Crown that he or some other public officer has the right to enter into a contract in respect of the property of the Crown when in fact no such right exists.'

There are three possibilities: A may reveal the identity of the P whom he represents; A may make it clear that he is acting as an agent but not reveal the identity of his P. A may in fact behave as if he was himself the P. English law has come to accept the doctrine of the undisclosed principal so that even though T thought he was contracting with A, it is possible for P to come in and take over the contract. It is hard to explain the rationale of this principle and the rule is not to be found in many other legal systems. Nevertheless it is well established. However, the consequences of transactions carried out by A are different.

10.2   Disclosed and undisclosed principals

Where P is disclosed, whether named or unnamed, the general rule is clear. P is liable and entitled to sue on the contract; A is neither liable nor entitled. If A acts outside his actual authority, but within his apparent authority, then P will be liable but will not be entitled to sue unless he ratifies the contract.

10.2.1   Disclosed principals

There are some cases where A is also liable and these are discussed below in s 3.

There are some special and complicated rules about bills of exchange, signed by agents: see ss 23 to 26 of the Bills of Exchange Act 1882. The general rule is that a principal is not liable on a bill of exchange, promissory note or cheque, unless his signature appears on it. However, it is not necessary that he should sign himself; it is sufficient that his signature is written by some person acting under his authority. Where P is a corporation, the bill or cheque will normally be signed by an agent. The critical question is whether the signature is that of the corporation or of the agent. Section 26(1) of the Bills of Exchange Act 1882 provides:

10.2.2   Bills of exchange

'(1) Where a person signs a bill as drawer, indorser, or acceptor, and adds words to his signature, indicating that he signs for or on behalf of a principal, or in a representative character, he is not personally liable thereon; but the mere addition to his signature of words describing him as an agent, or as filling a representative character, does not exempt him from personal liability.'

In *Brebner v Henderson* (1925) the promissory note was made out in the form:

'We promise to pay ... and signed 'CD, Director, EF, Secretary, the FE Ltd'.

It was held that the personal signatories were liable and the company was not, because although the signatures made it clear that CD and EF were officers of the company, they did not make it clear that they signed on behalf of the company.

10.2.3   Undisclosed principals

Where there is an undisclosed principal the general rule is that both P and A are bound. In principle, it is hard to see how there can be cases of ostensible authority in such a situation, since A has appeared to be acting on his own behalf.

However, in the controversial case of *Watteau v Fenwick* (1893), the defendants were the owners of a hotel. The hotel was managed for them by a man called Humble, whose name was over the door. The plaintiffs had supplied cigars to Humble and gave credit to Humble, and Humble alone. They had never heard of the defendants. The defendants had forbidden Humble to buy cigars on credit. The evidence was, however, that the cigars were the kind which would usually be supplied to and dealt with at an establishment of this kind. It was held that P was liable even though A had in fact been forbidden to do the act. One could in fact add together the doctrines of undisclosed principle and apparent authority, so that P was liable for acts of A which were within the usual authority of someone running a business of this kind. It did not matter that T thought they were dealing with a principal rather than an agent.

This has always been regarded as a doubtful case. It can be contrasted with *Koorangan Investments v Richardson & Wrench* (1982). In this case the plaintiffs lent money on mortgages. Mortgages were secured on properties which had been valued by Rathborne and it was accepted that the valuations were negligent. Rathborne was employed by the defendants, who were a firm of real estate agents and valuers. The valuations were on the defendant's notepaper but it was accepted that careful steps had been taken by Rathborne, in breach of the defendants' internal procedures, to make sure that nobody in the defendants company knew of the valuations. The valuations were prepared by Rathborne at the offices of another company and typed by a secretary employed by that company on headed paper of the defendant, supplied to her by Rathborne. None of the standard file copies were in the defendants' offices and the copy provided to the plaintiffs had been photocopied in such a way that the name of the person who had done the valuation was not contained. The plaintiffs did not deal with Rathborne or indeed know of his existence. There is no question, therefore, of apparent authority. The plaintiffs argued that what had been done was within Rathborne's actual authority. That argument was decisively rejected by the Privy Council. Lord Wilberforce said:

'In the present case, the defendants did carry out valuations. Valuations were a class of acts which Rathborne could perform on their behalf. To argue from this that any valuation done by Rathborne, without any authority from the defendants, and on behalf of the defendants but in his own interest, without any connection with the defendants' business, is a valuation for which the defendants must assume responsibility, is not one which principle or authority can support. To endorse it would strain the doctrine of vicarious responsibility beyond the breaking point and in effect introduce into the law of agency a new principle equivalent to one of strict liability. If one then inquires, as their Lordships think it correct to do, whether Rathborne had any authority to make the valuations in question, the answer is clear; it is given in clear and convincing terms by the trial judge. Rathborne was not authorised to make them; he made them during a period when the GB group were not in a client relationship with the defendants, when valuers were ordered not to do business with them. Rathborne did them, not as an employee of the defendants, but as an employee, or associate, in the GB Group and on their instructions. They were done at the premises of the GB Group, and using the staff of the GB Group: they were not processed through the defendants and no payment in respect of them was made to the defendants. Mr Hodgson, the responsible director, knew nothing of them. They had no connection with the defendants except through the use, totally unauthorised – to say nothing more – of the defendants' stationery. A clearer case of departure from the course or scope of Rathborne's employment cannot be imagined: it was total. The judge's conclusion on this part of the case was, in their Lordships' opinion, entirely correct.'

The doctrine of the undisclosed principal is obviously potentially onerous to T. So not surprisingly there are cases limiting its scope. In some cases it has been held that the express or implied terms of the contract in fact prevent the doctrine being applied.

In *Humble v Hunter* (1848) an agent executed a charterparty in his own name and was described in the document as the owner of the ship. It was held that P could not give evidence to show that A contracted on his behalf as this would be inconsistent with the statement that A was the owner of the ship. To modern eyes, this might be regarded as a rather extreme example of the 'parole evidence rule'.

In *F Drughorn Ltd v Rederiaktiebolaget Transatlantic* (1919) a charterparty described A as the 'charterer'. It was held that the evidence was admissible to show that A was in fact acting on behalf of P. Lord Haldane said:

'In accordance with ordinary business, commonsense and custom the charterers should be able to contract as agents for undisclosed principals who may come in and take the benefit of the charterparties.'

In *The Astyanax* (1985) Kerr LJ said:

> 'The description of Mr Pangagiotis (the purported agent) as "disponent owner" was admittedly in itself neutral. But the surrounding circumstances and the course of the negotiations clearly show that the intention was that he would conclude a time charter with the registered owners and that it was on this basis that he was described in the sub-voyage charter as "disponent owner". This was inconsistent with his contracting in the capacity of a mere agent on behalf of the registered owners, with the result that they cannot contend that they were in fact his undisclosed principals.'

There is also a small group of cases in which it has been said that the undisclosed principal cannot come in because it is clear that T would never be willing to contract with P. A good example is *Said v Butt* (1920), where A bought a theatre ticket on behalf of P in circumstances where there was a dispute between P and T, such as T would certainly not have sold a ticket directly to P. It was held that P could not intervene.

In these cases where T has a choice between suing P and suing A, it appears that if T decides to sue one and pursues the case so far as judgment against that one, he cannot later sue the other one. (This is obviously important where the one he chooses to sue turns out to be insolvent.) In *Priestly v Fernie* (1865), the master of the ship signed a bill of lading in his own name. The consignee sued and obtained judgment on him but the judgment was never satisfied. It was held that the consignee could not thereafter sue the shipowner.

Starting an action would not have this effect unless it was clear in all the circumstances that there had been a conscious election to look to one party only.

In *Clarkson Booker v Andjel* (1964) the plaintiffs sued for the price of 12 flights from Athens to London, which they had booked at the request of the defendant. The case was conducted on the basis that the defendant had acted as A for undisclosed principals. Some nine months after they issued tickets, the plaintiffs had written to both A and P demanding payment. Not having received payment they commenced an action against P and were told that P was insolvent and had gone into voluntary liquidation. The Court of Appeal held that it was not too late for the plaintiffs to sue A.

Suppose money is paid to A which he does not pay on. Does P or T bear the loss for A's dishonesty? It is necessary to distinguish between payments by T to A for transmission to P and payments by P to A for transmission to T.

In *Cooke v Eshelby* (1887) a broker entrusted with possession of goods by P sold them in his own name. The buyer knew the broker sometimes sold his own goods and sometimes those of P and that in both cases he sold in his own name. It was held that the buyer was not entitled in an action by P to set off against the sum due a debt which the broker owed him personally.

In *Irvine v Watson* (1880) the plaintiffs sold casks of oil and the contract named Conning as the purchaser but the plaintiffs knew that Conning was buying for P, though they did not know the identity of P. The defendants (P) had authorised Conning to pledge their credit and the invoice specified the goods to have been bought 'Per John Conning'. The defendants paid Conning but Conning did not transmit the money to the plaintiffs. The Court of Appeal was clear that the mere fact that the defendants had paid Conning would not discharge their obligation to the plaintiffs. Bramwell LJ said:

> 'It is impossible to say that it discharged them, unless they were misled by some conduct of the plaintiffs into the belief that the broker had already settled with the plaintiffs, and made such payment in consequence of such belief.'

In *Sorrell v Finch* (1977) a deposit was paid to an estate agent in respect of a 'subject to contract' agreement for the sale of a house. The prospective vendor had not expressly authorised the estate agent to receive such a payment. The House of Lords held that an estate agent would normally have no implied and therefore no apparent authority to take a deposit and that therefore he was holding the money on behalf of the prospective purchaser, who was the only person entitled to recover it.

The scope of A's authority is clearly very critical here.

A is liable to be sued in the following situations:

- where he acts for an undisclosed principal (see *Kelner v Baxter* (1886) discussed at 9.3.1 above).

- where the contract is so formulated that the court concludes that the intention was that A would be liable or that both A and P were liable (*Kelner v Baxter* (1866)) or that both A and P be liable (*The Swan* (1968)).

10.3   Cases where A is liable to be sued

A owned a shipping vessel and formed a company P to hire it from him and operate it. He ordered repairs, using the company's notepaper and signing with his name and the word director. It was held that although he had contracted as A for P, he had also undertaken personal liability. It is obviously of practical importance that in this situation the repairs had been carried out and that the company was insolvent, so that A would have had the benefit of the repairs without having to pay for them, unless he were liable on the contract.

Conceivably in some cases A may be liable in tort; see the difficult and complex case of *The Zephyr* (1984) discussed at para 11.1 below.

If A leads T to believe she has authority when she does not T may suffer loss, particularly where A is not acting within her apparent authority. In *Collen v Wright* (1857) it was established that in this situation A is liable on the grounds that he contracted that he does have authority. A describing himself as the agent of P agreed in writing to lease to T a farm which belonged to P. Both T and A believed that A had the authority of P to make the lease but this in fact was not the case. T having failed in specific performance against P took a course of action against A, claiming as damages the cost that he had incurred in suing P. It was held that the action succeeded. Willes J said:

'The obligation arising in such a case is well expressed by saying that a person, professing to contract as agent for another, impliedly, if not expressly, undertakes to, or promises the person who enters into such a contract, upon the faith of the professed agent being duly authorised, that the authority which he professes to have does in point of fact exist. The fact of entering into the transaction with the professed agent, as such, is good consideration for the promise.'

This is clearly what we would now call a collateral contract. A is liable on this even if he honestly and reasonably thinks he has authority.

In *Yonge v Toynbee* (1910) the solicitors were appointed to act for Mr Toynbee in litigation brought by the plaintiffs. The solicitors' appointment was brought to an end when, unknown to them, Mr Toynbee became of unsound mind. After this they took a number of further steps in litigation, which caused the plaintiffs to incur costs. It was held that the solicitors were liable for the plaintiffs' costs, which had been lost as a result of breach of the implied contract that they had authority to act on behalf of their client.

10.4 Cases where A is entitled to sue

• Undisclosed principal cases

A situation may arise where there is a contract both with P and with A. For instance, an auctioneer can usually sue on a collateral contract quite separate from that of the client whose goods have been auctioned. See Chelmsford Auctions v Poole (1973).

The External Relationship

This chapter deals with the rules governing the way in which A creates a contracts between P and T.

The two principal doctrines considered are:

1   Authority, actual and apparent;

2   Principals, disclosed and undisclosed.

The general principal is that A will bind P when he acts within the scope of his authority. It is therefore necessary to distinguish between different kinds of authority.

Authority

- Actual authority

  Actual authority may be either express or implied. The authority is express where P has given A express instructions. Authority is to be implied because what has been done is necessarily incidental to what was expressly instructed; or that A has been appointed to the position which is the natural course of things carries with it implied authority.

- Apparent authority

  Diplock LJ in *Freeman & Lockyer v Buckhurst Properties (Mangal) Ltd* (1964) said that there were four requirements:

  (a) that a representation that the agent had authority to enter on behalf of the company into a contract of the kind sought to be enforced was made to the contractor;

  (b) that such representation was made by a person or persons who had 'actual' authority to manage the business of the company either generally or in respect of those matters to which the contract relates;

  (c) that he (the contractor) was induced by such representation to enter into the contract, that is that he in fact relied upon it; and

  (d) that under its memorandum or articles of association the company was not deprived of the capacity either to enter into a contract of the kind sought to be enforced or to delegate authority to enter into a contract of that kind to the agent.

Disclosed and undisclosed principals

Where P is disclosed, whether named or unnamed, P is liable and entitled to sue on the contract; A is neither liable nor entitled. If A acts outside his actual authority, but within his apparent authority, then P will be liable but will not be entitled to sue unless he ratifies the contract.

Where P is undisclosed, the general rule is that both P and A are bound.

Chapter 11

The Internal Relationship

Where there is a contract A will obviously be liable for failure to carry out the contract. In some cases there will be elaborate express terms. In other cases it would be a question of what is to be implied. In most cases A will be expected to take reasonable care and skill in pursuit of what he has been appointed to do.

He will not usually be strictly liable successfully to carry out all his instructions but this must obviously depend on all the circumstances surrounding the contract.

In some cases there will be no contract, for instance, because the appointment is gratuitous. A would nowadays usually be liable in tort under *Hedley Byrne* for carelessly carrying out his instructions. The most difficult case would be where A carelessly fails to act. In this respect the important and difficult case of *The Zephyr* (1984) may give clues.

This case is concerned with the position of insurance placed on the Lloyd's maritime market. In this market insurance is normally placed with a number of syndicates. Brokers seeking to place insurance will normally first find a lead underwriter who will agree to take a part of the risk and indicate this by initialling a slip. Each underwriter would indicate what share of the risk he is prepared to take. It is common practice for brokers to carry on collecting initials on the slip after they have achieved 100% cover and indeed to indicate to underwriters as they are doing so that they intend to go to, say, 200%. The consequence of this would be that each underwriter would only have to take half the risk which he had indicated initially on the slip. Basically the case was concerned with whether undertakings by the broker as to how much he was going to over-provide were binding either contractually or tortiously. At first instance, Hobhouse J held that in principle the brokers would be under a tortious liability. On appeal Mustill LJ indicated that he did not agree with this view, though because of the procedural nature of the appeal it had to be assumed that it was at least arguable. This obviously leaves the question in some confusion, particularly as the area is in any case one which is still developing and where the precise boundaries between contract and tort cannot be drawn with any certainty.

11.1 Duties of agent towards principal

11.1.1 Contractual liability

11.1.2 Tortious liability

11.1.3   Fiduciary duties

Perhaps the most important and certainly the least understood by many principals and agents obligation are the fiduciary duties of A to P. It is clear that A must not put himself in a situation where his interests conflicts with that of P; she must not make a profit from her position or from any confidential information which she acquires, and similarly, A must not take commissions from T without revealing them to P. (In practice in some areas it has been extremely common historically for As to do this, particularly in relation to the formation of insurance contracts, where A nearly always receives a substantial commission from the insurer. This can only be justified if A is acting on behalf of the insurer but there is no doubt for other purposes A is treated as acting on behalf of the insured.)

There are difficult and complex cases on the remedies which P has in respect of this improper activity by A. Certainly P has a personal action in all cases, that is, he can sue for the money which A has improperly received. However, at least in some cases, P has a more extensive remedy based on constructive trust so that he can argue that property A holds is held on trust for him. This can be important where there are many claims against A, who is effectively insolvent and a constructive trust remedy might enable P to jump the queue. It can also be important where A has invested the proceeds and made further profits, which P can claim are really his. A very important case on this is *Phipps v Boardman* (1967).

A will created a trust, which included a shareholding in a private company. A1, a solicitor who had been acting for the trust, and A2, one of the beneficiaries, decided that the best way to protect the interests of the trust was to gain control of the company. Both A1 and A2 were commercially sophisticated and energetic. They bought shares in the company with their own money. These shares, together with the trust's holding constituted a controlling interest in the company. A1 and A2 led the directors of the company to think that they were acting on behalf of the trust. They therefore obtained substantial amounts of confidential information. A1 and A2 spent much time and ingenuity developing the interest in the company and the end result was that A1, A2 and the trust showed a handsome profit. It was held that A1 and A2 had to account for the profits which they had made on the shares which they had bought. They had made this profit partly by acting or appearing to act on behalf of the trust and partly out of access to confidential information, which they would not have obtained if they had not appeared to be acting on behalf of the trust and which, once they had obtained it, they could not use so as to enrich themselves. It is important to underline that in this case A1 and A2 were not subjectively dishonest. They thought that what they were doing was in everyone's best interests. They took risks with their own money and they do not appear to have reduced the value of the trust holding or indeed significantly to have risked doing so. Nevertheless, the House of Lords had no doubt that they were liable to account, though it did think that in the circumstances they were entitled to reasonable compensation for the work that they had put in.

In *Queensland Mines v Hodson* (1978), the Privy Council held that this reasoning did not apply where P (a company) had with full knowledge of the relevant facts, renounced all interest in the project and left A (its managing director) to carry on at his own risk and expense.

Historically the courts have appeared to hold that secret commissions and bribes only give rise to a personal action. In *Lister v Stubbs* (1890) A, who was employed to buy goods, accepted bribes from T (the seller of the goods) and invested part of the amount. It was held that although P could maintain an action for the amount of the bribes, it could not maintain an action for the proceeds of the profits for investing the bribes.

Even on the basis that the remedy is only personal, there will be situations in which P has a choice of remedies. P may bring an action for damages, based on the loss suffered by P from the transaction. Alternatively, P can bring an action claiming the amount of the bribe. In *Mahesan v Malaysian Government Officers CHS* (1979), the House of Lords held that the plaintiff may sue on either basis but cannot sue on both.

But the Privy Council recently disagreed with *Lister v Stubbs* in *Attorney General of Hong Kong v Reid* (1994). The respondent in this case had been convicted of accepting bribes which had been given to him while he was a public prosecutor in Hong Kong, so as to induce him to obstruct the prosecution of certain criminals. The Attorney General for Hong Kong brought an action in New Zealand, claiming that properties in New Zealand which the respondent had bought with the bribes were held on constructive trust in favour of the Crown. The Privy Council held that if property representing the bribe increased in value or if a cash bribe was invested advantageously, the fiduciary was accountable not only for the original amount of the bribe but also for the increased value of the property and accordingly the properties were indeed held in trust for the Crown. Lord Templeton said:

'The decision in *Lister v Stubbs* was not consistent with the principles that a fiduciary must not be allowed to benefit from his own breach of duty, that the fiduciary should account for the bribe as soon as he receives it and that equity regards as done that which ought to be done.'

11.1.4   Delegation

The general principle must be that the agent is not to delegate the task which has been entrusted to him. This is on the basis that P has chosen A relying on the agent's personal qualities and is not therefore required to accept someone else's performance. There will be many cases where delegation is expressly permitted and no doubt there are also cases in which it is impliedly permitted. So, for example, if the practice in a particular trade or profession is to delegate it can no doubt be inferred that delegation is permitted unless it is expressly prohibited. Similarly, there will be cases where the nature of the transaction will be such as to show that A can in practice not carry out his task without sub agents. So in *Bussche v Alt* (1878), Thesiger LJ said:

'A case like the present, where a shipowner employs an agent for the purpose of effectuating a sale of a ship at any port where the ship may from time to time in the course of its employment under charter happen to he, is pre-eminently one in which the appointment of substitutes at ports other than those where the agent himself carries on business is a necessity, and must reasonably be presumed to be in the contemplation of the parties; and in the present case, we have, over and above that presumption, what cannot but be looked upon as express authority to appoint a substitute ...'

Where an authorised sub-agent is appointed there will be questions regarding what rights P has against the sub-agent. Normally there will be no contract between P and sub-agent. P could recover an improper commission, taken by the sub-agent as in *Powell & Thomas v Evan Jones* (1905), where shipowners employed agents to obtain for them a loan secured by means of debentures on their ships. The agents with P's consent employed a sub-agreement employed a sub-agent who negotiated such a loan and accepted a commission from the lender. It was held that P could recover this commission from the sub-agent. The position in tort is very unclear. There are some old cases which appear to deny the possibility of a tort remedy but most of these were before *Hedley Byrne* and many before *Donohue v Stevenson*. There are modern cases holding that a sub bailee may be liable to the bailor, for example *Morris v C W Martin* (1966). But it may be that sub-bailment is a special case.

11.2   Rights of the agent against the principal

By far the majority of reported cases involve disputes about how much the agent is entitled to be paid. Of course some agents were not entitled to be paid, either because the appointment was gratuitous or because they had exceeded their authority (unless their acts were later ratified). It appears that in general most agents are entitled to be paid. Two main areas of dispute have arisen: one is the rate of payment and the other the conditions to be satisfied before payment is due.

The basic rule must be that the rate is whatever the parties have agreed. So courts have held that if the agent agrees to work for a commission to be left to P's discretion as in *Kofi v Strauss* (1951). A is only entitled to whatever P decides. Similarly a managing director who agrees to serve on such terms as the board may fix, as in *Re Richmond Gate* (1965).

If no express agreement is made it would be normal to imply a term that A is entitled to a reasonable payment, if it is clear that A is not to work for nothing (see *Way v Latilla* (1937)).

A reasonable payment would not necessarily be A's usual professional fees. This was decided in *Wilkie v Scottish Aviation* (1956) where A was a surveyor.

Obviously again this depends on the construction of the contract. It is extremely common for A to be paid on a commission basis and for the commission to be payable on the occurrence of an event such as the completion of the sale or the execution of a policy.

There have been vast numbers of cases concerned with the position of estate agents. In *Luxor v Cooper* (1941) the House of Lords held that P need not keep the commission open so as to give A the chance to earn his commission. Undoubtedly this case and others like it rest on an underlying assumption that an estate agent should expect to be paid from the proceeds of the sale and that if no sale is completed there are no proceeds to share with the estate agent. Estate agents commonly seek to improve their position by stipulating that the commission is payable not on completion of the sale but on some earlier event, such as the introduction of a purchaser or the introduction of a person 'reading, willing and able to purchase'. No doubt if estate agents had a sign in a prominent position outside their offices, saying 'we expect to be paid even if we do not sell your property', courts might be willing to construe such words as entitling an agent to payment if he finds a willing purchaser and the sale then falls through. However, in practice, agents do not express themselves with this brutal clarity, but rely on a document drafted by an estate agent and expressed in ambiguous terms. Courts have consistently held against constructions which result in commission being payable before the sale is complete, though

11.2.1   The rate of payment

11.2.2   The conditions to be satisfied before A is entitled to payment

it is clear that, in principle, it must be possible to find words which produce this result.

The agents' acts must be the effective cause of the event which triggers the right to payment. Where more than one agent is employed to sell a property, it would normally only be one of them who is the effective cause of the sale being completed, though there may well be scope for disputes in a case where the purchaser has actually got particulars of the house from two agents. In *Miller Son & Co v Radford* (1903), P employed A to find a purchaser of a property or failing that a tenant. A tenant was found and commission paid. Fifteen months later the tenant purchased the property. The Court of Appeal held that A was not entitled to commission.

In *Alpha Trading Ltd v Dunnshaw-Patten Ltd* (1981), the defendants P entered into a contract to sell 10,000 metric tons of cement C & F Bandarshapur to Mueller. P also agreed to pay a commission to A (the plaintiffs) for introducing Mueller to them as buyers. P never performed the contract with Mueller and argued that there was, therefore, no obligation to pay the commission to A, since commission was only payable on performance of the contract with Mueller. The Court of Appeal rejected this reasoning and held that in the circumstances it was an implied term of the contract between P and A, that P would in fact carry out its contract with Mueller. Note that in this case P had actually entered into a contract with Mueller; it would be much more difficult to imply a term that P would enter into such a contract, so it would usually be much easier for P to change its mind before the contract with T had come into existence.

| 11.2.3 | Losses incurred | The agent is entitled to be indemnified against all losses and liabilities incurred by her whilst acting within the scope of her authority. |
| 11.2.4 | Lien on goods | A will have a lien on any goods and chattels of P which are in his hands, so he need not release the goods until P has met all his legitimate claims. |

The Internal Relationship

This chapter considers:

1   The duties which the agent owes to the principal – contractual, tortious and fiduciary.

2   The agent's rights against the principal, particularly as to remuneration.

Duties of agent towards principal

Where there is a contract, A will be liable for failure to carry out the contract. Where there is no contract, for instance, because the appointment is gratuitous, A would usually be liable in tort under *Hedley Byrne* for carelessly carrying out his instructions.

Perhaps the most important obligations are the fiduciary duties owed by A to P. It is clear that A must not put himself in a situation where his interests conflict with those of P or that he must not make a profit from his position or from any confidential information which he acquires and, similarly, A must not take commissions from T without revealing them to P.

Rights of the agent against the principal

Unless the appointment was gratuitous, in general most agents are entitled to be paid. Two main areas of dispute have arisen: one is the rate of payment and the other the conditions to be satisfied before payment is due.

The Internal Relationship

PART III

CARRIAGE OF GOODS BY SEA

Chapter 12

Introduction to Carriage of Goods by Sea

Carriage of goods by sea may fit into a commercial law course in a number of different ways. It may be studied as a component standing on its own. It may also be studied as part of the study of the whole topic of carriage of goods, including carriage by land and by air. It may also be studied alongside the law relating to international sales. Although carriage of goods by sea and international sales are separate subjects and can be studied separately, they have a major practical overlap in that the reason for making most contracts of carriage of goods by sea is in order to perform an international sale contract. If you are studying a commercial law course, which includes international sales but does not include carriage of goods by sea you may find it helpful nevertheless to read this part as it will help you to understand what the seller and buyer are doing in order to perform the contract of sale. In the present work we have decided to concentrate on carriage of goods by sea and international sales as the most interesting and commonly taught elements.

In England most litigated and reported cases in carriage of goods are cases of carriage of goods by sea. This is because Britain is an island and has for centuries been one of the world's great trading nations. The result is indeed that many of the leading cases in general contract law are cases involving carriage of goods by sea.

The classical model involved a contract for the carriage of goods by road to a port, carriage of goods by sea from a port in England to a port in another country or vice versa and a land contract at the destination. Historically the land transport contracts gave rise to relatively few disputes as compared with the sea carriage contracts. Although it is possible today to carry goods by air, relative costs mean that it is usually only sensible to do so in the case of relatively small, high value items, where it is worth paying a significant premium for speed and delivery.

However, there have been two major changes in relation to sea transport, which enormously affect modern practice, although they have not yet had a very obvious impact on the sort of cases which come before the court. One is the development of the multi-modal contract, which embraces carriage by two or more modes. Historically a contract by a Birmingham

12.1 Nature of the subject

12.1.1 Multi-modal contracts

merchant to sell to a merchant in Frankfurt would have involved two land contracts and a sea contract. Today the Birmingham merchant would probably put the goods on board a lorry in Birmingham, which would drive to one of the channel ports, take a roll-on roll-off ferry and drive off on the other side down the Continental motorway network to Frankfurt. Although the goods will be carried by sea and there would be a contract between the lorry owner and the sea carrier, there will be no need for the Birmingham merchant to make a contract with the sea carrier (unless it was his lorry which was carrying the goods).

12.1.2   Containerisation

The other great development is containerisation. Traditionally goods were taken to a port and loaded into the hold of the ship. Although this is still done with certain types of cargo, it is nowadays common for many kinds of goods to be first of all loaded into a container and then for the container to be loaded onto a specially designed container ship. Because of historic difficulties with dockers, which are experienced in many countries, the container is often packed or 'stuffed' away from the docks at some inland centre and then carried in their loaded fashion to the docks. One important practical consequence of this practice is that the shipowner has, in practice, no means of knowing what is inside the container which typically arrives already sealed.

12.1.3   Statutory control

In the 19th century the doctrine of freedom of contract was applied to contracts of carriage of goods by sea, so that there was little or no attempt to protect weaker parties. In practice, this meant that shipowners had a wide ability to trade on standard terms, which served to limit their liability. Some countries, such as Britain, were predominantly ship owning countries. Their ships carried goods of goods owners from many other countries. Other countries, particularly the United States, were predominantly goods owning countries. Although they owned ships, many of the goods which they imported and exported were carried in ships which did not fly the Stars and Stripes. Ship owning countries were naturally much more relaxed about the practice of shipowners excluding much of their liability than were cargo owning countries. This distinction is still important today. In the late 1890s, the United States was the first country to react to this situation by passing the Harter Act in 1893, which substantially restricted the freedom of shipowners to limit their liability. This led to a series of international conferences to see whether an acceptable compromise between the interests of shipowners and cargo owners could be reached. This was done in the early 1920s by the adoption of the Hague Rules, which were enacted into

English law by the Carriage of Goods by Sea Act 1924. The Hague Rules and the 1924 Act had laid down a mandatory regime for contracts where the goods were carried under a bill of lading but not for carriage under charter-parties (this distinction is explained below). A revised version of the Hague Rules, The Hague-Visby Rules were adopted into English law by the Carriage of Goods by Sea Act 1971. Some countries are still operating under the Hague Rules; some countries, including Britain, under the Hague-Visby Rules and some under an even newer set of Rules, the Hamburg Rules, which have not been adopted in Britain. There are similar international conventions for International Carriage of Goods by road and by rail. There is no international convention for multi-modal transport and there are major theoretical and practical problems concerned with damaged goods, which are being carried in multi-modal transport, particularly as in many cases the goods may arrive at their destination damaged, without one being able to say with confidence where the damage took place and with separate legal regimes applicable to the land and sea carriage.

If the owner of goods wishes to arrange for his goods to be carried by sea, he has three alternatives. The first is to buy a ship. This would only be a sensible alternative if the owner knew that he had a long-term and continuing need to move goods around the world. An example of such a goods owner would be a major oil company. Even with such a goods owner, however, it would be very unlikely that all the carriage of goods by sea needs would be met by buying ships, because this would be a very inflexible solution. A second alternative is to make a contract for the use of a whole ship, either for a voyage or series of voyages or for a period of time. Such a contract is called a charterparty. Charterparties are discussed more fully in Chapter 3. The third possibility is to put a cargo on board a ship which is available to take cargo to the destination port, which the cargo owner wishes his goods to reach. Such a contract is called a bill of lading contract. The bill of lading is the name of the document which is normally issued by the shipowner to the cargo owner to show that the goods have been put on board and will be carried to the destination. Bill of lading contracts are considered in Chapter 13.

In practice, bills of lading are very commonly issued, even in relation to charterparty contracts. The problems of bills of lading in charterparty contracts are considered in Chapter 14. The provisions of the mandatory regime for bill of lading contracts laid down by The Hague and Hague-Visby Rules are considered in Chapter 5.

Introduction to Carriage of Goods by Sea

This chapter explains the general structure of contracts for the carriage of goods by sea. It notes the major changes arising from the adoption of multi-modal transport and containerisation. It considers the relationship between carriage of goods and international sales.

Chapter 13

Bills of Lading

A typical bill of lading is a document which acknowledges that goods have been shipped by a particular person, normally attesting to their apparent order and condition upon shipment, upon a particular ship, for carriage to a particular place, for delivery to another person 'or order' or 'or assigns'. There usually follows a large space for particulars of the goods, and a space for signature preceded by a statement that the master has signed a number of originals of the bill, 'one of which being accomplished the other shall stand void'. The reverse is usually covered by contractual terms in small print.

The bill of lading in English law, when issued by or for a shipowner, has the following three features:

- as evidence of a contract of carriage;

- as a receipt for goods;

- as a document of title.

It is usually said that as between the shipper of the goods and the shipowner the bill of lading is evidence of the contract of carriage but is not the contract itself. The reason for this is that because of standard offer and acceptance principles the contract will have been formed before the bill of lading is issued. The bill of lading is normally issued shortly after the ship has set sail. Clearly there will be a contract by then because the goods will be safely on board. The contract will have been formed either when the goods are tendered to the ship on the docks and accepted for loading by being allowed on board, which was historically the usual analysis or perhaps when space is booked on the ship as would nowadays be much more usual. It is sometimes said that booking space is non contractual, because shipowners typically put into their documentation a 'shut out clause', that is, a clause saying that they are not liable if there is no room for the cargo and it is therefore not loaded. However, on general offer and acceptance principles it is probably more plausible to argue that there is a contract but that the contract contains an exemption clause covering a case where the goods are not loaded.

In practice, however, its terms will often constitute the contractual terms, either because the shipper will be regarded as knowing the terms by virtue of a course of dealing, or as

13.1 What is a bill of lading?

13.1.1 Evidence of contract of carriage

agreeing to the goods being carried on the terms of the bill of lading whatever they are: the more so where he fills in the bill of lading as often happens. But it is always possible to call evidence that a prior arrangement was made inconsistent with the terms of the bill of lading subsequently issued; and sometimes to argue that unusual and unexpected terms were not contemplated at the time of contracting and do not bind.

In *The Ardennes* (1951) the plaintiff wished to ship a cargo of mandarin oranges from Cartagena to London and was anxious that they should arrive before 1 December. He was orally assured that if the cargo was loaded on 22 November, the ship would sail direct to London. In fact the ship went first to Antwerp and did not arrive in London until 4 December. By this time there had been an increase in import duties on mandarin oranges and a fall in the market price. The plaintiff relied on the oral assurance that the ship would go direct to London; the defendant argued that the bill of lading permitted the ship to go via Antwerp. It was held that the oral undertaking was binding and was not superseded by the bill of lading.

However where, as will often be the case, the bill of lading is transferred by indorsement to a third party, it is clear that the contractual relationship between that third party and the shipowner is governed by the bill of lading. In other words, the bill of lading is now the contract and not merely evidence of the contract. The leading case is *Leduc v Ward* (1888). In this case the bill of lading had been indorsed to the plaintiff who sought damages in respect of a cargo of rape seed which had been shipped from Fiume to Dunkirk but which had been lost off the mouth of the Clyde. It was clear that to go to Glasgow as part of a journey from Fiume to Dunkirk was, in principle, an unjustified deviation. But the shipowners argued that the shippers had known at the time of entering into the contract that the vessel intended to go to Glasgow. The Court of Appeal held that although this knowledge might have effected the rights of the original shipper, the rights of the indorsee and shipowner were governed by the bill of lading and nothing but the bill of lading.

| 13.1.2 | Receipt for goods |

Since the bill is (typically) signed on behalf of the owner, it is therefore evidence against him that goods were shipped as described. Thus if the goods do not arrive, or arrive damaged the inference will be that they were lost or damaged on the voyage. Not all statements on the bill, however, do more than raise a *prima facie* case against the owner; some statements, eg as to quality, are inserted by the shipper and refer to matters as to which the owner cannot attest. He may, therefore, on a subsequent dispute, prove that the goods on loading were not as indicated. However, it has long been established that the owner is 'estopped', that is prevented, from denying statements as to the apparent order and condition on loading, at any rate against an indorsee of the bill who has no knowledge of the circumstances of loading and takes up the bill on the assumption that what is says is correct. (It would be more difficult for a shipper to rely on such an estoppel.) It might well be assumed that the shipowner is also estopped by statements as to the fact that goods were loaded, and as to their quantity on loading. But by virtue of the ancient decision in *Grant v Norway* (1855) it was until recently possible in England for the owner to prove that the goods were never loaded in whole or in part. In that case the master signed a bill of lading acknowledging a shipment of 12 bales of silk, none of which had in fact been loaded. It was held that it was open to the shipowners to show that no bales had been shipped on the grounds that the captain had no authority to sign bills of lading, unless the goods had been shipped. The same principle has been applied to a bill of lading which incorrectly states the quantity. The reasoning was that the master or other signatory has no authority to sign for goods not shipped, so that his signature does not bind the owner.

In the case where no goods at all have been loaded, as opposed to the case where goods have been loaded but the quantity is incorrectly stated, there is a separate argument based on the case of *Heskell v Continental Express* (1950) that there is no contract at all if no goods are loaded because in many cases the contract is formed by the tendering and acceptance of goods. An agent who signs a bill of lading without authority may of course be warranting his authority and there may therefore be an action by the shipper or indorsee against the person who signs the bill of lading. This would probably not be a very profitable action if brought against the master but in modern practice bills of lading are quite often signed by loading brokers, who are worth suing (*Rasnoimport v Guthrie* (1966)).

This highly inconvenient rule in *Grant v Norway* was partly abolished by the Hague-Visby Rules (Article III.4) which made statements as to quantity in a bill of lading, conclusive evidence in favour of a consignee or indorsee who takes the bill in good faith. Not all bills of lading are subject to the rules, however, and the anomalies which survived were substantially removed by s 4 of the Carriage of Goods by Sea Act 1992, under which representations in a bill of lading as to the quantity of goods shipped or received for shipment are conclusive evidence against the carrier in favour of the lawful holder of the bill, that is, someone who has taken the bill in good faith.

Since the Hague Rules of 1924, owners have been required to attest in the bill to the number of packages or pieces or quantity or weight, and as to the apparent order and condition of the goods on shipment (Article III.3). Reservations can be inserted where there is no means of checking quantity, or where there is a defect in apparent order and condition: but a bill containing blanket reservations (eg 'shipper's load and count') may be rejected where the Hague or Hague-Visby Rules are applicable.

13.2   Document of title

In the great case of *Lickbarrow v Mason* (1784) the courts recognised that by commercial custom bills of lading had become documents of title. This notion of the bill of lading as a document of title is central to the understanding of international sales law. It means that by transferring the bill of lading the transferor can transfer rights in the goods. What rights are transferred? Strictly speaking it is not necessary to transfer the bill of lading in order to transfer ownership. If I have a cargo of 1000 tons of western white wheat on board the SS *Chocolate Kisses* which is in mid-Atlantic on route to Liverpool, I can sell it to you and if we agree property can pass by agreement, provided that the goods are ascertained. In practice, however, you would have difficulty in collecting the goods off the ship when it arrives at Liverpool. If, however, I have transferred to you the bill of lading with appropriate indorsements, you will have no difficulty in getting goods off the ship because the master will deliver the goods to someone who holds a bill of lading in the appropriate form. What the bill of lading transfers, therefore, is the right to possession. Possession is usually being transferred as part of the act of transferring ownership, but not necessarily so. If you were a bank I might give you the bill of lading as security for a loan. This would not make you the owner of the cargo but it would make you a pledgee and enable you if I did not repay the loan to take delivery of the cargo and sell it to redeem the loan. So the fact that the bill of lading is a document of title enables sophisticated dealings in the goods to be made by transferring the bill of lading, while it is impossible to transfer the goods because they are on the high seas.

People sometimes talk about the bill of lading being 'negotiable'. Strictly speaking this is inaccurate. A bill of lading cannot be negotiable in the way that a bill of exchange can be. A bill of exchange like money can be transferred so that a *bona fide* purchaser for value can get a better right than the transferor had. This is not possible with bills of lading. The transferee will not get a better right than the transferor had. Nevertheless, the fact that a bill of lading is transferable is of critical importance. The bill of lading will be transferred by indorsing it.

As in the case of cheques, the indorsement may be general or special, and its effect of the indorsement of a bill of lading depends on the circumstances in which it is done, just as in the case of the handing over of a chattel. The indorsement may transfer the ownership of the goods represented thereby; or possession but not ownership (ie when the goods are pledged to a bank by indorsement of the bill); both these require that the goods be ascertained, namely not part of a larger bulk. But an indorsement may merely facilitate collection and have no effect on property or possession. A seller will normally consign goods to her own order and only indorse the bill away against payment, whether direct or through a bank. Indorsement to the buyer's bank will usually make the buyer owner of the goods and the bank pledgee.

The shipowner should in general only deliver to a person producing the bill, and indeed may lose his P & I cover if he does otherwise. However, in some trades it is common for there to be many sales of the goods while they are at sea. In such cases the paperwork often falls behind and when the ship arrives the latest buyer may well not have the bill of lading. In practice, the shipowner in this situation will often deliver the goods to someone who plausibly appears to be the buyer against an indemnity from that person against the consequences of mis-delivery.

It is normal in many trades for bills to be issued in sets of several 'originals' (apart from copies) which can be sent to a consignee by different means of transport. The purpose of this was once to reduce the risk of loss – it may be of less value now.

The fact that more than one original is used gives rise to problems, since each original ranks of itself as the symbol of the goods. There are two aspects to this. As regards transferees, it is possible for a holder of a set to pledge one and collect the goods with the other, or to pledge all three successively. In general, the persons holding originals rank in the order in which dispositions were made to them (a bankruptcy point). But the shipowner is protected if he delivers to the first person presenting an apparently regular bill unless he has grounds for suspicion – this is the significance of 'one of which being accomplished the others shall stand void'. For these reasons banks financing a sale by documentary credit or otherwise taking a pledge of documents normally insist on having the full set.

13.3 The bill of lading as a transferable contract

The transfer of a bill of lading may transfer the goods, but it does not at common law transfer the contract of carriage. Thus a position could arise where the transferee, at whose risk the goods were, was not able to sue the shipowner, with whom he had no contract, when the goods were lost or damaged in transit. There was some possibility of the transferor doing so, but this might not be easy to procure, and the argument was always possible that he had suffered no loss. Hence the Bills of Lading Act 1855 provided that the transferee of the bill of lading could sue and be sued on the contract contained therein as if it had been made with himself. In point of fact despite the wording of the Act, it is clear that he sues on a new contract on the terms appearing on the bill of lading; for him (as compared with the shipper) the bill of lading is the contract. However, the actual wording of s 1 of the Bill of Lading Act 1855 is:

> 'Every consignee of goods named in a bill of lading and every endorsee of a bill of lading, to whom the property in the goods therein mentioned shall pass upon or by reason of such consignment or endorsement, shall have transferred to and vested in him all rights of suit, and be subject to the same liabilities in respect of such goods as if the contract contained in the bill of lading had been made with himself.'

This wording presented problems because it only transferred the contractual rights where the property in the goods passed by consignment or indorsement, and so did not apply where it passed before consignment or indorsement (eg on shipment) or after (as where there is a bulk cargo not separated until arrival). In *The Delfini* (1990) there were *dicta* in the Court of Appeal suggesting that it was not necessary for property to pass simultaneously with indorsement, provided that there was a causal link between indorsement and the passing of property. Most of these difficulties have been removed by the Carriage of Goods by Sea Act 1992.

Since the transferee can sue, it has been held that the transferor cannot, unless he can prove loss: *The Albazero* (1977) (where the indorsee was time-barred). The House of Lords refused to apply its earlier decision in *Dunlop v Lambert* (1839) on the ground that that case only applied where there was no contract between the shipowner and the person who suffers the actual loss. In *The Albazero* there was a contract with the indorsee but the indorsee was not able to enforce it because he had failed to start the action within the one year time limit laid down by the Hague Rules.

It has long since been held, however, that where a consignee presents a bill of lading and seeks delivery of the goods, an implied contract may arise under which the shipowner is deemed to agree to deliver on bill of lading terms in consideration of payment of freight and/or other outstanding charges. This is usually referred to as a *Brandt v Liverpool* contract, from a leading case on it, *Brandt v Liverpool, etc Steam Navigation Co* (1924). It was extremely important where a consignee wished to sue the shipowner but could not take advantage of the 1855 Act, eg because he had no bill of lading but some other document such as a delivery order, or because he did not acquire property by his indorsement, as when he was a pledgee seeking to collect the goods and realise his security. Such a contract cannot usually be found, however, where the goods never arrive. In *The Aramis* (1989) a quantity of goods covered by several bills of lading had been shipped in bulk but by the time the final bill was presented there was no cargo on board. The bill of lading holder could not sue under the 1855 Act because property had not passed on the indorsement of the bill of lading. The Court of Appeal held that there was no *Brandt v Liverpool* contract because there had been nothing done by the shipowner which amounted to an acceptance of the bill of lading holders' offer.

Bills of lading should be distinguished from the following:

13.4 Other documents used for sea carriage

(a) Short form bills of lading

These are simply bills of lading in a standard, abbreviated form which can be reproduced on plain paper by an overlay transmitted by visual display, etc. Their purpose is simplification of documentation, and their main difference from an ordinary bill of lading is that they do not set out the contractual terms on the reverse (indeed this is left blank), but purport to incorporate the shipowner's terms by reference to standard terms elsewhere available, as has been done on railway tickets for more than a century. They have all the features of bills of lading, though the standard form appears to be a 'received' bill and thus does not acknowledge shipment. There may be problems as to which of the standard terms are incorporated, and if the standard terms are changed.

(b) Mate's receipts

These are issued in some situations preparatory to the issue of a bill of lading. They provide *prima facie* evidence that the goods described are on board, but usually no more. In particular, they are not usually evidence of the contract terms, and are not a document of title – at any rate unless a custom to use them as such is proved, a plea which nearly succeeded in *Kum v Wah Tat Bank* (1971). Wharf and dock receipts are similar documents which, however, do not even evidence shipment.

(c) Delivery orders

The term delivery order is not a term of art. Those that attract most legal consequences appear to be those used to break up larger quantities on one bill of lading. They are not documents of title at common law; they do not evidence a contract of carriage nor provide a receipt for the goods; and their transfer does not transfer any contract. Delivery under such a document may however create a *Brandt v Liverpool* contract (*Cremer v General Carriers* (1973)). In some cases transfer of a delivery order may evidence intention to transfer property in the goods to which it relates. If the delivery order is presented and attorned to by the holder of the goods the transferee may acquire constructive possession of them.

(d) Through and combined transport bills of lading

These vary enormously in their format. Some are simply ordinary bills of lading with provisions for transshipment and forwarding. Some are issued by an organisation which itself undertakes combined transport. If the organisation acts as carrier, the legal results are easier to analyse, though difficulties are still caused by the fact that the modes of transport involved have different regimes (CIM, CMR, Hague-Visby Rules) and efforts at harmonisation have not so far had much success. It should, however, be possible to establish (though this has not yet been done) that such a document is a document of title: and perhaps that it is a bill of lading for the purposes of the 1855 Act. Other types of document cause much more trouble, and it is necessary to scrutinise each document carefully to see what it purports to achieve.

(e) Non-negotiable sea waybills

These are a comparatively recent introduction. Their purpose is to provide a simpler document in respect of sea carriage which is not transferable and does not have to be presented when the goods are collected. Such documents are likely to be in short form also, namely to incorporate contractual terms by reference, and to be in 'received' form. They are therefore evidence of the contract and receipts for the goods, but not documents of title, nor can the contract of carriage be transferred by dealings with them. Conceivably a *Brandt v Liverpool* contract may arise when goods are collected under such documents; but the waybill confers few rights in respect of goods afloat and thus is very like the delivery order in that problems may arise if such a document is sought to be used as a bill of lading. In particular, the shipper appears to retain a right to redirect the goods. Waybills are intended for situations where it is not desired to retain control of the goods after shipment nor to finance the sale on the security of the goods, and where the buyer does not require a document of title for his own purposes.

Major changes in the status of documents other than bills of lading are made by the Carriage of Goods by Sea Act 1992. Under this act title to sue is now vested in the lawful holder of a bill of lading, the consignee identified in a sea waybill or in the person entitled to delivery under a ship's delivery order, whether or not they are the owners of the goods which are covered by the document. Title to sue is divorced from the passing of property in the goods.

The present law is dominated by pieces of paper. This is out of line with modern business practice, which is very strongly in favour of moving from document based transfers to electronic transfers. Under the Carriage of Goods by Sea Act 1992 the Secretary of State is empowered to draft regulations extending the provisions of the Act to cover electronic transmission of information.

Bills of Lading

The bill of lading has three functions: to act as evidence of the contract of carriage; to act as a receipt for the goods; and as a document of title.

Introduction

The bill of lading is evidence of the contract of carriage but is not the contract itself. The reason for this is that the contract will have been formed before the bill of lading is issued. In practice, however, its terms will often constitute the contractual terms, either because the shipper will be regarded as knowing the terms, either because the shipper will be regarded as knowing the terms by virtue of a course of dealing, or as agreeing to the goods being carried on the terms of the bill of lading whatever they are. However, where the bill of lading is transferred by indorsement to a third party, it is clear that the contractual relationship between the third party and the shipowner is governed by the bill of lading (*Leduc v Ward* (1888)).

Evidence of contract of carriage

Since the bill is (typically) signed on behalf of the owner, it is evidence against him that goods were shipped as described. Thus if the goods do not arrive, or arrive damaged, the inference will be that they were lost or damaged on the voyage.

Receipt for goods

A transfer of the bill of lading acts as a transfer of rights in the goods (*Lickbarrow v Mason* (1784)). What rights are transferred? Strictly speaking it is not necessary to transfer the bill of lading in order to transfer ownership. In practice, however, the transferee would have difficulty in collecting the goods off the ship without a bill of lading with appropriate indorsements. What the bill of lading transfers, therefore, is the right to possession. Possession is usually being transferred as part of the act of transferring ownership but not necessarily so.

Document of title

The transfer of a bill of lading may transfer the goods, but it does not at common law transfer the contract of carriage. Hence the Bill of Lading Act 1855 provided that the transferee of the bill of lading could sue and be sued on the contract contained therein as if it had been made with himself. However, the wording of s 1 of the 1855 Act because it only

The bill of lading as a transferable contract

transferred the contractual rights where the property in the goods passed by consignment or indorsement, and so did not apply where it passed before consignment or indorsement (eg on shipment) or after (as where there is a bulk cargo not separated until arrival). Most of these difficulties have been removed by the Carriage of Goods by Sea Act 1992.

Other documents used for sea carriage

Other documents which are used for sea carriage include the following:

- short form bills of lading;
- mate's receipts;
- delivery orders;
- through and combined transport bills of lading;
- non-negotiable sea waybills.

Chapter 14

Charterparties

In general, charterparties are contracts for the carriage of goods by sea (sometimes called contracts of affreightment), ie contracts for the services of the shipowner and his equipment. They are of three types,

(a) Voyage charterparties

Here a ship is chartered to proceed on a particular voyage or series of voyages (a 'consecutive voyage charterparty'), the freight payable being either a lump sum or calculated in some way by reference to the size of the cargo (eg so much per metric ton). Since the shipowner has in effect quoted a fixed price he includes in this a certain period for loading/unloading ('laytime') and a charge for keeping the ship waiting beyond this time ('demurrage'), which in theory represents agreed damages for breach of contract. The calculation and applicability of these provisions can obviously involve large sums of money, the difference between profit and loss on the voyage.

(b) Time charterparties

The ship is chartered for a particular period for use by the charterer, often within stated geographical limits with a place for re-delivery. Hire is calculated on a time basis. Although this may look like the hire of a ship it is in fact still the hire of the services of the shipowner and his equipment. It is important to see that the distinction between voyage and time charterparties is not merely a matter of fashion but has important consequences for the allocation of the risks. To take a simple example, suppose the charterer wishes to secure the use of a ship for a voyage from Yokohama to New York. Under modern conditions someone who knows the capacity of the ship could make a pretty accurate estimate of how long the voyage would take. Someone might charter the vessel for this period. The effect of delaying the voyage would be quite different, depending on whether it is a voyage or time charterparty. If the ship takes another five days to reach New York under a voyage charterparty, this is simply a loss to the shipowner; conversely, under a time charterparty the shipowner will be paid for an extra five days. Here it is the charterer who needs protection against delay by the shipowner; hence a hallmark of the time charter is the 'off-hire' clause, under which the charterer does not pay freight when the ship is not working for him, eg because undergoing repair. Again, claims involving this clause can be considerable.

Sometimes a ship is chartered for a particular voyage, but to be paid for on a time basis (a 'trip charter'). This is predominantly a time charter. So the allocation of risks and the payment provisions are those characteristic of time charters. It is however a term of the contract that the voyage be made (*Temple v Sovfracht* (1945)).

Conversely, a consecutive voyage charterparty, for example, for as many consecutive voyages as can be completed within the period of 12 months is predominantly a voyage charterparty, that is, the scheme of payment and allocation of risks is predominantly modelled on that of voyage charterparties.

It is permissible and indeed common for a charterer to sub-charter the ship and not unusual for the sub-charterer to sub-sub-charter. It is important to remember that these transactions will be controlled by the doctrine of privity of contract, so that a sub-charterer will only have contractual rights against the charterer and not against the shipowner, and so on. It is also common for the owner to borrow money against the charter payments and so you will come across many cases in which the owner has assigned to the bank the payment which is due under the charter.

(c) Demise or bare boat charters

The third type of charter is the demise or bare boat charter, under which the charterer actually hires the ship and employs the crew. This is analogous to a lease of land. It is not a contract for the carriage of goods by sea and is used for different purposes (eg financing operations).

A demise charterer has possession of the ship and it is probable that in appropriate cases the rights of the demise charterer would be protected by an action of specific performance. So if the shipowner were to sell the demised ship over the demised charterer's head, it is likely that the demise charterer would be protected. On the other hand, if the shipowner sells a ship which is the subject of a voyage or time charterparty over the charterer's head, although this would clearly be a breach of contract and give rise to a damages action by the charterer against the original owner, it is not clear whether the charterer would have any rights against the new owner, even if the new owner knew of the charterer when he bought the ship. See the conflicting views expressed by the Privy Council in *The Strathcona* (1926) and by Diplock J in *Port v Ben Line* (1958).

Voyage charterparties are today less common than time charters. The basic rules are important, however, because historically the duties of a shipowner under a voyage charterparty and under a bill of lading contract are the same (except that under a bill of lading contract the duties often cannot be excluded because of the Hague Rules, while there was no such limitation in voyage charterparties). Bill of lading contracts often incorporate charterparty terms. The problems caused by this are discussed later.

14.2   Voyage charterparties

Standard forms are used which may have biases towards one or the other party. They may be the subject of considerable negotiation, often through shipbrokers. The ship is likely not at the time of chartering to be at the place where it is required. The charter will require it to proceed there: this stage may be called the 'preliminary' or 'approach voyage'.

14.2.1   Creation

At common law (ie if no written terms are agreed) the duties of the carrier are normally taken to be strict: to deliver the goods at the place designated in as good a condition as he received them unless prevented by Act of God, the Queen's enemies, inherent vice in the goods, defective packing or by a general average sacrifice.

14.2.2   Duties of carrier

Since the mid-19th century at least carriers have generally sought to protect themselves by elaborate written terms. Unlike bills of lading, to which the Hague Rules are normally applicable, charterparty terms are subject to no statutory control: but the courts interpret them where possible so as to be consistent with the main duties of the carrier, which are regarded as being as follows:

(a) Seaworthiness: to provide a ship which is cargoworthy on loading and seaworthy on sailing (but not later). The duty is at common law (not under the Hague Rules) absolute (ie not discharged by using all reasonable care) and difficult to exclude. If it is broken the shipper can sue for loss caused by unseaworthiness; and can take the cargo off or refuse to load if he acts in time. Problems arise as to whether containers must be cargoworthy as part of the ship, or whether they are merely the shipper's packaging;

(b) To take reasonable care of the goods;

(c) To proceed with reasonable despatch (mostly relevant to the approach voyage);

(d) Not to deviate. The ship must proceed by the usual and direct route from the starting port to the destination. The charterparty may, and indeed often does, contain a liberty to deviate, that is, a permission to the shipowner to call at intermediate ports. Such a liberty to deviate will be construed so as not to permit fundamental departures from the route (*Glyn v Margetson* (1893)).

For historical reasons the rule has become established that if the ship deviates from the normal commercial route the shipowner loses the benefit of all exclusions in her favour, at any rate from the moment of deviation onwards – unless she can prove that the trouble would have occurred anyway (as where it was caused by defective packing). Her exclusions are not restored when she reverts to course. This rule, said to be based on the fact that the ship was not insured after deviating, may provide a windfall for the cargo owner since it applies even though the deviation is immaterial to him and the cargo arrives undamaged. The leading case is *Hain SS Co v Tate & Lyle* (1936).

In this case the ship had been chartered to load a cargo of sugar at two ports in Cuba and one Port in San Domingo to be nominated by the charterer. The charterer made the nomination but the owner's agent did not inform the master of the nominated port in San Domingo. The ship loaded at the two Cuban ports and proceeded to Queenstown for orders. The mistake was quickly discovered and the ship ordered back to San Domingo to load the remaining cargo. However, on leaving the port in San Domingo the vessel ran aground and part of the cargo was lost and the balance had to be transshipped in order to complete the voyage. Shortly before the vessel arrived at its destination the bills of lading were indorsed to Tate & Lyle, who took delivery in ignorance of the deviation.

The House of Lords held that what had happened constituted a deviation. The position of the charterers and the indorsees of the bill of lading was different. The charterers had, with full knowledge of the deviation, ordered the ship back to San Domingo. By doing so they had waived their rights in respect of the deviation. However, the charterers waiver did not bar the rights of Tate & Lyle and Tate & Lyle had not waived their rights themselves, since they did not know of the deviation when they took delivery of the cargo.

This decision still leaves some theoretical questions in the air. Suppose the ship deviates but no harm is done and the cargo is safely delivered. If the contract is at an end, it would appear that the shipowner cannot sue for freight. However, it appears to be the case that although the shipowner cannot sue for contractually agreed freight she can recover on a *quantum meruit* basis for having actually carried the goods.

(e) To contribute in general average. By very ancient maritime law where a shipowner makes a necessary sacrifice or incurs special expenditure to avoid peril, all the interests involved in the adventure (ship, cargo, freight) may be required to contribute.

Numerous clauses usually found in standard form charters vary these duties. For example the shipowner is regularly exempted from liability for 'perils of the sea', which can have very wide effect. Even where the shipowner is in principle liable, the rules as to the burden of proof may make it difficult for the cargo owner to establish this, for the shipowner can often produce a *prima facie* defence such as perils of the sea which it may be difficult for the cargo owner to acquire the information to displace.

The charterparty will often contain statements as to the position of the ship at the time of chartering. Stipulations as to the position of the ship and its expected readiness to load have long been regarded as conditions (*The Mihalis Angelos* (1971)). This is probably still the case, even in the light of modern developments in such cases as *Hong Kong Fir v Kawasaki* (1962).

14.2.3   Sequence of operations

On the approach voyage the duty is one of reasonable dispatch. Terms may be inserted into the charter to make arrival or departure by certain dates conditions. More commonly however there is a cancellation clause, which gives the charterer the right to cancel if the ship does not arrive by a certain date. This is a facility for the charterer which he can and often does exercise ruthlessly: he can exercise it even though the late arrival is excused by the terms of the contract, or causes him no prejudice, and unless it is otherwise provided the charterer may refuse to tell a shipowner who is plainly going to be late whether or not he intends to cancel on the stated date.

The traditional distribution of duties on loading is that the shipper lifts the goods to the ship's rail and the shipowner takes from there. This is in effect however modified by the nature of the cargo, the facilities and custom of the port and the terms of the contract, which may provide for stowage, stevedoring etc, often by the use of trade terms. This has the consequence that in a free on board (fob) contract where the seller owes the buyer the duty to put the goods on board, he may be unable to do more than deliver them alongside or to the wharf, because the shipowner operates from that point onwards; but the risk and property will still be in him, at least until loading (as opposed to the case of a free alongside ship (fas) contract). The matter is discussed at length in the leading case of *Pyrene v Scinda* (1954).

In this case a number of fire tenders were sold on fob terms. While one of them was being loaded it fell onto the dockside and was seriously damaged. All the other tenders were safely loaded and a bill of lading was issued covering the fire tenders which had been safely loaded and not mentioning the one which had been damaged. An action was brought against the shipowner by the fob seller, that is, the shipper. The shipowner argued that he was entitled to limit his liability in accordance with the Hague Rules (see below para 16.4). The shipper argued that this was not possible because there was no contract between him and the carrier. Devlin J held that the carrier was entitled to rely on the Hague Rules immunity which would have been contained in the bill of lading if it had been issued. This decision raises or assumes a number of very important points. First, all the parties assumed that as between seller and buyer the risk of damage to the fire tender was still on the seller. This was despite the fact that at the time of the damage the fire tender was swinging at the end of the ship's tackle to and fro across the ship's line. It is sometimes said that risk for an fob contract passes when the goods pass the ship's rail but the decision in this case makes much better sense if we say the risk passes only when the goods are safely loaded (see discussion under International Sales, para 20.5).

Second, the case assumes that everybody is proceeding on the basis that the the contract is on bill of lading terms even though at the end of the day a bill of lading was not issued to cover the relevant goods (see above, para 13.1.1).

Thirdly, if a bill of lading had been issued it would have been issued to the buyer and not to the seller. Devlin J however thought that the shipowner was entitled to the protection of the Hague Rules limitations as against the seller, even when the bill of lading contract was with the buyer. He may have thought that there was an exception to privity of contract in such a situation, but this view would be difficult to reconcile with the later decision of the House of Lords in *Scruttons v Midland Silicones* (1962). A better explanation would be that there was a collateral contract covering the seller, at least up until the moment when risk passed to the buyer. Devlin J's decision that the allocation of the risk of damage should be the same whether the risk is on the seller or the buyer at the moment when the goods are damaged, seems commercially entirely sensible.

The shipper is normally entitled to a bill or bills of lading, either by custom of the trade or the terms of the charter. In general, he may not demand a bill containing terms inconsistent with the charter, which will lead to bills incorporating charterparty terms. However, the matter becomes more difficult where, as usually, the Hague Rules apply, for provisions permissible in charters may not be allowed under the Rules.

The charterparty will often empower the charterer to designate a discharging port or ports within a certain range, and may sometimes provide for the ship to deliver 'as near thereto as she may safely get' or similar wording, which can cause difficult problems in cases of low rivers, ice, congested docks, etc. The charterer must normally designate a safe port. Safety includes political as well as physical characteristics of the court. It must be judged in relation to the particular vessel. So a port which is inaccessible to a large ship, may be perfectly safe for a smaller ship. A port is not unsafe because in certain weather conditions it presents dangers. In *The Khian Sea* Lord Denning MR said:

> 'First there must be an adequate weather-forecasting system. Second, there must be an adequate availability of pilots and tugs. Thirdly, there must be adequate sea room to manoeuvre. And fourthly, there must be an adequate system for ensuring that sea room and room for manoeuvre is always available.'

In general the critical question is whether the port is safe when the ship has to use it, rather than whether it was safe when nominated. In *The Evia (No 2)* (1982) *The Evia* had been chartered to load a cargo in Cuba for carriage to Basrah at a time when there was no reason to believe that Basrah was unsafe and was likely to become so. *The Evia* arrived in the Shatt al Arab on 1 July, but because of congestion it had to wait until 20 August before a berth was available in Basrah. The cargo was not completely unloaded until 22 September. On that day the Iran-Iraq war broke out and navigation on the Shatt al Arab ceased. An arbitrator held that as from 4 October the contract was frustrated, because by that date it was clear that the ship had become indefinitely trapped in the port and that the war was likely to be, as indeed it proved to be, of indefinite duration. The shipowners argued that if the contract was frustrated this was an example of self-induced frustration, because the charterers were in breach of contract in ordering the ship to Basrah. The House of Lords held that although the safety of the port was to be tested at the time the ship was there so that it did not matter that the port was unsafe for reasons unknown to the charterer, the charterer was not liable if the port became unsafe because of some 'unexpected abnormal event (which) occurred ... where conditions of safety had previously existed.' It seems important to note that in this case the port was still perfectly safe when the ship arrived. It would appear that in the case of ships which were still sailing towards Basrah on 22 September, the charterer would have been under a duty to nominate an alternative port.

The situation as to unloading is the same as that as to loading but in reverse. The shipowner should in principle deliver the goods only against a bill of lading (if such was issued) and does so otherwise (eg under an indemnity) at his peril; indeed he may lose his P & I cover if he does so. He is however normally entitled to deliver to the first person who presents a valid bill apparently in order (even though by virtue of dealings with other originals of the bill the presenter's claim may not in fact be valid).

| 14.2.4 | Duties of charterer |

The duties of a charterer are: not to ship dangerous goods (including goods dangerous politically, eg cargo liable to seizure); to have his cargo ready so that delay is not caused to the ship, eg by inability to berth because cargo is not available; and to load a full cargo (a lesser one would reduce the freight earned; problems arise regarding designations of the ship's capacity) of the specified merchandise (other merchandise might attract a different rate of freight); and to designate in reasonable time a discharging port where appropriate.

Delays in loading or unloading are very common and frequently expensive. Such delays may be the fault of either shipowner or charterer but they are often the result of congestion in the port of loading or discharge. Does the loss thus caused fall on shipowner or charterer? In practice, this normally depends on the provisions for laytime and demurrage. The charterparty will normally provide for a number of days called 'laydays' in which loading or unloading is to take place and for payment of 'demurrage' that is, a sum to be paid by way of liquidated damages for delay beyond this. Litigation on this topic is very common.

| 14.2.5 | Laytime |

When does laytime start? Usually (but see below for 'time lost' clause) when:

- the vessel is an 'arrived ship';

- she is ready to load or discharge;

- shipowner has given notice of readiness to load.

Most difficulty surrounds the question of when a ship is 'arrived'. This depends on the destination named in the charterparty. If a berth or wharf are named the ship arrives when she gets alongside that berth or wharf (*Tharsis Sulphur and Copper v Morel Brothers* (1891)); if a dock is named then the ship is arrived on entering that dock (*Tapscott v Balfour* (1872)).

Much more difficulty surrounds a port charterparty, that is, one where a port is named as destination, since the chances of the ship being in some sense in the port quite unable to unload are much higher. Four cases of the many litigated on this issue must be considered in detail.

In *Leoniss SS Co Ltd v Rank Ltd* (1908), a charter to carry wheat to 'one or two safe loading ports or places in the River Parana ... with option of loading the entire cargo at Bahia Blanca'. Loading was to begin 12 hours after notice. The ship was ordered to Bahia Blanca and anchored in the river within port a few ships length off the pier. The Master gave notice of readiness to load but the ship was delayed getting a berth because of congestion. The Court of Appeal held that laytime began 12 hours after notice and not from the time the vessel obtained berth. In so doing the court referred to the 'commercial area of the port' and 'the master effectively placing his ship at the disposal of the charterer'.

In *The Aello* (1961) a ship had been chartered to load maize 'at one or two safe loading ports or places in the River Parana ... and the balance of the cargo in the port of Buenos Aires'. The traffic control system in the River Plate prevented maize ships proceeding beyond the free anchorage near a point in the roads called intersection without a permit. The permit was issued by the customs authority when the Grain Board certified that the cargo had been allocated. Owing to congestion the Port Authority decided that not only must a Grain Board certificate be obtained but a cargo must be available. *The Aello* arrived in free anchorage on 12 October; charterers obtained a Grain Board certificate on 13 October but did not have cargo until 29 October. House of Lords held 3–2 that the ship was not within the commercial area of the port. The House also held 4–1 that the charterer was in breach of contract by failure to provide a cargo.

In *The Johanna Oldendorff* (1973) the ship was chartered 'to the Port of Liverpool/Birkenhead (counting as one port)'. The ship arrived at the Mersey Bar on 2 January; proceeded to Prince's Bar Pier landing stage Liverpool on 3 January and cleared customs. She was then ordered to proceed to Bar Light vessel. She did so and gave notice of readiness to load. She did not reach a berth in Birkenhead until 20 January. The Bar Light anchorage was 17 miles from Prince's Pier and was within the geographical, fiscal, legal and administrative area of the port of Liverpool/Birkenhead. The House of Lords held that the ship had arrived when she was at the Bar Light anchorage. In so doing they either overruled or at least severely restricted *The Aello*. Most importance was attached to the Bar anchorage being the usual waiting place for vessels awaiting berth and to the vessel being, with improved communications, at the effective disposition of the charterer.

In *The Maratha Envoy* (1977) the vessel was chartered to 'one safe port German North Sea in charterer's option'. The vessel arrived at Weser lightship on 7 December and anchored. On 10 December charterers nominated Brake but as no berth was available the vessel remained at the lightship. The Weser lightship was the usual waiting place for ships awaiting a Weser river berth but was 25 miles seaward of the mouth of the Weser and outside the legal, fiscal and administrative limits of the Port of Brake. The Court of Appeal held that the ship arrived when she reached the lightship since that was the usual waiting place and she was there at the effective disposition of the charterers but the House of Lords reversed this decision on the grounds that these conditions were not sufficient if the ship was outside the area of the nominated port.

It should be noted that the giving of notice of readiness may depend not merely on the physical position of the ship, but also on such matters as clearing customs and obtaining free pratique. In some ports this can be done at the waiting place but in others it may not be possible before getting into berth.

The master may give an invalid Notice of Readiness. Usually if the notice is bad on its face it should be rejected to avoid arguments that the invalidity has been waived.

- How long does laytime run?

  This will normally be stated in the charterparty. Note that this may define length in 'days', 'working days' or 'weather working days'.

- Extent of delay

  In principle, the provisions for demurrage represent an agreed damages clause. In practice, the amount of demurrage fixed is often below the real loss to the shipowner so that the clause operates in fact to limit the charterers' liability. This raises the difficult question of whether the shipowner can ever recover more than the amount of demurrage. In the *Suisse Atlantique* case the House of Lords accepted, in principle, that delay might be so prolonged as to entitle the shipowner to terminate the contract and recover damages at large.

- The 'time lost' clause

  Delay in loading might be caused either by the fault of the shipowner (the ship's tackle does not work) or because of the fault of the charterer (no cargo is available). In a case such as this the decision as to when the ship has arrived is not the end of the matter because there may be a damages action, which will in practice reverse the result (see *The Aello* above). However, in many cases the delay in loading or unloading is not the fault of either the shipowner or the charterer but is the result of congestion, which in many ports in the world is endemic. In such cases what the rule is doing is to allocate the risk of delay caused by congestion. Obviously the parties are free to allocate the risk in some other way. If, as if often the case, both parties are commercially astute and aware of the risks, allocation of the risks would be reflected in the number of laydays or the rate of demurrage or the amount of freight charged. It is very important to remember, therefore, that all of these rules are subject to the contrary agreement of the parties. So, many Weser river charters contain a 'Weser lightship' clause by which arrival at the lightship is sufficient. An important example is the 'time lost' clause. So the Gencon charterparty contains the expressions 'time lost in waiting for berth to count as loading (discharge) time'. These clauses also give rise to their problems.

In *The Darrah* (1978) there was a Gencon charter with time lost clause. Another clause provided for a rate of discharge 'per weather working day of 24 hours, Friday and holidays excepted'. The shipowners claimed demurrage on the basis that the entire time spent waiting for a berth including Fridays, holidays, etc, counts as laytime. This was rejected by the House of Lords (previous authority had supported shipowners' contention).

In *Dias Compania Navia v Louis Dreyfus* (1978) there was a Baltimore Grain charterparty with added time lost clause. There was a further added clause 'At discharging charterers/receivers have the option at any time to treat (ie fumigate) at their expense ships ... cargo and time so used not to count'. The ship was ordered to discharge at HsinKang and on arrival anchored in roads awaiting a berth. Laytime expired on 26 October. On 9 November the receivers began fumigating on board, a process which lasted 16 days. Discharge started on 30 November. The shipowners claimed demurrage for the whole period after 26 October. The charterers argued that the 16 days spent on fumigation should not count, but the House of Lords held that in context fumigation was only not to count for purpose of calculating laytime and since laytime had elapsed before fumigation began, demurrage was due.

14.3   Time charterparties

Parties usually employ one of the standard forms eg 'Baltime' with additions and amendments.

The following clauses would be among those usually found:

- An agreement to provide a vessel for a period of time and a statement of her size, speed, fuel consumption, etc.

- An agreement by the charterer to pay a sum by way of hire. Such sums are often payable at intervals, eg monthly in advance and it is common to insert a withdrawal clause enabling the shipowner to withdraw the ship failing prompt payment. If charter rates have gone up, the shipowner will be likely to take advantage of such a clause and the House of Lords has held a shipowner entitled to take advantage of a trivial breach in *The Laconia* (1977).

In this case payment of hire was due on a Sunday. The charterers paid in a form equivalent to cash across the counter of the shipowner's bank at 3.00 pm on Monday. It was held by the House of Lords that the payment was late; that the shipowners were entitled to exercise their right to withdraw for late payment and that the bank had no authority to waive the shipowner's right to terminate by collecting payment in this way.

Conduct of the owner after the charterer's failure to pay promptly may amount to a waiver of the right of withdrawal.

In *The Mihalios Xilas* the charterers were entitled to deduct bunker costs and other dispersements from the final month's hire. Payment was due on 22 March. The charterers apparently thinking that this was the final payment, indicated that they intended to deduct $31,000 without explaining the calculations on which this figure was based. On 20 March the shipowners indicated their objection to the deductions but did not instruct their bankers to refuse payment which was in fact made on 21 March. On the following day the shipowners were supplied with details of deductions, which made it clear that the charterers were treating the ninth month as the last month of the charterparty. The shipowners asked for further details, which were not supplied. Eventually the shipowners withdrew the vessel on 26 March. The charterers argued that the withdrawal of the ship was wrongful but the House of Lords did not agree. The House of Lords held that the charterers were not entitled to make the deductions which they did because the relevant month was not the last month of the charter. Nevertheless, when the charterers underpaid on 21 March the shipowners were not entitled to withdraw at that stage because the charterers had until midnight on 22 March to pay the balance and there was therefore no default at that stage. The House of Lords agreed that there was a question whether by waiting until 26 March the owners had waived their rights to terminate, but held that the arbitrator's finding that it was reasonable in the circumstances to take this time to consider the position could not be disturbed. In a case of this kind the owner is entitled to reasonable time to investigate the facts and make up his mind what to do.

- An 'off-hire' clause, ie a clause that in certain events no hire is to be payable, eg 'In the event of drydocking or other necessary measures to maintain the efficiency of the vessel, deficiency of men or owner's stores, breakdown of machinery, damage to hull or other accident, either hindering or preventing the working of the vessel and continuing for more than 24 consecutive hours'. It should be noted that a breakdown does not take a ship 'off-hire' if it causes no loss of time, eg an engine-room failure while the ship is loading.

  Different off-hire clauses may be operated differently, eg whether calculation is 'net loss of time' or 'period off-hire'.

- A cancelling clause, ie a clause entitling the charterer to cancel in certain events.

- Delivery and re-delivery. With a time charter there is an obvious problem about getting the last voyage to fit in with the end of the period of charter. If the charter goes overtime, the charterer will have to pay for the use of the ship, but will he have to pay at the contract rate or the market rate? The first question is to ask whether the charterer is in breach of contract. This obviously depends on the terms of the contract. The charter may simply define the terms as, say, '12 months'. In such a case the courts are usually prepared to imply a commercially reasonable tolerance. On the other hand, where the length contains an express tolerance, for instance, '12 months, 15 days more or less'. This would usually be treated as the only tolerance so that there will be no room for further leeway on top of the express tolerance and re-delivery 16 days late will be a breach of contract. In *The Dione* (1975) the vessel had been chartered for a period of six months, 20 days more or less in charterer's option'. When sent on its final voyage the charterers could not reasonably have expected re-delivery by the end of this period, which would have fallen on 28

September. The vessel was in fact re-delivered on 7 October. It was held that the charterers should pay hire at the contract rate up to 28 September and at the market rate thereafter (in this case the market rate had gone up above the contract rate). Obviously if the market rate fell below the contract rate the charterer who overlapped would not be entitled to take advantage of this, but in practice the owner would be very unlikely to complain in such a situation.

The key concept in this context is that of the 'legitimate last voyage'. A charterer should not order a last voyage, which a reasonable charterer would expect to end after the express or implied tolerance. If such an illegitimate last voyage is ordered, the shipowner would be entitled to refuse the order and call for the charterer to order a legitimate last voyage. If the charterer refused to do so the owner would, in principle, be entitled to terminate.

Charterparties

Charterparties are contracts for the carriage of goods by sea (sometimes called contracts of affreightment).

The ship is chartered to proceed on a particular voyage or series of voyages (a 'consecutive voyage charterparty'), the freight payable being either a lump sum or calculated in some way by reference to the size of the cargo. Since the shipowner has in effect quoted a fixed price, he includes in this a certain period for loading/unloading ('laytime') and a charge for keeping the ship waiting beyond this time ('demurrage'), which in theory represents agreed damages for breach of contract.

Voyage charterparties

At common law, the duties of the carrier are normally taken to be strict: to deliver the goods at the place designated in as good a condition as he received them unless prevented by Act of God, the Queen's enemies, inherent vice in the goods, defective packing or by a general average sacrifice.

Duties of carrier

The main duties of the carrier include:

- to provide a ship which is cargoworthy on loading and seaworthy on sailing;

- to take reasonable care of the goods;

- to proceed with reasonable despatch;

- not to deviate;

- to contribute in general average.

The duties of the charterer include:

Duties of charterer

- not to ship dangerous goods;

- to have his cargo ready so that delay is not caused to the ship;

- to load a full cargo;

- to designate in reasonable time a discharging port where appropriate.

The ship is chartered to proceed on a particular period for use by the charterer, often within stated geographical limits with a

Time charterparties

place for re-delivery. Hire is calculated on a time basis. A hallmark of the time charter is the 'off-hire' clause under which the charterer does not pay freight when the ship is not working for him (eg because the ship is undergoing repair).

Demise or bareboat charters

The charterer hires the ship and employs the crew. This is analogous to a lease of land. It is not a contract for the carriage of goods by sea is used for different purposes (eg financing operations).

Chapter 15

Bill of Lading for Goods in Chartered Ship

Even where the goods are put on board the ship by a charterer, it is common to issue a bill of lading. This can be useful to the charterer if he wants to deal with the goods. In addition, a charterer may procure a cargo from other merchants or allow the ship to act as a general ship so that bills of lading are issued to other shippers.

15.1 Introduction

(a) In hands of charterer

Where there are differences between bill of lading and charterparty, the relation of shipowner and charterer continues to be governed by the charterparty (see *President of India v Metcalfe* (1970)).

It is quite likely that the charterparty and bill of lading terms will be different since a bill of lading would usually be subject to The Hague or Hague-Visby Rules, whereas these would not apply to charter-parties. There are also often different provisions about arbitration.

(b) In hands of transferee

If the charterer indorses the bill of lading over, its terms will govern the relationship between the shipowner and transferee except in so far as the charterparty terms have been incorporated into bill of lading. If the goods are lost the charterer will still have a claim in contract against the shipowner, but will only recover substantial damages if he has himself suffered loss (see *The Albazero* (1976)).

15.2 Bill of lading given to charterer

If other shippers put their goods on board the ship, the question will be whether they are contracting with the shipowner or charterer. This depends on whether the master signs the bill of lading on behalf of the shipowner or charterer. Usually the natural inference will be that she acts for the shipowner since he is employed by the shipowner (particularly where the shipper is ignorant of the charter), but this will not always be so.

In the case of *Elder Dempster v Paterson Zochonis* (1924) the charterer was itself a shipping line which had chartered ships from the shipowners in order to increase its capacity. The master was equipped with standard bills of lading, which were in use by the charterer on its own ships and which

15.3 Bills of lading given to other shippers

contained a statement that the master was signing for the company which in this case was the charterer.

Some bills of lading include the so-called 'demise clause' designed to make sure that the contract is between shipowner and shipper only. Such clauses can cause significant practical difficulties for the goods owner who wishes to make a claim, particularly where, as under The Hague or Hague-Visby Rules, he only has a year to do so. In some jurisdictions such clauses have been held invalid or very strictly construed, but in *The Berkshire* (1974) such a clause was held valid in English law.

15.4 Incorporation of charterparty terms

Some bills of lading issued in respect of a chartered ship contain the phrase 'and all other conditions as per charterparty'. There has been much litigation on such expressions. Under general contract law such expressions would probably be effective to incorporate into the bill of lading all the terms of the charterparty. In practice, however, courts have been extremely reluctant to construe expressions in that way, because in practice people receiving the bills of lading will have no real opportunity of discovering what the terms of the charterparty are. The general result of the cases is to incorporate only those conditions which are to be performed by the consignee of the goods or which relate in the mode of delivery to him by the shipowner.

15.5 Cesser clause

Where the ship is to be loaded with cargo not belonging to charterer, clauses are often inserted designed to relieve him from liability for demurrage, eg 'charterer's liability to cease when the ship is loaded, the captain having a lien on the cargo for freight, dead freight and demurrage'. Such clauses are again unattractive from the point of the shipowner. They are an attempt to make the shipowner accept in place of his action against the charterer a right against the cargo which may, in practice, be difficult to exercise. In *The Sinoe* (1971) Donaldson J said:

> 'Cesser clauses are curious animals because it is now well established that they do not mean what they appear to say, namely, that the charterer's liability shall cease as soon as the cargo is on board. Instead, in the absence of special wording ... they mean that the charterer's liability shall cease if, and to the extent that, the owners have an alternative remedy by way of lien on the cargo.'

Bill of Lading for Goods in Chartered Ship

This chapter considers the problems which arise where a bill of lading is issued in respect of goods put on board a chartered ship either to the charterer or to another shipper.

Chapter 16

The Hague and Hague-Visby Rules

The breadth and efficacy of the exceptions regularly used by shipowners led to concern among countries which were primarily cargo-owning, rather than ship-owning, namely the United States and the former British Dominions. The first step towards controlling such clauses was taken in the United States by the Harter Act of 1893, which imposed certain duties on the shipowner and forbade certain types of exclusion. The division of responsibility on which it was based was this: the shipowner could not contract out of a duty to use reasonable care to provide a seaworthy ship and in care of the cargo, and in return was exempted from liability for loss caused by his negligence in navigation and management of the ship (a concession partly based on the hazards of maritime adventures and partly on the assumption that the shipowner is likely to look after his own ship). Similar legislation was soon adopted in New Zealand (1903), Australia (1904) and Canada (1910).

16.1 Origin of the Hague Rules: the Harter Act

Various factors, including continued dissatisfaction by cargo-owning countries, commercial problems caused by the handling of bills of lading containing differing terms, and the UK government's wish to introduce uniform legislation throughout the then British Empire, led to the formulation of the Hague Rules, so-called because an initial draft was settled at a meeting at The Hague in 1921. These were actually adopted at an international convention at Brussels in 1924. In general, the Rules adopt the same division of risks as the Harter Act, but seek to provide something nearer to a complete code for carriage by sea under bills of lading.

16.2 The Brussels Convention of 1924: the Hague Rules

Under the 1924 Act the Rules apply as follows:

(a) To outward shipments from UK ports (other than coastal trade). Problems arise where the law of another country is selected for such a shipment (the so-called 'Vita Food' gap, a problem of the conflict of laws traditionally associated with *Vita Food Products Inc v Unus Shipping Co* (1939)).

(b) Covered by a bill of lading – even when such is never issued (wrongfully, in error, or because the shipowner lost the goods while loading them).

16.3 Application of the Rules

(c) To those loading and unloading operations which the contract places upon the carrier 'before and after' problem, discussed in *Pyrene v Scindia* (1954).

(d) They do not cover deck cargo and live animals.

(e) Such provisions as protect the carrier do not protect his employees or independent contractors (eg stevedores). This was the problem of *Midland Silicones v Scruttons* (1962), perhaps partly solved by the 'Himalaya clause'; see *The Eurymedon* (1975) and *The New York Star* (1980).

(f) They are displaced, as are other contractual terms, by deviation.

16.4 Provisions of the Rules

The basic provisions of the Rules are that the shipowner owes a duty to exercise due care (only) as to seaworthiness and care of cargo (Article II, III.1.2; IV.1). In return, he is exempted in 17 ways (Article IV.2(a)–(g)) of which the most conspicuous are negligence in navigation and management of the ship, fire unless caused by his actual fault, perils of the sea, war, seizure, strikes, inadequate packing, and any other cause arising without his fault (eg pilferage). These duties cannot be varied except to increase the shipowner's responsibility.

The important limits are that suit must be brought within one year (Article III.6); and that the shipowner's liability is limited to £100 gold value per 'package or unit' unless a higher value is declared (which would lead to higher freight). Great difficulty is caused in determining what ranks as a package or unit, especially with containerised or palletised cargo.

16.5 The Hague-Visby Rules

The Hague Rules did not satisfy everyone, and one school of thought sought to procure fairly minor amendments of detail to them, so as to eliminate certain well-known problems. This led to the Hague-Visby Rules, a draft of which was adopted in Stockholm in 1963. The final protocol was adopted at Brussels in 1968 and enacted here as the Carriage of Goods by Sea Act 1971. The protocol did not however receive sufficient ratifications to be brought into force until 1977 (the UK not ratifying until 1976): it came into effect here on 23 June 1977. About 14 countries (including the Scandinavian countries and France) now give effect to them: other countries still retain the old Hague rules.

The changes made in the Visby Rules are comparatively slight. They are as follows:

(a) English courts must apply them to all international carriage where the bill of lading is issued in a contracting state, the carriage is from a port in a contracting state, or the bill of lading contract provides directly or indirectly that the Rules are to apply (Article X). This was the view taken by the House of Lords in *The Morviken*.

In this case machinery had been shipped aboard a Dutch vessel at Leith for carriage to the Dutch Antilles under a bill of lading which included a Dutch choice of law clause and provided that the Court of Amsterdam should have an exclusive jurisdiction over any dispute arising under the bill. The machinery was damaged on arrival in the Antilles and the shippers started proceedings in England. The shipowners contended that the contract was subject to an exclusive jurisdiction of the Dutch courts and to Dutch law. Dutch law was still subject to The Hague Rules and therefore liability was limited to a lower figure than under The Hague-Visby Rules. The House of Lords had no doubt that The Hague-Visby Rules applied, since the bill of lading had been issued in Scotland and carriage was from a Scottish port and the United Kingdom was a contracting state.

(b) The shipowner's protections cover his servants and agents – but not his independent contractors such as stevedores (a partial solution only to the problem of *Midland Silicones v Scruttons*). The Rules also apply to claims in tort as well as in contract (Article IV *bis*).

Both these changes are assisted by the words 'shall have the force of law' in s 1(2) of the Act.

(c) New monetary limits are set (Article IV.5(a)). It is sought to solve the problem of containers by specifying that 'the number of packages or units enumerated in the bill of lading as packed in such article of transport shall be deemed the number of packages or units' (Article IV.5(c)). Considerable problems obviously still exist in this area.

(d) Article III.4 prevents a shipowner proving against a good faith transferee of the bill of lading that goods signed for as loaded in the bill of lading were not loaded (the problem of *Grant v Norway* discussed above).

(e) The Rules are no longer excluded from the coastal trade (s 1(3), 1971 Act).

The Hague and Hague-Visby Rules

This chapter considers the mandatory régime laid down for bill of lading contract by the Hague Rules and Hague-Visby Rules.

The Hague Rules were adopted by an international convention at Brussels in 1924. The Rules apply as follows:

The Hague Rules

- to outward shipments from UK ports (other than coastal trade);

- covered by a bill of lading;

- to those loading and unloading operations which the contract places upon the carrier 'before and after' problem;

- they do not cover deck cargo and live animals;

- such provisions as protect the carrier do not protect his employees or independent contractors (eg stevedores);

- they are displaced, as are other contractual terms, by deviation.

The basic provisions of the Rules are that the shipowner owes a duty to exercise due care as to seaworthiness and care of cargo. In return, he is exempted in 17 ways (such as negligence in navigation and management of the ship, perils of the sea, inadequate packing). These duties cannot be varied except to increase the shipowner's responsibility.

The Hague-Visby Rules were adopted at Brussels in 1968 and enacted in the UK as the Carriage of Goods by Sea Act 1971. The protocol did not however receive sufficient ratifications until 1976 (it came into effect in the UK on 23 June 1973). The changes made in the Visby Rules are as follows:

The Hague-Visby Rules

- English courts must apply them to all international carriage where the bill of lading is issued in a contracting state, the carriage is from a port in a contracting state, or the bill of lading contract provides that the Rules are to apply;

- the shipowner's protections cover his servants and agents but not his independent contractors (eg stevedores);

- new monetary limits are set;

- the shipowner is prevented from proving against a good faith transferee of the bill of lading that goods signed for as loaded in the bill of lading are not loaded;

- the Rules are no longer excluded from the coastal trade.

Chapter 17

Freight

The rules here are complex and only explicable, if at all, in the terms of their ancient history. Nevertheless, they are for the most part well settled.

17.1 Introduction

The *prime facie* rule is that freight is payable on delivery of the goods. So if the goods are not delivered, even through an excepted peril, the carrier cannot sue. This was held in *Hunter v Prinsep* (1808).

17.2 Freight payable on delivery

On the other hand if the goods arrive, though damaged, freight is due in full and the claim for damage must be the subject of a separate action (*Dakin v Oxley* (1864) (see further set-off below)), but the goods must still be commercially the same as those shipped (*Asfar v Blundell* (1896)).

If the contract provides for freight in a lump sum, it is not necessary for the full cargo to arrive for freight to be due. It is sufficient that part of the cargo arrives even though the vessel never completes the voyage (see *Thomas v Harrowing* (1915)) and even though it is the shipowner's fault.

17.3 Lump sum freight

Although the ship may fail to complete the voyage and the goods are not delivered, there may be an express or implied agreement to pay all or part of the freight eg parties may agree to discharge at a different port as a substituted performance (*Christy v Row* (1808)), but this is dependent on proof of an agreement (*St Enoch Shipping v Phosphate Mining* (1916)).

17.4 *Pro rata* freight

Where freight is paid, or payable in advance, then it is due even though goods do not reach their destination. In practice, freight is often made payable in advance and in certain trades it may be desirable or even essential to obtain bills of lading stamped 'freight pre-paid'.

17.5 Advance freight

Normal delivery may sometimes by prevented by some cause outside the master's control. The master may then take reasonable steps to deal with goods and shipowners may charge cargo-owners 'back freight' to cover expenses so incurred.

17.6 Back freight

17.7	**Dead freight**	If a charterer fails to keep his contract to provide cargo, the shipowner may have action against him for 'dead freight'.

17.8	**Set-off**	The shipowner may have a claim for freight and the cargo owner may have a claim against the shipowner for delivering only part of the cargo or delivering it in damaged form. One might expect that the cargo owner could set-off his claim against the claim to freight but it is clearly established that this is not so (see *Dakin v Oxley* (1864)). This is of considerable practical importance since the time limit for the two claims will frequently be different.

The Aries (1977) involved a voyage charterparty where there was an alleged short delivery. The charterers paid their freight less $30,000. It was held by the House of Lords that the shipowners could sue for the balance. The Hague Rules applied to the claim for short delivery, but that claim was barred after a year. In other words, in such a situation the cargo owner must pay in full and issue a writ in respect of his own claim within a year.

It is unclear whether these rules apply equally to time charters. In the leading case of *The Nanfri* (1979) the majority of the Court of Appeal thought that they did not, but the House of Lords expressed no view. Most time charters would include some express power to deduct for off-hire but it seems probable that under the general rules of set-off the charterer can also deduct reasonable claims made in good faith, arising out of conduct by the shipowner which has deprived him of the use of the ship.

17.9	**Who is liable for freight**	There may be claims for freight against:

- the shipper of the goods;

- the consignee or indorsee of the bill of lading;

- a seller who stops goods *in transitu*;

- the charterer.

Note that changes are made here by s 3 of the Carriage of Goods by Sea Act 1992.

Freight

The usual rule is that freight is payable only on delivery. This chapter considers this and associated rules and the rules relating to set-off of cargo claims against freight.

PART IV

INTERNATIONAL SALES

Chapter 18

General Problems

Not all international sale contracts will be governed by English law. Some will be governed by the law of France or the law of Germany or the law of the State of New York and so on. The present notes are concerned with English rules for international sales, that is for those international sale contracts which are governed by English law. What law governs any particular contract is a matter for another subject called the 'conflict of laws'. The details of this are outside the scope of the present work but it may be said that, roughly speaking, English law will be applied either where the transaction is more closely connected with the English legal system than any other or where the parties have chosen English law as the governing law. Both in English law and in the conflict of law rules of most other countries, the parties enjoy great autonomy in choosing their own law. So many international sale contracts which have little or no connection with England will contain express choice of English law. Such choices would usually be effective in the eyes of both English and foreign courts.

During the 19th century, when most of the basic laws of international sale contracts were developed, problems with the conflict of laws appeared less important because a substantial body of trade was within the commonwealth and all relevant countries had rules as to contract and sale of goods which were substantially very similar. This is no longer the case today and many international sale contracts involve English buyers and sellers dealing with continental sellers and buyers. One solution to reduce the practical problems which arise from this is to move towards uniform rules for international sales in the main trading countries. Obviously, if all the major countries actually have the same rules it will matter much less in practice which country's rules are formally being applied. There is in fact a major project to this end which is called the Vienna Convention on International Sales. This was adopted by the UN Congress at Vienna in 1980. The United Kingdom took part in negotiation of the Vienna Convention but it seems in practice unlikely that it will ratify the Convention and bring it into force in English law in the near future. It has been brought into force in most of the other major trading countries in the world.

18.1   Conflict of laws

18.2	**The Sale of Goods Act**	When an international sale contract is governed by English law, it will be subject to the Sale of Goods Act. This means that conceptual structure of domestic and international sales is largely the same. However, whoever drafted the Sale of Goods Act appears to have had problems presented in domestic sales mainly in mind and this meant that the practical solutions adopted for international sales are often not the same as those adopted for domestic sales. The following features are particularly inappropriate to international sales:

(a) sales presumed to be for cash;

(b) risk *prima facie* passes with property (s 20);

(c) property *prime facie* passes on agreement where goods specific (s 18 r 1);

(d) seller's duty to deliver goods (s 27);

(e) payment and delivery concurrent conditions (s 28);

(f) unpaid seller normally only protected by lien, namely the right to retain possession (ss 41–43).

International sales raise special problems for the parties because of the considerable period which may elapse between dispatch of the goods and their arrival. During this period the parties are subject to dangers of three types – financial (seller wishes to be paid before parting with the goods, buyer does not wish to pay till he sees goods); physical (goods may deteriorate en route); and legal (there may be governmental interference on export or import). To provide for this the special cif and fob terms have been evolved which (except where used simply as price terms) vary the *prima facie* duties of the parties as expressed in the Sale of Goods Act. They are well worked out in English law, especially the cif contract, partly because all import and export contracts involved (until air transport) the use of sea transport, and much of it (eg the Far East trade) very long sea transport.

The rules thus established refer to older methods of ship operation: it is not always clear how they operate in respect of modern methods, eg containerisation.

18.3	**Finance**	In domestic contracts payment terms are often of the nett monthly kind. Such terms are not unknown in international sales, particularly between various branches of multinational companies but the risks are obviously greater in international sales, where the creditworthiness of the buyer is more difficult to verify. In many countries the prospect of suing the buyer in the local courts may also be unattractive.

The seller may commonly stipulate for cash against documents. The buyer then agrees to pay on presentation of the documents and usually property will pass at this moment. Payment might be made in cash (unlikely), by banker's draft or by acceptance of a *bill of exchange*.

A common procedure is for the documents to be forwarded together with a bill of exchange attached to them drawn by the seller on the buyer. Such a *documentary bill* has the effect of ensuring that the buyer will not receive the goods unless he accepts the bill of exchange. Under s 19(3) Sale of Goods Act 1979 if the buyer does not accept the bill of exchange, she has to return the documents and if she wrongfully fails to do so, property will not pass to her.

The seller might instead stipulate that the buyer will accept a bill of exchange payable at 30 or 60 days, before he ships the goods, but then the buyer would be exposed to the risk that the seller would not ship the goods.

Bills of exchange have a number of advantages from the seller's point of view. In particular they can be converted into cash by discounting with a bank thereby avoiding the problem of the solvent but slow paying buyer and the buyer cannot set up defences to the bill of exchange based on defects in the goods. On the other hand, they do not protect against the buyer's insolvency. It is very common therefore to stipulate instead for payment by *banker's commercial credit*. This involves introduction of a bank (often two or three) between buyer or seller.

In its simplest form the credit transaction has three parties and there are three contracts. The sale contract contains a term requiring payment by credit; the buyer then makes a contract with his bank for the opening of a credit and the bank then writes to the seller informing him of the opening of the credit and promising to pay against presentation of the documents. In practice there may often be a second bank doing business in the seller's place of business since the first bank may prefer to deal with another bank rather than directly with the seller. Sometimes, indeed, the buyer's bank will deal with its correspondent bank in the seller's country which will then deal with the seller's own bank. Those other banks may simply act as channels of communication or they may themselves undertake that the credit will be honoured. They are then said to *confirm* it. The original undertaking of the buyer's bank may be *revocable* or *irrevocable*. If it is irrevocable then the bank binds itself from the moment the seller receives notice of the credit.

18.3.1   Mechanics of the credit

18.3.2   Some points to note

The following points should be noted:

(a) The opening by the buyer of a credit in conformity with the contract of sale is a condition precedent to the seller's obligation to ship the goods. So if the buyer opens a non-conforming credit it is open to the seller to call on her to rectify the omission and, if she fails to open a conforming credit within the time limit, to terminate the contract. If the seller does so he may be able to recover profits which he has lost where it was within the buyer's contemplation that the credit would be used by the seller to complete his own purchase of the goods (*Trans Trust v Dambian Trading* (1952)).

(b) If the buyer opens a non-conforming credit, the seller may decide, notwithstanding, to go ahead with performance. This may well amount to a consensual variation of the contract or a waiver of his rights (*Alan v El Nasr* (1971)).

(c) If the buyer opens a conforming credit, the seller's primary remedies will be against the bank. But the opening of the credit does not extinguish the buyer's secondary obligation to pay the price. So in principle the buyer would be liable to pay if the bank became insolvent or if the buyer receives the goods but the bank lawfully refused to pay because the documents are defective. See *Saffron v Cafrika* (1958); *Alan v El Nasr* (1971); and *Man v Nigerian Sweets and Confectionery* (1977).

(d) In practice it is very important that the terms of the three contracts are carefully tied together and consistent. The courts will construe the three contracts separately. If the bank stipulates for payment against documents different from those required by its instructions from the buyer then it will be bound to the seller but unable to seek indemnity from the buyer.

(e) In practice virtually all credits are now issued subject to the Uniform Customs and Practice for documentary credits (UCP) (1993 revision). These are normally incorporated either by express reference in the documents or by banking practice in the country concerned.

(f) It is a fundamental principle of banking practice in relation to credits that the transactions are in documents and not in goods. So if the bank pays against the precise documents specified in the buyer's instructions it is entitled to be indemnified and if it pays against other documents it is not; as Lord Summer said in *Equitable Trust Company of New York v Dawson Partners* (1927) 'There is no room for documents which are almost the same or which will do just as well.'

(g) In the same way the bank is liable to the seller if he presents a document in conformity with the terms of the credit. If the seller does this the bank is not entitled to refuse payment nor is the buyer entitled to instruct the bank to withhold payment on the grounds that the goods are defective (*Malas v British Imex Industries* (1957); *Discount Records v Barclays Bank* (1975)).

The only exception to this appears to be where there is clear and unequivocal evidence of fraud on the part of the seller (*Sztejn v Henry Schroeder Banking Corporation* (1941); *United City Merchants v Royal Bank of Canada* (1983)).

(h) It will be seen that there is a not insubstantial risk that the seller will be able to present documents which qualify for payment even though he has shipped goods which are not up to contract. This is particularly so where the goods sold are of a kind defects in which would not be expected to be revealed by the bill of lading. It is open to the buyer to increase his protection against this danger by stipulating for extra documents, eg consular certificates of inspection and quality. This is undoubtedly a sensible step but it is essential to specify the nature of the extra documents with care and accuracy (*Commercial Banking Co of Sydney v Jalsard* (1972)).

There are other methods of financing cif and fob sales, eg the use of confirming houses or export factoring, or operating through associations of finance houses which have entered into reciprocal agreements with their opposite numbers in other countries such as the Amstel Club. There is also the possibility of making use of the facilities of the *Export Credits Guarantee Department*. This department in effect offers a policy of insurance against the risk of default by the foreign buyer where the risk is of a nature which could not be commercially insured.

18.3.3   Other methods of payment

Performance bonds are an increasingly common requirement insisted on by foreign buyers. They are in many respects a mirror image of the system of credits. Again there is a triangular relationship between buyer, seller and bank. In this case the bank guarantees to the buyer payment of a sum, usually 5% or 10% of the price, to guarantee the seller's performance. Commonly there are in fact two or more banks, the actual guarantee being given by a bank in the buyer's country which has received a guarantee in its turn from the bank in the seller's country, which in turn no doubt has obtained an undertaking from the seller to indemnify it against loss. In many cases these guarantees are payable simply on demand and there have been a series of cases before the

18.3.4   Performance bonds

English courts, such as *RD Harbottle (Mercantile) Ltd v National Westminster Bank* (1977), *Howe Richardson Scale Company Ltd v Polimex* (1978) and *Edward Owen Engineering Ltd v Barclays Bank International Ltd* (1978).

In each case the court has held that where the performance bond was stated to be payable on demand, the bank must honour it even though there has in fact been no failure to perform by the seller unless there was clear and unequivocal evidence of fraud. In coming to this conclusion the courts have relied heavily on the analogy of documentary credits and on the principle that in both cases banks deal only in documents and do not enquire into the rights and wrongs of the dispute between buyer and seller unless there is clear evidence of fraud. If the buyer wrongfully calls up the performance bond when there has in fact been no breach by the seller, then it is open to the seller to sue but in many cases this would require an action in the buyer's country which may appear difficult or even impossible. In the *Owen* case it would have involved suing a branch of the Libyan government before the Libyan courts.

| 18.4 | **Export and import licences** |

In many international sale contracts, performance will depend on obtaining an export and/or import licence. Obviously if a necessary licence is not obtained, lawful performance of the contract will normally be impossible but this is not the end of the matter. Questions may arise as to whether one of the parties is at fault in having failed to obtain a licence. This question divides itself into two limbs: who should obtain the licence and is the duty to obtain the licence absolute? As to who should obtain the licence, it is tempting to suggest that export licences should be obtained by the exporter and import licences by the importer, but this is clearly too simple a view. Much will depend on the nature of the licence and the purpose for which the licensing system exists. Often the purpose of the export licence has been to prevent goods going to a specific undesired destination, eg strategic goods to Eastern European or Indian goods to South Africa. In such a case the importer may know much more about the ultimate destination of the goods than the exporter and it may be incumbent on him to obtain the licence. Again it may be that only one of the parties would be an acceptable applicant for a licence to the Government Licensing Office (see *AV Pound v MW Hardy & Co* (1956)).

Obviously a well-drafted contract may well expressly state on which party the duty to obtain the licence rests. Similarly, it may say whether he is simply to use his best endeavours to obtain a licence or whether the duty is absolute. Where the contract is silent the courts have sometimes inferred that the duty is simply one of reasonable diligence as in *Re Anglo Russian Merchant Traders* (1917) and sometimes that it is absolute as in *KC Sethia v Partabmul Rameshwar* (1951). See also the problem in the *Polish Sugar* (1979) case where the sellers had obtained a Polish export licence which was later revoked because of the decision of the Polish government not to permit export of sugar to meet the contract.

The duty of insurance by the seller fall under two different types of contract: the fob contract or the cif contract.

18.5   Insurance

In fob contracts the seller is normally under no duty to insure for the benefit of the buyer (unless the contract expressly requires him to do so). The seller is however under a duty to give such notice to the buyer as may enable him to arrange insurance of goods during transit. He should also provide all the necessary information to enable the buyer to obtain the necessary cover. If the seller fails to give this notice (and the necessary information) the goods remain at the seller's risk.

18.5.1   The fob contract

As a general rule the seller has an insurable interest in the goods until the goods pass the ship's rail, whereupon the buyer acquires an insurable interest. In some cases, however, the seller retains an insurable interest in the goods even though they have been loaded on to a vessel – for example if the seller has a right to stop the goods *in transitu.*

In cif contracts the seller is under a duty to insure the goods during shipment, for in a normal cif contract, the sale price of the goods includes the cost of the goods, their insurance and the freight. The seller is bound to tender to the buyer a policy of insurance – a certificate or cover note may not be sufficient. The policy must cover the goods from the time of shipment until delivery, and must be a policy which is usual in the trade in question (unless the contract otherwise provides).

18.5.2   The cif contract

If the goods are lost in transit, the buyer must pay the seller but can then sue on the policy or sue the shipowner for the loss of the goods.

Practical operation of cif and fob contracts depends heavily on the use of bills of lading. Even if you are studying a course which does not include carriage of goods by sea, you will find it helpful therefore to read the account of bills of lading given in Chapter 13.

18.5.3   The bill of lading

In the account of cif and fob contracts which follows, it is assumed that the material on domestic sales has been read and mastered. The concepts are not explained again and the relevant sections of the Sale of Goods Act are not set out in full. You may need therefore to refresh your memory about the law relating to domestic sales.

General Problems

This chapter considers a number of general problems which arise in relation to international sales which do not occur at all, or at least to the same extent, in domestic sales. These include problems as to which legal system should govern; as to payments, particularly by letter of credit; performance bonds; export and import licences and insurance.

Conflict of laws

Not all international sales contracts will be governed by English law. Roughly speaking, English law will be applied either where the transaction is more closely connected with the English legal system than any other or where the parties have chosen English law as the governing law.

When an international sale contract is governed by English law, it will be subject to the Sale of Goods Act.

Finance

In its simplest form the credit transaction has three parties and there are three contracts. The sale contract contains a term requiring payment by credit; the buyer then makes a contract with his bank for the opening of a credit and the bank then writes to the seller informing him of the opening of the credit and promising to pay against presentation of the documents.

The following points should be noted:

- the opening by the buyer of a credit in conformity with the contract of sale is a condition precedent to the seller's obligation to ship the goods;

- if the buyer opens a non-conforming credit, the seller may decide, notwithstanding, to go ahead with performance;

- if the buyer opens a conforming credit, the seller's primary remedies will be against the bank although the opening of the credit does not extinguish the buyer's secondary obligation to pay the price;

- in practice, virtually all credits are now issued subject to the Uniform Customs and Practice for documentary credits (1993 revision);

- it is a fundamental principle of banking practice in relation to credits that the transactions are in documents and not in goods;

- the bank is not entitled to refuse payment nor is the buyer entitled to instruct the bank to withhold payment on the grounds that the goods are defective where the seller presents shipping documents in conformity with the terms of the credit.

Performance bonds

The bank guarantees to the buyer payment of a sum, usually 5% or 10% of the price, to guarantee the seller's performance. In many cases, these guarantees are payable simply on demand and the bank must honour the performance bond even though there has in fact been no failure to perform by the seller unless there was clear and unequivocal evidence of fraud.

Export and import licences

As to who should obtain the licence, much will depend on the nature of the licence and the purpose for which the licensing system exists. Often the purpose of the export licence has been to prevent goods going to a specific undesired destination. In such a case, the importer may know much more about the ultimate destination of the goods than the exporter and it may be incumbent on him to obtain the licence. Again, it may be that only one of the parties would be an acceptable applicant for a licence to the Government Licensing Office (*AV Pound v MW Hardy & Co* (1956)).

The contract may well expressly state on which party the duty to obtain the licence rests. Similarly, it may say whether that party is simply to use his best endeavours to obtain a licence or whether the duty is absolute. Where the contract is silent, the courts have sometimes inferred that the duty is simply one of reasonable diligence (*Re Anglo Russian Merchant Traders* (1917)) and sometimes that it is absolute (*KC Sethis v Partabmul Rameshwar* (1951)).

Insurance

In fob contracts, the seller is normally under no duty to insure for the benefit of the buyer (unless the contract expressly requires him to do so). The seller is however under a duty to give such notice to the buyer as may enable him to arrange insurance of goods during transit. If the seller fails to give this notice, the goods remain at the seller's risk.

In cif contracts, the seller is under a duty to insure the goods during shipment for, in a normal cif contract, the sale price of the goods includes the cost of the goods, their insurance and the freight.

Chapter 19

CIF Contracts

'A cif contract is an agreement to sell goods at an inclusive price covering the cost of the goods, insurance and freight. The essential feature of such a contract is that a seller, having shipped, or bought afloat, goods in accordance with the contract, fulfills his part of the bargain by tendering to the buyer the proper shipping documents. If he does this, he is not in breach even though the goods have been lost before such tender. In the event of such loss the buyer must nevertheless pay the price on tender of the documents, and his remedies, if any, will be against the carrier or against the underwriter, but not against the seller.'

19.1   Definition

The duties of a seller are:

19.2   Duties of seller

(a) to ship goods or (where this duty is appropriate) buy goods afloat;

(b) which are conforming (strict duties, eg as to title, description and quantity; date of shipment, which is part of the description; satisfactory quality, fitness for purpose and conformity with sample – SGA ss 12–15, 30);

(c) to appropriate contractually goods to the contract;

(d) to procure and tender documents which (though the contract may provide otherwise) are as follows:

   (i) invoice (problems of extent to which goods must be described);

   (ii) bill of lading, which
   - is transferable ('or assigns')
   - provides continuous documentary cover
   - is 'shipped' not 'received'
   - provides for carriage to specified destination by
   - specified or customary route
   - is issued on shipment
   - is genuine
   - is valid and effective
   - is clean (*The Galatia* (1980))
   - covers the contract goods only;

   (iii) policy (not certificate) of insurance, which
   - is assignable by indorsement
   - is effective

- covers contract goods only
- is usual at time and place effected (problems of war risks)
- problems as to delivery orders, mates receipts, non-negotiable waybills, which are not documents of title
- time of tender (*Toepfer v Lenersan-Poortman NV (1980)*).

19.3   Duties of buyer

The duties of the buyer are:

(a) to pay the price against documents (whether personally or through bank)

- 'blind', without seeing the goods (*Horst v Biddell Bros* (1912))
- in many cases, even if goods known to have deteriorated or perished (*Groom v Barber* (1915); *Manbre Saccharin v Corn Products* (1919)).

(b) to perform other contract duties, eg specify destination.

19.4   Passing of property

Most cif contracts are for the sale of unascertained goods. It is an overriding rule that property cannot pass until the goods are ascertained. Subject to this, where the contract is for the sale of specific goods or for the sale of unascertained goods which have been ascertained, the rule is that property passes when it is intended to pass. On the whole, express provisions as to when property is to pass seem to be unusual so the court has to infer the party's intention from the circumstances.

Undoubtedly the most common inference is that property is intended to pass only on the taking up of the documents, that is by the transfer of the documents from seller to buyer and of the price from buyer to seller. Payment need not in this sense mean payment in cash as eg where the buyer accepts a bill of exchange payable at 30 days. In such a situation the seller would usually be treated as giving credit to the buyer so the property would pass on acceptance of the bill and not on its payment. The reason why the seller is not normally thought to intend to transfer property before he parts with the documents was explained by Lord Wright in *Ross T Smyth v Bailey* (1940). The seller in modern conditions is usually not content to rely on his rights of lien and stoppage in *transitu* but wishes to reserve a right of disposal. This is so where the seller has taken a bill of lading to the order of the buyer but retained it in his possession. The situation is even clearer where the seller has taken a bill of lading to his own order or to the order of the bank which has financed the transaction.

The general rule is that risk *prime facie* passes with property. (Sale of Goods Act s 20). This general rule will not normally apply however in a cif contract. In the absence of an express contrary provision, it will normally be inferred that risk in a cif contract passes 'on shipment or as from shipment' *per* Lord Porter in *The Julia*. The reason for this is that it is the seller's duty to insure as from shipment and the buyer will therefore enjoy the benefit of the policy of insurance as from this date. It should be noted that the rule has two branches. If the contract precedes shipment, then risk will pass on shipment. If shipment precedes the contract then the risk will pass as from shipment; the seller's obligations as to quality will also operate as from shipment.

This statement probably requires some qualification in the case of total loss. In *Couturier v Hastie* (1856) there was a contract for the sale of a cargo of corn cif to be carried on a particular ship. In fact unknown to the parties the cargo had already been sold before the contract by the master because it was fermenting. It was held that the buyer was not bound to pay the price so if total loss precedes the contract it would seem that risk will not pass, but this would not be true of partial loss or deterioration.

The following may be classed as remedies for the seller: termination, action for the price and damages.

The seller may be able to terminate the contract because of the buyer's repudiation or because of some serious breach by the buyer of his obligations. The most likely example would be a breach by the buyer of his obligations as to payment, eg failure to open a conforming credit.

This is governed by Sale of Goods Act s 49. The seller may bring an action for the price either 'where the property in the goods has passed to the buyer, and the buyer wrongfully neglects or refuses to pay for the goods in accordance with the terms of the contract' or 'where the price is payable on a day certain irrespective of delivery.' In the most common case where the payment provision is for cash against documents, neither limb of s 49 will apply. The first limb will not apply because if the buyer does not pay, property will not have passed to the buyer and the second limb will not apply because the date of payment is not a day certain irrespective of delivery.

19.5   Passing of risk

19.6   Remedies of the seller

19.6.1   Termination

19.6.2   Action for the price

19.6.3	Damages

Under the Sale of Goods Act s 50 the seller is entitled to damages 'where the buyer wrongfully neglects or refuses to accept and pay for the goods'. *Prima facie* the damages are measured by the difference between the contract price and the market price though they may include consequential loss if this is not too remote. The relevant time would probably be that for the contractual date for delivery of the documents or if there is no such date, the date on which the buyer refused to take up the documents.

19.7   Remedies of the buyer

The following may be classed as remedies of the buyer: rejection; damages; specific performance.

19.7.1	Rejection

The cif buyer receives two deliveries, one of goods and one of documents and he therefore has in principle two rights to reject. This gives rise to considerable complexities.

(i) He may reject the documents if they are defective (probably even if the defect is slight, because exact documentary compliance is required). They may be defective in two ways. First, they may not conform on their face with the contract requirements, eg contract requires October shipment, bill of lading dated November; contract requires first grade carcasses, bill of lading shows second grade carcasses. But second, and less obviously, a bill of lading may be defective because false – eg bill shows October shipment, goods actually loaded in November; bill of lading shows hard amber wheat, wheat actually soft white wheat.

But he may also lose the right to reject by waiver of it; and sometimes he may be estopped from saying that he has not waived it (*Panchaud Frères* (1970)).

(ii) He may reject the goods if they are defective.

He may not, however, do so if the defect in the goods was apparent on the face of the bill of lading and he accepted the bill; for by doing so he may be held to have waived his right to reject (but not his right to damages). As in the case of documents, he may lose the right to reject by waiver and sometimes other conduct or inactivity (see above).

If he has the right to reject, his motives in exercising it are irrelevant; it does not matter that his reason for doing so is that the market has fallen.

(iii) He may not, however, reject good documents merely because he can prove that the goods shipped were defective: he must pay against documents and then (if he wishes) reject the goods and claim his money back (*Gill & Duffus v Berger* (1984)). Obviously this involves risks.

False (eg falsely dated) documents may deprive the buyer of the opportunity to reject them: had he known shipment was really in November and not (as stated) in October he would have rejected them. In such a case he may be entitled to damages for the loss caused to him by false documents – usually that he was deprived of an opportunity to reject altogether on a falling market (*Kwei Tek Chao v British Traders & Shippers* (1954)). The damages are such as to put the buyer in the position in which he would have been had the statements been true. So if, had the statements been true, the buyer could not have rejected, he cannot calculate his damages on this basis (*Proctor & Gamble v Becher* (1988)).

The buyer may recover damages for non-delivery, Sale of Goods Act s 51(3). The amount of recovery is *prima facie* 'the difference between the contract price and the market or current price of the goods at the time or times when they ought to have been delivered or if no time was fixed then at the time of the refusal to delivery' (see *Sharpe v Nosawa* (1917)). He may also recover damages for defective delivery (Sale of Goods Act s 53).

Prima facie 'in the case of a breach of warranty of quality the difference between the value of the goods at the time of delivery to the buyer and the value they would have had if they had answered to the warranty'. He may also recover damages for the loss of the right to reject (see above).

19.7.2   Damages

Under Sale of Goods Act s 52 the court has discretion to order specific performance 'in any action for breach of a contract to deliver specific or ascertained goods.' The most important practical application for this in a cif context would be an attempt to assert priority over other creditors in the seller's insolvency where property in the goods had not passed the buyer (see *Re Wait* (1927)).

19.7.3   Specific performance

CIF Contracts

The c(ost) i(nsurer) f(reight) form of contract is the most popular form of international sale contract. This chapter considers the duties of seller and buyer under this form of contract; the rules as to passing of property and risk and as to the remedies of seller and buyer.

The duties of the cif seller are:

Duties of seller

- to ship goods;

- which are conforming under the terms of the contract;

- to appropriate contractually goods to the contract;

- to procure and tender proper shipping documents (usually invoice, bill of lading and policy of insurance).

The duties of the buyer are to pay the price against documents and to perform other contract duties (eg specify destination).

Duties of buyer

Most cif contracts are for the sale of unascertained goods. It is an overriding rule that property cannot pass until the goods are ascertained. Subject to this, where the contract is for the sale of specific goods or for the sale of unascertained goods which have been ascertained, the rule is that property passes when it is intended to pass. On the whole, express provisions as to when property is to pass seem to be unusual so the court has to infer the party's intention from the circumstances.

Passing of property and risk

Undoubtedly the most common inference is that property is intended to pass only on the taking up of the documents, that is by the transfer of the documents from seller to buyer and of the price from buyer to seller.

The general rule is that risk *prima facie* passes with property (Sale of Goods Act s 20). This general rule will not normally apply however in a cif contract. In the absence of an express contrary provision, it will normally be inferred that risk in a cif contract passes 'on shipment or as from shipment' *per* Lord Porter in *The Julia*.

The cif seller may:

Remedies of the seller

- terminate the contract because of the buyer's repudiation or because of some serious breach by the buyer of his obligations;

- bring an action for the price either 'where the property in the goods has passed to the buyer, and the buyer wrongfully neglects or refuses to pay for the goods in accordance with the terms of the contract' or 'where the price is payable on a day certain irrespective of delivery' (s 49 Sale of Goods Act);

- be entitled to damages 'where the buyer wrongfully neglects or refuses to accept and pay for the goods' (s 50 Sale of Goods Act).

Remedies of the buyer

The cif buyer may recover damages for non-delivery (s 51(3) Sale of Goods Act) or for defective delivery (s 53). Under s 52, the court has discretion to order specific performance 'in any action for breach of a contract to deliver specific or ascertained goods'.

The cif buyer has, in principle, two rights to reject. This gives rise to considerable complexities:

- he may reject the documents if they are defective (either because they may not conform on their face with the contract requirements or because a bill of lading may be false);

- he may reject the goods if they are defective (but not if the defect in the goods was apparent on the face of the bill of lading and the buyer accepted the bill);

- he may not, however, reject good documents merely because he can prove that the goods shipped were defective (he must pay against documents and then reject the goods and claim his money back).

Chapter 20

FOB Contracts

'In an ordinary fob contract ... "free on board" does not merely condition the constituent elements in the price but expresses the seller's obligations additional to the bare bargain of purchase and sale' (*Wimble v Rosenberg* (1913)).

20.1 **Definition and classification**

Devlin J in the case of *Pyrene v Scindia Navigation Co Ltd* (1954) said:

20.1.1 The 'classic' fob contract

'The fob contract has become a flexible instrument.

[1] In what counsel called the classic type as described, for example, in *Wimble, Sons & Co Ltd v Rosenberg & Sons,* the buyer's duty is to nominate the ship, and the seller's to put the goods on board for account of the buyer and to procure a bill of lading in terms usual in the trade. In such a case the seller is directly a party to the contract of carriage at least until he takes out the bill of lading in the buyer's name. Probably the classic type is based on the assumption that the ship nominated will be willing to load any goods brought down to the berth or at least those of which she is notified. Under present conditions, when space often has to be booked well in advance, the contract of carriage comes into existence at an earlier point of time.

[2] Sometimes the seller is asked to make the necessary arrangements, and the contract may then provide for his taking the bill of lading in his own name and obtaining payment against the transfer, as in a cif contract.

[3] Sometimes the buyer engages his own forwarding agent at the port of loading to book space and to procure the bill of lading; if freight has to be paid in advance this method may be the most convenient. In such a case the seller discharges his duty by putting the goods on board, getting the mate's receipt and handing it to the forwarding agent to enable him to obtain the bill of lading. The present case belongs to this third type; and it is only in this type, I think, that any doubt can arise about the seller being a party to the contract.'

Note in particular (a) seller's obligations with regard to delivery and appropriation; (b) cost of transportation and insurance; (c) risk of fluctuation in cost of these items (see the case of *The Parchim* (1918)).

20.1.2 Distinction between fob and cif contracts

20.2 Duties of the seller	The duties of the seller are:

(a) to put the goods on board a ship nominated or designated by the buyer. He may not tender delivery elsewhere; nor does it seem that he can be required to deliver elsewhere even though the alternative method is less expensive;

(b) to bear expenses up to the point of shipment;

(c) to obtain such shipping documents as are required by the terms of the contract. These may require him to obtain a bill of lading, or only some other document, such as a mate's receipt;

(d) to ship the goods at the appropriate time within the shipment period (if any) specified in the contract. The exact time of shipment within that period is normally at the buyer's option so that shipment must be made between receipt of shipping instructions and the end of the period. The time may, however, also be at seller's option. Stipulations as to the time of 'delivery' refer to the time of shipment;

(e) to perform the duties imposed by s 32 of the Sale of Goods Act 1979, to the extent that they apply to fob contracts.

20.3   Duties of the buyer

The duties of the buyer are:

(a) to give shipping instructions – ie to name or designate a ship;

(b) to ensure that these instructions are 'effective' (as a matter of law, it is not necessary to make an advance reservation of shipping space);

(c) to give shipping instructions in due time. The time for giving such instructions depends on whether the time of shipment is at the seller's or buyer's option, and on other provisions in the contract;

(d) to bear expenses after shipment;

(e) to pay the price – usually on tender of the documents specified on the contract. The time and place for payment are (unless the contract otherwise provides) those of tender of documents.

20.4   Passing of property

The passing of property –

(a) On shipment

Property in goods passes when those goods are unconditionally appropriated to the contract – ie when the last decisive act has been performed by the seller. Property in unascertained goods cannot pass before shipment, because until shipment takes place there are no particular goods which the seller is bound irrevocably to ship.

(b) Documents

However, even though shipment has taken place, property in the goods will not have passed if the seller has reserved a right of disposal. He may do this:

(i) when the bill of lading makes the goods deliverable to the order of the seller or his agent;

(ii) when the only shipping document in the seller's hands is the mate's receipt made out in the seller's name, and when the ship will only hand over to the buyer the bill of lading on delivery of that mate's receipt;

(iii) when the bill of lading makes the goods deliverable to the order of the buyer, but it is agreed that the seller will retain possession of the bill of lading until payment is made.

When the seller retains a right of disposal property will not normally pass until the conditions of the contract as to payment are met.

20.5 Passing of risk

The general rule is that risk passes from the seller to the buyer on shipment. There are two views on what amounts to shipment:

(i) the traditional view – when the goods cross the ship's rail;

(ii) when the seller's duty with respect to loading has been performed.

The latter is preferable. If, therefore, the sale were on 'fob and stowed' terms, the risk would not pass until the goods were stowed.

Thus, if the goods are destroyed before delivery, the seller must deliver other goods or pay damages for non-delivery. If the goods are destroyed after delivery, the buyer must nevertheless pay the price.

20.6 Remedies of the buyer

The remedies of the buyer are:

(a) Rejection

(i) of goods

An fob buyer may reject goods when they are not in accordance with the contract in a way which amounts to a breach of an important term, or if they are not of the agreed quantity. Breach by a seller of a contractual provision as to shipment date is a ground of rejection.

(ii) of documents

An fob buyer may reject documents which do not comply with the contract.

The right to reject may be lost by waiver or acceptance. A buyer is deemed to have accepted goods if, (1) he has had a reasonable opportunity of examining them to see whether they are in accordance with the contract, or (2) he has done some act inconsistent with the ownership of the seller (such as reselling the goods) provided he has had a reasonable opportunity of examination.

In most fob contracts, the point of examination is the place of destination.

These rights of rejection are cumulative not alternative.

(b) Damages

(i) for non-delivery

The quantum of damages is the difference between the contract price and the market price of the goods at the time when they ought to have been delivered or, if no time was fixed, then at the time of refusal to deliver.

The *prima facie* rule is that the time of delivery is the time of shipment, and the place is the place of shipment. In the case of an anticipatory breach when no time of delivery has been fixed, the price is the market price at the time the goods ought to have been delivered. Consequential damages – eg dead freight – are recoverable.

(ii) for defective delivery

The quantum is the difference between the value of the goods at the time of delivery, and their value had they not been defective.

20.7 Remedies of the seller

The remedies of the seller are:

(a) Termination

The seller can normally rescind,

(i) where the buyer fails to comply with stipulations as to time of payment which are of the essence of the contract; or

(ii) where the buyer refuses to accept and pay for the goods.

(b) Action for the price

Where property has passed, and the buyer wrongfully refuses to pay in accordance with the contract, the seller can sue for the price. Similarly where property has not passed but the price is payable on a day certain irrespective delivery.

(c) Action for damages

For non-acceptance the quantum is the difference between the contract price and the market price at the time and place at which the goods ought to have been accepted. If no time was fixed, the relevant time is the time of refusal to accept (subject to the rule relating to anticipatory breach).

Where the goods have been shipped, damages will usually be assessed by reference to the market at the destination. When the goods have not been shipped, the relevant market is at the place of shipment. Consequential damages are recoverable.

The seller has the right of stoppage in transit. If this right is exercised the seller may resell the goods.

Summary of Chapter 20

FOB Contracts

The f(ree) o(n) b(oard) form of contract is the second most popular form of international sale contract. This chapter considers the duties of seller and buyer; the rules as to the passing of property and risk and as to the remedies of seller and buyer.

The duties of the fob seller are:

Duties of the seller

- to put the goods on board a ship nominated or designated by the buyer;
- to bear expenses up to the point of shipment;
- to obtain such shipping documents as are required by the terms of the contract;
- to ship the goods at the appropriate time within the shipment period specified in the contract;
- to perform the duties imposed by s 32 of the Sale of Goods Act 1979.

The duties of the buyer are:

Duties of the buyer

- to give effective shipping instructions;
- to give shipping instructions in due time;
- to bear expenses after shipment;
- to pay the price (usually on tender of the documents specified in the contract).

Property in goods passes when those goods are unconditionally appropriated to the contract. It is clear that property in unascertained goods cannot pass before shipment because, until shipment takes place, there are no particular goods which the seller is bound irrecovably to ship.

Passing of property and risk

However, even though shipment has taken place, property in the goods will not have passed if the seller has reserved a right of disposal.

The general rule is that risk passes from the seller to the buyer on shipment.

Remedies of the buyer   The remedies of the buyer are:

- rejection of goods or of documents;
- damages for non-delivery or for defective delivery.

Remedies of the seller   The remedies of the seller are:

- termination;
- action for price;
- action for damages.

Chapter 21

Other Forms of Contract

The 1990 edition of Incoterms provides for 11 other standard forms other than fob and cif. Obviously there is no theoretical limit to the parties' freedom to devise their own arrangements and with modern methods of multimodal transport it is no doubt increasingly common either for the seller to take the goods all the way to the buyer or for the buyer to collect the goods and take them all the way home. Nevertheless the standard provisions are of great practical importance and because they enable the parties by shorthand to incorporate many general understandings. It is perhaps convenient to list some of the main possibilities in what one might call geographical order starting with the case where the buyer comes to collect.

21.1   Introduction

In the case of ex works the seller's only responsibility is to make the goods available at his premises for collection. He is not even responsible for loading the goods unless that should be expressly agreed.

21.2   Ex works

FOR/FOT means free on rail/free on truck and the terms are synonymous since the words truck is used to relate to railway wagons. This term is to be used only where the goods are to be carried by rail. A named departure point should be given.

21.3   FOR/FOT

FAS means free alongside a ship. A named port of shipment needs to be given. This is similar to an fob contract except that the seller assumes no obligation as to loading so that he has performed the contract when the goods have been placed alongside the ship on the quay or in lighters.

21.4   FAS

C&F means cost and freight and with a named port of destination. This is very similar to cif except that the seller assumes no obligation as to insurance. Some importing countries in the third world object to cif contracts and use C&F contracts as a means of supporting their own domestic insurance industry.

21.5   C&F

Ex ship with a named port of destination means that the seller must make the goods available to the buyer on board the ship at the destination named in the contract, has to pay all cost and risk involved in bringing the goods there. Obviously this contract also has a good deal in common with the cif contract and indeed some difficult cases have arisen as to where a particular contract is properly classified as a cif or ex ship contract.

21.6   Ex ship

21.7   Ex quay

Ex quay means that the seller makes the goods available to the buyer on the quay at the named destination and has to bear the full cost and risk involved in getting the goods there. The contract should make it clear whether the contract is 'duty paid' or 'duties on buyers account'.

Other expressions which are used in Incoterms are delivered at frontier; delivered duty paid; fob airport; free carrier (this is similar to fob except that it is seller's obligation not to put the goods on board a ship but to put them safely into the hands of the carrier at the named point. This would be an appropriate form where the carriage was going to be in a container from an inland point or by use of a role on role off truck); freight carriage paid to; freight carriage and insurance paid to.

Other Forms of Contract

This chapter briefly considers some other popular forms of international sale contract including:

- ex works;
- FOR/FOT;
- FAS;
- C&F;
- ex ship;
- ex quay.

PART V

CONSUMER CREDIT

Chapter 22

Introduction to Consumer Credit

The availability and use of credit greases the wheels of developing consumer economies. Logically, therefore, government will be interested in regulating its use. This regulatory framework will cover such matters as:

(a) precontractual statements – both in the terminology and display of advertising to the general buying public and in disclosure to individual prospective debtors;

(b) control over pricing and the other terms used in consumer credit contracts;

(c) control over the mechanisms of enforcement that are available to creditors to force apparently recalcitrant debtors back into contractual line;

(d) control over the nature, quality and respectability of those who engage in the 'consumer credit industry'.

It is important to note that these are only aspects of a whole landscape and they are interrelated. For example, the ways in which the mechanisms of control over the enforcement activities of disappointed creditors are regulated will be reflected in their decision-making processes when selecting debtors.

The business of consumer credit has expanded rapidly in scope since the early years of this century and in extent since the 1960s. The trade moved from pawnbroking, tallymen and moneylenders to instalment credit from retailers and a huge growth in hire-purchase finance. Huge finance houses have developed. Manufacturers have set up 'in-house' finance schemes to facilitate the purchase of their own products. Mail order houses have grown to massive size and importance, (particularly to low-income families).

More recently, the emphasis has shifted slightly. Hire-purchase is now only centrally important in the car trade and for the more expensive of electrical goods. Pawnbrokers have staged a partial revival, although their premises are usually carpeted nowadays and their clientele are more likely to pledge candelabra and wedding rings for weekend 'fun-money' than Sunday suits to feed the children.

The increasing role of the clearing banks, having diversified beyond their 'traditional' business of lending to industry and commerce, and the building societies, now

22.1 Nature of the subject

deregulated, in the provision of consumer credit has further complicated the trade, although some might argue that the consumer benefits from greater choice and the impact of 'market forces' forces down the cost of credit to consumers.

The key development in consumer credit has been the rapid expansion of the credit card industry in all its various forms. Credit and charge cards have appeared from many directions, mostly supplied by banks and building societies, and with many organisations apparently endorsing or benefiting from them. There are 'in-house' credit and charge cards. There are cards where every transaction in which they are used gives a donation to a charity or a token for air travel or a discount from the price of a car, and so on. These are the days of easy credit – particularly for those who can, or who are able to appear as if they can, afford to repay the considerable cost of borrowing in this manner, not having cleared the account within the 'statement period'.

It seems from figures such as those published from time to time by agencies such as the Central Statistical Office that consumer credit is used mostly by adults between, say, 25 and 45, and in the middle socioeconomic groupings. Cars account for at least a third of the money borrowed. There are significant differences in the costs of various types of credit. This is a reflection of the risks carried by the creditor. The cheapest forms tend to be bank loans and overdrafts, whereas the most expensive seem to be from moneylenders who are prepared to lend against little or no security and perhaps despite the debtor's less-than-glowing credit reference.

22.2 The DGFT's report 'Overindebtedness'

From time to time surveys and reports on credit are prepared and published. They usually concern themselves with the developing consumer credit 'industry', and the evolving attitudes of consumers in the light of those developments.

One of the most important reports on consumers' attitudes in recent years was presented by the then Director General of Fair Trading (DGFT) in the summer of 1989. It was simply entitled 'Overindebtedness'.

Introducing the report, he described it as

'probably the most wide-ranging review for many years of attitudes to and opinions on credit and debt – and particularly the problems of over-commitment. The Consumer Credit Act requires me to keep the provision of credit in this country under review. There has been considerable public debate in the past few years on this subject. Most recently attention has focussed on those who found themselves borrowing to an extent that caused them all sorts of problems. Much of this debate has been based on opinion, hunches and horror stories. I therefore decided it was high time that some hard facts were injected, to give a basis for reasoned discussion.'

The report was based on the findings of three pieces of research: a survey commissioned by the Office of Fair Trading (OFT) and conducted in Autumn 1987 by PAS Business Surveys Ltd; unpublished data made available from the Family Expenditure Survey (a continuous survey of households carried out by the Office of Population Censuses and Surveys for the Department of Employment); and findings from questions included in the PAS Omnibus Survey carried out in January 1989.

The main findings quoted in the report are discussed below.

Spontaneous awareness of different types of credit was understandably greatest among those people most likely to use it. Only 3% of members of the age group most likely to use credit (the 25–44 year olds) were unable to name any type of credit, compared with over one quarter of the age group least likely to use it (the over 65s). Spontaneous awareness of individual forms of credit was again highest in those groups who used that type – for example, among the AB social classes, 76% of respondents spontaneously named credit cards as a type of credit. Young people were only a little less aware of credit than their elders. Groups least likely to use credit (such as the elderly and those in social classes DE) were most likely to admit ignorance.	22.2.1 Awareness of credit
While many people were aware of the advantages and disadvantages of different types of credit, there was also a high level of ignorance. Although 52% of people rightly thought they could lose their houses if they failed to keep up payments on a second mortgage, only 20% realised that a loan from a finance company could take the form of a second mortgage.	22.2.2 Awareness of the pros and cons of different types of credit
Only 9% of respondents were unable to name the most expensive form of credit, and 19% were unable to name the cheapest. Half of 16–17-year-olds questioned were able correctly to name the tallyman/moneylender as the most expensive form of credit. Over one third of this age group thought that buying on instalments from a mail order catalogue was the cheapest.	22.2.3 Awareness of the expense of different types of credit
Only 20% of all respondents (11% of 16–17 year olds) could correctly state what the initials APR stood for; 62% could not even hazard a guess. When told what the initials stood for, only 15% could give a completely accurate explanation of the	22.2.4 Awareness of the meaning and purpose of APR

phrase's meaning – again, 62% would not even attempt to give an explanation. Less than one in 20 young people could give an accurate answer, with 76% unable even to attempt an explanation.

Just over one third of adults and one tenth of young people took the APR into account when considering credit arrangements. Even those who took the APR into account were not very knowledgeable about the APR applied to bank, credit card and finance company loans, tending to underestimate the true cost of credit.

22.2.5	Attitudes towards credit

Taken overall, the groups most favourably disposed towards credit and most likely to use it were: those aged 25–44; those with children; social classes AB; those whose full-time education ended when they were aged 17 or over; higher income groups; those with assets; and those with existing high credit commitments. Surprisingly, those who had experienced difficulties with payments were more favourably disposed to credit than non-users.

22.2.6	Reasons for using or not using credit

The better-off listed as a reason for using credit that it was a convenient method of payment (61% of social classes AB compared with 43% of social classes DE). The least well-off were more likely to be impelled by necessity (49% of social classes DE gave this as a reason compared with 26% of social classes AB). Nearly two thirds of those who had been unemployed for six months or more gave 'necessity' as a reason for using credit. As a reason for not using credit, 'principle' was almost equally important to all social classes, but 'peace of mind' and 'cannot afford' were more important to the less well-off. For those aged 18–24, 'necessity' was the leading reason for using credit (58% of this age group compared to 10% for those aged 65 and over). For the oldest group, 76% listed convenience as a main reason for using credit, compared with 32% of 18–24 year olds. Half of those aged 65 and over were against the use of credit 'on principle', compared with 26% of 18–24 year olds.

22.2.7	Attitudes to different types of credit

Eight-six per cent of all respondents would never dream of using a loan from a tallyman/moneylender. Only 8% would not use a mortgage.

22.2.8	The use of credit

The use of credit increased with incomes rising to £20,000 per annum, and then tended to fall off slightly. People with mortgages were more likely than either renters or outright owners to use other forms of credit.

The peak age range for most forms of credit was between 25 and 44. The over 65s were least likely to use any form of credit. Over one third of 16 and 17-year-olds had used some form of credit and 97% expected to have used at least one form by the time they were 25. The use of credit rose with educational level, except for mail order catalogues which peaked among those whose education finished at the age of 16.

The percentage of households which paid both mortgage instalments and credit repayments rose from 17.1% to 22.7% in the period 1982-86.

22.2.9 Changes in the use of mortgages and credit

The percentage of households which made neither type of payment decreased from 50.4% to 46.3%. In the same period, the level of principal and interest mortgage repayments rose by 30% and the level of interest only mortgage payments rose by 11%; the level of credit repayments rose to 50%; the Retail Price Index rose 20% and the Index of Average Earnings rose by 35%.

There was therefore a rise in real terms of credit repayments. It is likely that changes in the adult population over the next few years may well change the use of credit. The current 65 and over group (most of whom were not credit users, and who had a tendency to be against the use of credit on principle) will be replaced by the current 55–64-year-olds who are far more likely to be credit users. Young people entering adult life are more likely to be heavy users of credit. An increase of 5% in the percentage of adults using credit can reasonably be forecast over the next few years.

In autumn 1987, 32% of all households were using credit cards. By 1989, 39% of all heads of households and housewives were using this type of credit. The 1989 survey showed that overall, 38% of credit card users incurred interest charges. It is interesting to note that 45% of those aged 44 and under incurred interest charges, compared with 19% of those aged 45 and over. Income was also a significant factor: 29% of those with annual incomes of less than £9,500 paid interest compared with 48% of those with annual incomes of £9,500 and over.

2.2.10 The use of different types of credit

The leading purpose for which bank and finance house loans were used was to buy cars. Home improvements, household appliances and furnishings were also high on the list. Hire-purchase and credit sales were used mostly for the purchase of electrical goods and domestic appliances. The leading use of mail order was to buy clothing. Over 90% of credit purchases made by 16 and 17-year-olds were of clothing. The leading purchases using credit cards were of clothing and petrol.

22.2.11 The purposes for which credit is used

22.2.12	Heavy commitment and difficulties with credit	The report details for the first time an objective measure of heavy commitment, based on disposable income left after satisfying credit and mortgage commitments.

The report details for the first time an objective measure of heavy commitment, based on disposable income left after satisfying credit and mortgage commitments.

Using this measure, the percentage of households having heavy mortgage commitments was identified as 0.9% in 1982 rising to 1.4% in 1986, and those identified as having heavy credit commitments rose from 4.1% to 8.6%.

Virtually all households with heavy commitments had incomes below the national average. Estimates based on the findings of the surveys indicate that the number of households in the United Kingdom having heavy mortgage commitments is in the region of 300,000, and the number having heavy credit commitments in the region of 1,800,000. The number of adults who had had difficulties with repayments in the previous five years is probably about 4,450,000.

22.2.13 Types of credit with which people had difficulty

Of all those who experienced difficulties, 31% had difficulty with credit card repayments and 16% with mortgage repayments. Nine per cent of all credit card users and 5% of all mortgagees, had experienced difficulties with the respective forms of credit.

22.2.14 Reasons for difficulties

When asked what had caused repayment difficulties, 33% mentioned unemployment of themselves or their spouses; 21% mentioned a fall in earnings; 18% said that they had taken on too many commitments; 8% said that they had overspent; 8% mentioned sickness; and 7% blamed marital problems.

22.2.15 Outcome of difficulties

Of those with problems, 37% had at some point stopped making repayments; 55% had approached their creditors for help; 78% of these people were offered the opportunity to make smaller repayments. 40% said that creditors had been very understanding, but 17% said that their creditors had been not very understanding or worse. Sixty seven per cent had turned to no one for advice, while 16% had turned to friends or relatives, 9% to a bank manager and 8% had approached a Citizens Advice Bureau.

For one fifth of those who had experienced repayment difficulties (ie 2% of all adults in the United Kingdom) there had been no satisfactory outcome, although the difficulties of 48% had been satisfactorily resolved.

22.3 Mintel's 'Debt!' report

In May 1993, the Mintel International Group, a leading UK market and consumer research analyst, published a report entitled 'Debt!'. Introducing the work (a snip at £795) they said:

'It used to be called credit and was acceptable, but now it is called debt and reflects a new attitude to borrowing which may take a long time to reverse. According to 'Debt!', consumers' attitudes to credit have changed dramatically due to the recession. And despite the fact that figures show that people are starting to borrow again, a cautious attitude is likely to prevail for some time to come.

Last time we looked at this market we called the report 'Consumer Credit'. It is a reflection of how much things have changed that in 1993 we felt we must call it 'Debt!', when in fact credit and debt are really the same thing. However, one is much easier to sell than the other, which is bad news for lenders. Today's financial marketers are facing an uphill task with the cautious consumer of the nineties.'

Mintel's research reveals that borrowing showed a significant decline in the first three years of the 1990s. Even so there are an estimated 1.8 million households in debt in the UK – owing a total of around £2 billion to 3.3 million creditors. Perception of credit for anything other than a mortgage has changed since the heady days of the late 1980s. Discussion groups held by Mintel for the report revealed that while some people still think of loans as credit the perception changes when people start to struggle with repayments. As two people put it:

'You're not in debt as such unless you fall behind with the repayment.'

'It's only when it becomes a problem that I think of it as debt, if it was to become a problem then I'd call it debt.'

Perhaps more disturbingly for the lenders, some people appear to have developed a rather 'devil may care' attitude to debt, showing a very relaxed attitude about being unable to pay it back:

'Well, if you can't pay it back what can you do, what can they do?'

Mortgages are seen as a necessary source of debt and quite separate from other forms of borrowing, a sort of unavoidable evil. Even so, those who had not yet taken out a mortgage were not in a hurry to jump on the mortgage treadmill, preferring in some cases to live with parents (even returning home after a marriage break-up) rather than take on the burden. Some were discouraged by friends caught in a negative equity trap.

The report is not all doom and gloom for the lenders. Mintel does not expect the demand for credit to vanish. Consumers are still in favour of owning their own homes and will need credit to smooth out the peaks and troughs in personal finances. And even more positively, recent movements in the housing market indicate that some of the factors that potential borrowers were waiting for, notably the bottoming out of the housing market, are now actually starting to occur.

However, we believe that consumers will increasingly become more sensible as borrowers, using debt as tool, but treating it with the same care as they would a very sharp knife.

22.4   Types of credit

There are many forms of credit. They have developed over the years, presumably as those who market financial services have spotted potential customers. No 'one size fits all' in this industry. There is a type of credit to fit almost everyone who needs it.

22.4.1   Fixed-sum loans

Fixed sum loans can be obtained from banks and finance companies of various kinds, and also from shops. The banks may like to see the loan spent in a particular way. The finance company will not usually be interested in how it is spent. The shop will be very anxious that the loan be spent on their goods. The loan is usually for a fixed sum at a fixed rate of interest. Finance companies usually charge quite a high rate. The scheme with shops is not usually like this, but of a type called 'revolving credit' where you pay in a fixed sum each month (usually by standing order from your bank account), and this maintains your ability to borrow up to a value in goods which is equivalent to a fixed multiple of your monthly payment. Banks provide revolving credit too.

22.4.2   Loans of a varying sum

The common example is the bank overdraft. Here, the amount of the loan varies with the customer's demands. The bank will agree that any amount can be borrowed up to an agreed limit by drawing more money from the bank account than it holds. Interest is paid only on the excess amount. The interest rate may well vary. The number of occasions on which money can be drawn up to the amount agreed is not usually fixed.

22.4.3   Trading checks or vouchers

Trading checks or vouchers are a type of fixed sum credit which is quite popular in the north of England (and in Scotland) although it is not unknown in the south. A company makes arrangements with a number of shops whereby any of these will accept a particular card or voucher produced by customers, mark it with the amount spent in the store, and recover this money from the company. The customer will hold the card until its total value has been gradually used up in this way, and then apply for another. Alternatively, the company may issue the customer with a number of checks, each of a small denomination (eg £5), which are later redeemed by the company. Meanwhile the debtor is paying either weekly or monthly (and usually to a company representative who calls at the door) instalments which together represent the face value of the card, plus interest. Often an initial payment, over and above the value of the card, is made when it is issued.

A trading voucher is normally one document for one purchase from one store, or chain of stores. The amount is usually much larger than on a trading check.

Credit cards are widely known and used. It has aspects in common with each of the types already mentioned. The card holder shops at places which have agreements with the company issuing the card. The accumulated debt is paid off either at the end of the month or gradually in whatever instalments are convenient (or possible!). There is a minimum. There is a maximum amount of credit available to him. It is a form of revolving credit, since the debtor is allowed to repay and reborrow as often as he chooses. This represents an extremely flexible way of obtaining instant credit for goods, services and cash from banks. However, it is rather expensive, particularly if the debtor allows his debt gradually to mount up towards his personal credit limit.

22.4.4   Credit cards

Unsecured loans are not unknown, particularly in family or social contexts, but a creditor will rarely be satisfied with a simple promise from the borrower to repay the debt. There will usually be some form of security required.

22.5   Protecting against the risk of being left unpaid

With unsecured loans, no security is given. The debtor just promises to repay the money lent. If he does not, or cannot, then the creditor is left to sue him on his promise. Since the risk involved may be high, the interest rate is also likely to be high. There is usually no restriction on how the money may be spent.

22.5.1   Unsecured loans

Unsecured credit is similar to unsecured loans but here there are usually particular goods involved. The debtor is allowed time to pay on a particular purchase. Still no security is demanded to protect the creditor's risk.

22.5.2   Unsecured credit

With secured credit perhaps a lower rate of interest will be charged, since the creditor (eg a bank) has obtained some kind of security to protect his risk. He will be entitled to realise (sell) the security if the debtor fails to repay. Types of secured credit are:

22.5.3   Secured credit – types of security

(a) Mortgage of goods

These are quite rare. They must comply with the technicalities of the Bills of Sale Acts 1878 and 1882. The transaction must be written, witnessed and registered. Otherwise the security may be void and the creditor left in the same position as if the loan were unsecured. The Acts do not, however, apply to registered companies. The debtor, in effect, allows the creditor to sell certain of his property if the loan is left unpaid. It is sometimes called a 'chattel mortgage'.

(b) Mortgage of land

If you own your house then you may be an attractive person to the professional creditor. Land is of great and, in the long term, increasing value. You will probably mortgage your ownership initially in order to secure a loan to buy the house. If this is paid off, and the house is now free of such a charge, it is a very valuable asset. Even if it is still charged to one mortgagee, there are many companies who specialise in giving loans on the security of 'second mortgages'. However, some building societies, fearful of the extra burden on your income, will insist that you do not take on a second mortgage, even if the value of your house has increased since you bought it, thus giving you a margin of extra value over the amount that you owe them.

This extra value is sometimes referred to as the 'equity' in the house. Some of those that bought houses during the so-called 'boom' years of the late 1980s have found themselves in possession of what journalists and others refer to as 'negative equity'. That is, that the market value of the house has fallen so much since it was bought that it is now worth less than the outstanding loan for which it it was put up as security.

(c) Guarantee or indemnity

Briefly, a guarantee is an arrangement whereby someone else promises to repay the loan if the debtor does not. His promise must be evidenced in writing (s 4 Statute of Frauds 1677).

An indemnity is a promise made by another to repay a loan made to you. You are not required to pay the loan back at all. Hire-purchase transactions and bank loans often involve the need to find guarantors, particularly where the debtor has little security to offer.

When a finance house sets up a business relationship with a supplier – say to facilitate the use of credit cards – then it is normal for there to be a 'recourse' agreement such that if the debtor defaults then there is a recourse to the supplier for the creditor. Thus the supplier is a sort of guarantor, even though the debtor will probably be unaware of the fact.

(d) Pledges

These are often called 'pawns'. They arise where the possession of goods of some value is transferred to the creditor as security for the repayment of the loan made. The pawnbroker is likely to lend rather less than he feels he could easily realise by selling the goods pledged. The Consumer Credit Act (CCA) has replaced much of the old law relating to pledges (ss 114–122). Briefly, provided the loan is less than £15,000 and is a commercial agreement, then a 'pawn receipt' must be issued in exchange for the goods:

'114 (1) At the time he receives the article, a person who takes any article in pawn under a regulated agreement shall give to the person from whom he receives it a receipt in the prescribed form (a "pawn-receipt").'

Pawnbrokers should not deal with children:

'114 (2) A person who takes any article in pawn from an individual whom he knows to be, or who appears to be and is, a minor commits an offence.'

The goods are redeemable within six months, or longer if agreed:

'116 (1) A pawn is redeemable at any time within six months after it was taken.

(2) Subject to subsection (1), the period within which a pawn is redeemable shall be the same as the period fixed by the parties for the duration of the credit secured by the pledge, or such longer period as they may agree.'

Even after the expiry of the agreed period the right to redeem is largely protected:

'116 (3) If the pawn is not redeemed by the end of the period laid down by subsections (1) and (2) (the 'redemption period'), it nevertheless remains redeemable until it is realised by the pawnee under section 121, except where under section 120(1)(a) the property in it passes to the pawnee.

(4) No special charge shall be made for redemption of a pawn after the end of the redemption period, and charges in respect of the safe keeping of the pawn shall not be at a higher rate after the end of the redemption period than before.'

To redeem the goods the 'pawn receipt' must be produced:

'117 (1) On surrender of the pawn-receipt, and payment of the amount owing, at anytime when the pawn is redeemable, the pawnee shall deliver the pawn to the bearer of the pawn-receipt.'

Unless, of course, the 'bearer' has, or seems to have, improper possession of the receipt:

'117 (2) Subsection (1) does not apply if the pawnee knows or has reasonable cause to suspect that the bearer of the pawn-receipt is neither the owner of the pawn nor authorised by the owner to redeem it.'

Naturally, some people lose their receipts as easily as they lose their lottery tickets. Section 118 of the Act provides:

'118 (1) A person (the "claimant") who is not in possession of the pawn-receipt but claims to be the owner of the pawn, or to be otherwise entitled or authorised to redeem it, may do so at any time when it is redeemable by tendering to the pawnee in place of the pawn-receipt –

(a) a statutory declaration made by the claimant in the prescribed form, and with the prescribed contents, or

(b) where the pawn is security for fixed-sum credit not exceeding £25 or running-account credit on which the credit limit does not exceed £25, and the pawnee agrees, a statement in writing in the prescribed form, and with the prescribed contents, signed by the claimant.

(2) On compliance by the claimant with subsection (1), section 117 shall apply as if the declaration or statement were the pawn-receipt, and the pawn-receipt itself shall become inoperative for the purposes of section 117.'

The usual intention of the parties to an agreement like this is to set up a secured loan and to pay it off as agreed. However, it may well be (and in the past it often was) the intention of the debtor to ignore the right to redeem the property and leave the goods with the creditor. The law must provide for the title in the goods to pass so that the security can be 'realised'. That is, the pawnbroker must be able, in defined circumstances, to sell the goods in order to get paid. Section 120 of the Act provides:

'120 (1) If at the end of the redemption period the pawn has not been redeemed –

(a) ... the property in the pawn passes to the pawnee where the redemption period is six months and the pawn is security for fixed-sum credit not exceeding £25 or running-account credit on which the credit limit does not exceed £25; or

(b) in any other case the pawn becomes realisable by the pawnee.'

'121 (1) When a pawn has become realisable by him, the pawnee may sell it, after giving to the pawnor (except in such cases as may be prescribed) not less than the prescribed period of notice of the intention to sell, indicating in the notice the asking price and such other particulars as may be prescribed.

(2) Within the prescribed period after the sale takes place, the pawnee shall give the pawnor the prescribed information in writing as to the sale, its proceeds and expenses.

(3) Where the net proceeds of sale are not less than the sum which, if the pawn had been redeemed on the date of the sale, would have been payable for its redemption, the debt secured by the pawn is discharged and any surplus shall be paid by the pawnee to the pawnor.

(4) Where subsection (3) does not apply, the debt shall be treated as from the date of sale as equal to the amount by which the net proceeds of sale fall short of the sum which would have been payable for the redemption of the pawn on that date.

(5) In this section the 'net proceeds of sale' is the amount realised (the "gross amount") less the expenses (if any) of the sale.

(6) If the pawnor alleges that the gross amount is less than the true market value of the pawn on the date of sale, it is for the pawnee to prove that he and any agents employed by him in the sale used reasonable care to ensure that the true market value was obtained, and if he fails to do so subsections (3) and (4) shall have effect as if the reference in subsection (5) to the gross amount were a reference to the true market value.

(7) If the pawnor alleges that the expenses of the sale were unreasonably high, it is for the pawnee to prove that they were reasonable, and if he fails to do so subsections (3) and (4) shall have effect as if the reference in subsection (5) to expenses were a reference to reasonable expenses.'

So, if the loan is £25 or less, after the period of the pawn property passes to the creditor and he can sell the goods. If it is more, then the right to sell is subject to a prescribed period of notice of intention to sell. After sale, any money realised over and above the loan must be paid to the debtor. If the sale realises less than the loan, the debtor must pay the balance. If it is alleged that the proceeds were less than the market value of the goods in the circumstances, it is for the pawnbroker to disprove it.

(e)   Assignment of life assurance policy

The debtor may be required to assign the entitlement to a lump sum payment when an endowment policy matures. This will be much more than the surrender value of the policy during its life and often represents very considerable security value.

Introduction to Consumer Credit

Credit is an increasingly important fact of everyday life. The credit industry has grown rapidly and is now subject to considerable regulation, covering such matters as pre-contractual statements (in the terminology and display of advertising to the general buying public and in disclosure to individual prospective debtors), control over pricing and the other terms used in consumer credit contracts, control over the mechanisms of enforcement that are available to creditors to force apparently recalcitrant debtors back into contractual line and control over the nature, quality and respectability of those who engage in the 'consumer credit industry'.

The reality of the credit industry is considered in the light of the Report of the Director General of Fair Trading called 'Indebtedness' which was based on the results of three surveys carried out in the 1980s. They concentrated on the public's perception of credit, its varying types, costs and implications. They also studied the nature and extent of the problems that debtors had experienced using credit.

The more recent Report from Mintel shows significant changes in debtors' attitudes in the early years of the 1990s.

Chapter 23

The Consumer Credit Act 1974

The CCA is the legislature's implementation of many of the recommendations of the Crowther Committee on Consumer Credit. Changing social habits and attitudes in the 1950s and 1960s led to a rapid growth in consumer credit. But existing legislation had developed in a rather piecemeal way within several distinct statutes, and concerns were expressed over the possible social and economic effects of credit as the so-called 'consumer society' grew during those decades.

23.1   Introduction

In September 1968 a committee under the chairmanship of Lord Crowther was appointed to carry out a wide-ranging review of consumer credit. The Crowther Report, published in March 1971, found that there was no justification for concerns about the economic and social effects of consumer credit, but recommended a new and comprehensive legal framework to regulate it including a licensing system. The then government responded in 1973 with a White Paper, *The Reform of the Law on Consumer Credit*, which confirmed its intention to implement the recommendations of the Crowther Report with only a few modifications. The resulting Consumer Credit Bill received Royal Assent on 31 July 1974, having been reintroduced unchanged by the new government that had taken office earlier in 1974.

23.2   The Crowther Report

Since then there have been considerable developments in the market for consumer credit. These were listed in a document from the OFT in August 1993, as part of their extensive consultative exercise:

'The main sources of consumer credit at the time of the Crowther Report [were such that] in terms of loans outstanding, over 40% was provided by retailers, are just under 50% by banks and finance houses.

By 1981 the position had changed substantially with banks and finance houses directly providing over 65% of all consumer credit. Credit cards provided another 12%, so giving banks (including finance houses) nearly 80% in total. Over the next 10 years the banks (as widely defined and now joined by the building societies) consolidated their position with 82% of all credit outstanding by 1990. The expansion was due to a further increase in credit card and finance house lending at the expense of retailer credit which fell to less than 5% of the amount outstanding, compared with 40% before Crowther.

At the time of the Crowther Report, the average consumer credit debt was equivalent to about two weeks' disposable income. Over the next 10 years the figure had risen to 4.5 weeks and 20 years after Crowther it had reached 7.5 weeks.

Another way of looking at the development of the credit market over this period is through the types of credit commitment entered into. In its 1989 report, the Policy Studies Institute (PSI) repeated a survey undertaken by National Consumer Council 10 years earlier. The figures relate to credit sources and are unweighted by the value of credit which the different sources may offer. So for example the decline in the number of instalment credit and loan arrangements may reflect a switch to revolving credit (credit or store cards) for smaller value purchases. At any one time not all these sources will be activated; over 50% of credit card accounts are paid in full and under present card operators' rules fail to attract interest. PSI estimated in 1989 that whereas nearly three quarters of households had access to some form of consumer credit, at any one time only around half had amounts outstanding. The proportion with access to credit is broadly consistent with the proportion of adults with bank accounts.

For the most part finance houses grew up as providers of hire-purchase in specialist retailing sectors, notably cars and household durable goods. More recently finance houses have diversified into a wide range of personal finance and consumer credit products. These now include:

a) hire-purchase (their traditional product);

b) personal loans both for specific items and revolving credits (eg budget accounts);

c) credit and store cards;

d) cheque and savings accounts.

Some of these products may be operated on behalf of particular retailers and marketed by them. Others will be marketed through banks and building societies to current account customers. Finance houses have built up systems of credit marketing, credit referencing and credit scoring which enable them to respond rapidly to consumer demand.

As already noted, some finance houses are owned by retailers or manufacturers. Otherwise finance houses are generally subsidiaries of UK or overseas banks.

The shift towards banks (and building societies) as providers of credit mirrors the changes in banking habits over the last 20 years which have significantly affected the availability of credit. In 1969 only one third of adults had a bank account. For the unbanked the only sources of credit were retailers – hire-purchase agreements or other forms of "putting it on the slate", pawn-brokers and money lenders. Even for the third with bank accounts, there was a much narrower range of credit products than the banks offer today.

By 1979, the proportion of adults with bank accounts had risen to three-quarters and it is now over four-fifths (including building society cheque accounts). The growth in the use of banks has mirrored the decline in the payment of wages and salaries in cash. Less than 10% of those in work and only around 25% of pensioner households are now without a bank or building society account.

Another major development is credit cards, which were just beginning in 1969. By 1980 nearly 12m Visa and Access cards were in use. By 1990 the number of cards in use had risen to 30m, covering some 14m individual cardholders who between them operated 22m accounts. Between 1980 and 1990, the number of retail outlets accepting credit cards trebled.

The result of these developments in banking has been to give a large proportion of the population access to new forms of credit from the mainstream lenders. In addition to hire-purchase these include overdrafts, personal loans, credit cards and store cards. Bank and building society customers are now exposed to credit marketing both from banks and their associated finance houses.

These new products have changed the way retailers offer credit. Previously, the retailer would have operated instalment credit through his own accounts department or by introducing purchasers to a finance house offering hire-purchase. Now retailers are able to offer credit simply by accepting credit cards or by operating a store card through a finance house (often a bank subsidiary). For higher value purchases, the retailer may still offer hire-purchase agreements, again through a finance company. '

The 1980s saw the dismantling of the many and various forms of credit control which had been in operation and a general liberalisation and deregulation of financial services. Previously, governments had operated controls over the balance sheets of financial institutions, over non-priority lending and over the down-payment and repayment conditions of hire-purchase and other forms of instalment credit. Minimum deposits and maximum repayment periods were used as economic regulators until 1982. Mortgage lenders were under instructions to limit advances as far as practicable to house purchase and not to allow equity stakes to be withdrawn to finance other spending on the favourable and subsidised terms intended for housing loans, though this is not to say that no such leakage occurred.

'Generally, control of the volume of credit as a macro-economic instrument stopped at the beginning of the 1980s. Instead reliance was placed on the price of credit, that is to say, interest rates.

This liberalisation has had major effects. Since 1980 there have been no direct limits on the volume of credit advanced by the banks. Those with existing mortgages found that rising house prices (up to 1988) led to increases in the equity stakes held in their properties. Secured loans were marketed positively to "unlock the equity tied up in your house", initially in particular by the clearing banks which had also moved into the provision of first mortgages. Finance houses also diversified away from their traditional hire-purchase business into personal loans and revolving credit. Following the Building Societies Act 1986, the societies began to offer overdrafts associated with cheque accounts, credit cards and other unsecured lending in addition to a wide range of other financial products.

Probably the most striking change in the market since the Crowther Report is the reduction in consumer credit provided by retailers direct. The key development lies perhaps with finance houses and their status under the Banking Acts. Over 80% of credit, measured in terms of balances outstanding, is now provided by institutions covered by the Banking Acts.

Moreover, the environment of credit and consumer sophistication has changed stepwise since Crowther. At the time, consumers were primarily faced with hire-purchase deals. The normal interface with the retailer is now the running account. Credit is now used as a discretionary instrument by many consumers (shown by bank and building society account switching, paying off credit card bills in full, and the constant development of new products).'

| 23.3 | Scope of the CCA | In December 1986 a European Community Directive on consumer credit (87/102/EEC) was adopted by the European Council. The Directive reflects a variety of the CCA's key features, although its information requirements are less prescriptive than those of the Act. Harmonisation of the method of calculating APRs was addressed in an amending Directive adopted in February 1990 (90/88/EEC). Once again this was to a degree modelled on UK legislation, although there are some differences whose apparently technical nature perhaps belies their importance. The government has not yet |

implemented the latter Directive, relying upon a transitional provision in it permitting implementation to be postponed until 1 January 1996.

The Crowther Committee found that English law in this area had developed in a rather haphazard way, so that the rights, duties, and so on of the parties depended more on the legal technicalities in which a particular credit transaction was framed, than on the real substance of that transaction. The Committee was concerned at 'the serious anomalies arising from the division of credit transactions into a variety of legally distinct 'boxes' and the consequent lack of a uniform treatment of what are in essence very similar transactions.

The provisions of the Act were brought into force in stages over a period of years, the process not finally being completed until 19 May 1985.

An important element of the Crowther Report, subsequently reflected in the Act, was the concept of 'truth in lending': consumers were to be helped to protect themselves through the prescription of given levels of information to be made available at all the stages of credit and hire transactions.

The CCA itself is only a framework. It has been 'filled out' with many detailed regulations, although in the current climate of 'deregulation' the trend seems to be to re-examine such sets of regulations as these with a view to simplification. There is, of course, a danger in such activity that the 'baby goes out with the bathwater' and whilst the legal framework may be simpler and the pressure upon business enterprises lighter, the protection afforded to consumers is reduced.

The regulations concern such matters as advertisements, quotations and the total charge for credit, documentation in all its various forms, the rebate of interest liability when agreements are paid early, and so forth. The Act often refers to the 'prescribed form', the 'prescribed limit', and suchlike. The regulations state such 'prescriptions'.

This statute is very complicated. It has been described as 'an Act of unrivalled technicality'. Be that as it may be, the Act will be cited here wherever possible. It is a crafted piece of draftsmanship. It means what it says, not necessarily what writers say it means!

It contains 193 sections and 5 schedules.

23.4   Aims of the CCA

The aims of any statute are set out right at the beginning in an explanatory paragraph, or 'long title' before the actual statute law itself is quoted. The 'long title' of the CCA is:

'An Act to establish for the protection of consumers a new system, administered by the Director General of Fair Trading, of licensing and other control of traders concerned with the provision of credit, or the supply of goods on hire or hire-purchase, and their transactions, in place of the present enactments regulating moneylenders, pawnbrokers and hire-purchase traders and their transactions, and for related matters.'

The Office of Fair Trading has also issued an explanation. Their motto for the CCA is 'Fair deal on Credit':

'Credit, in its various forms, plays an increasingly important part in daily life. Hire-purchase, credit cards, bank overdrafts, credit sales, mortgages, trading checks and cash loans are examples.

Before the introduction of the Consumer Credit Act the credit laws were in a tangle. Different forms of credit had different rules. Some gave customers adequate protection, others not. A rogue minority of traders were able to bring the industry into disrepute. People lost money or even their homes through dealing with unscrupulous traders.

The Act seeks to ensure that both traders and customers get a fair deal. It allows for stricter control of the various businesses that collectively make up the credit industry. Similar rules are applied to all kinds of credit. A system of licensing is being used to weed out people unfit to be in the business.

Customers are to be given more information, including full details of the cost of any credit offered to them.'

Professor Aubrey Diamond quotes an anonymous judge complaining about how much of his time is taken up with 'people who are persuaded by persons whom they do not know to enter into contracts that they do not understand to purchase goods that they do not want with money that they have not got.' The CCA sets out to reduce such a workload.

Professor Royston Goode has written, 'The ... Act has many interesting and original features. Not the least of these is the new terminology coined by the draftsman in a highly successful endeavour to encompass not only the extraordinary diversity of forms of consumer credit currently used but also forms not yet conceived which may one day appear on the English financial scene.' This reflects the fact that the variety of forms of providing credit, many of which have already been noted, grew out of the activities of those sharp-witted enough to devise ways around the restrictions which had been placed upon their last creations. The CCA seeks to cover the lot, and those yet to come along. Consequently there is an apparently difficult terminology to master. It is not as bad as it seems, at least not quite. For example, the first few definitions mentioned below are those relating to regulated agreements - to those agreements which will be affected by the CCA generally, and by regulations made under the CCA in particular.

These regulated agreements are divided into various types, as follows. It is necessary to master a few of the main terms used in the CCA before a proper understanding of its enormous impact on the consumer credit industry can be obtained.

One of the most innovatory aspects of the Act is that it includes a series of 'worked examples' in Schedule 2, illustrating by a full analysis the use of the terminology employed by the Act.

In the case of conflict between Schedule 2 and any other provision of the Act, that other provision prevails: s 188(3). Some of these 'examples' will be incorporated into this text.

23.5   The main terms

The Act contains a 'definition' section, s 189, which contains much of the 'new' terminology:

23.6   Regulated agreements

> '"regulated agreement" means a consumer credit agreement, or consumer hire agreement, other than an exempt agreement, and "regulated" and "unregulated" shall be construed accordingly.'

This is the key concept in the Act, for the Act controls only regulated agreements (except for the controls over advertising and extortionate credit bargains, which are of wider application).

Now to unpick the terms within the definition:

Section 189 provides that a:

23.6.1   Consumer credit agreements

> " 'consumer credit agreement' has the meaning given by section 8, and includes a consumer credit agreement which is cancelled under section 69(1), or becomes subject to section 69(2), so far as the agreement remains in force.'

and s 8 provides:

> '(1) A personal credit agreement is an agreement between an individual ("the debtor") and any other person ("the creditor") by which the creditor provides the debtor with credit of any amount.
>
> (2) A consumer credit agreement is a personal credit agreement by which the creditor provides the debtor with credit not exceeding £15,000.

(3) A consumer credit agreement is a regulated agreement within the meaning of this Act if it is not an agreement (an "exempt agreement") specified in or under section 16.'

So these are agreements whereby credit which does not exceed £15,000 is provided to an individual. Credit, as mentioned above, means virtually any financial accommodation:

- The figure of £15,000 relates only to the net credit advanced, not to the price of any goods supplied. Thus charges and deposits are deducted.

- The credit itself might be 'fixed sum' credit, that is, a definite amount, eg a bank loan. The fact that it is advanced in instalments does not matter. The credit might be 'running-account' credit, eg bank overdrafts or credit cards. Here the credit limit must not exceed £15,000 or if it does, then, when it does (or when it exceeds some lesser fixed amount), it must cost more.

- The credit may be 'restricted-use' credit, where it is lent for a particular purpose eg hire-purchase of a motor bike or a budget account at the high street tailors. It may be 'unrestricted use' credit where the debtor is free to spend the loan as he chooses eg personal loan from a bank or from a pawnbroker.

Section 11 provides:

'11 (1) A restricted-use credit agreement is a regulated consumer credit agreement –

(a) to finance a transaction between the debtor and the creditor, whether forming part of that agreement or not, or

(b) to finance a transaction between the debtor and a person (the "supplier") other than the creditor, or

(c) to refinance any existing indebtedness of the debtor's, whether to the creditor or another person,

and "restricted-use credit" shall be construed accordingly.

(2) An unrestricted-use credit agreement is a regulated consumer credit agreement not falling within subsection (1), and "unrestricted-use credit" shall be construed accordingly.

(3) An agreement does not fall within subsection (1) if the credit is in fact provided in such a way as to leave the debtor free to use it as he chooses, even though certain uses would contravene that or any other agreement.

(4) An agreement may fall within subsection (1)(b) although the identity of the supplier is unknown at the time the agreement is made.'

Credit cards are an interesting example here. If they are used to buy goods or services then the credit is 'restricted-use'. If they are used to obtain cash from a bank, then the credit is 'unrestricted-use'.

Consumer credit agreements fall into two categories:

(a) Debtor-creditor-supplier agreements (DCSA)

This is a daunting phrase defined by s 12 as:

'A debtor-creditor-supplier agreement is a regulated consumer credit agreement being –

(a) a restricted-use credit agreement which falls within section 11(1)(a), or

(b) a restricted-use credit agreement which falls w i t h i n section 11(1)(b) and is made by the creditor under pre-existing arrangements, or in contemplation of future arrangements, between himself and the supplier, or

(c) an unrestricted-use credit agreement which is made by the creditor under pre-existing arrangements between himself and a person (the "supplier") other than the debtor in the knowledge that the credit is to be used to finance a transaction between the debtor and the supplier.'

So a DCSA will be made where the creditor is connected in a business sense with the transaction. This may be because she is herself the supplier. This would be the case with a hire-purchase agreement where the creditor buys the goods and lets them out to the debtor (with an option to purchase). It would also arise with a conditional sale, where the debtor would be given possession of the goods and time to pay. Until she pays, ownership does not pass. The passing of ownership is, therefore, conditional on the payment of the price. Finally, it would arise with a credit sale where the ownership does pass but the price is paid in instalments.

Thus, a DCSA arises where the creditor is the supplier. It also arises where the creditor is connected with the supplier. That is, there is (or there is expected to be) a business arrangement between them whereby the creditor has agreed to finance transactions between the supplier and his customers.

An illustration of this is the use of a credit card or trading check to buy goods. The creditor who has provided the debtor with the card or check has an agreement with the supplier of the goods, usually evidenced by the display of a sign of some kind in the shop window. The agreement under which the credit is granted, that is, under which the card or check is issued, is a DCSA. The use of the card or check is a 'linked transaction' (see below).

b) Debtor-creditor agreements (DCA)

Section 13 provides that:

> 'A debtor-creditor agreement is a regulated consumer credit agreement being –
>
> (a) a restricted-use credit agreement which falls within section 11(1)(b) but is not made by the creditor under pre-existing arrangements, or in contemplation of future arrangements, between himself and the supplier, or
>
> (b) a restricted-use credit agreement which falls within section 11(1)(c), or
>
> (c) an unrestricted-use credit agreement which is not made by the creditor under pre-existing arrangements between himself and a person (the "supplier") other than the debtor in the knowledge that the credit is to be used to finance a transaction between the debtor and the supplier.'

All regulated agreements must fall into one of these two categories. Thus, if it is not a DCSA, it must be a DCA (so to speak). If there is no business relationship between the creditor and supplier then the deal is a DCA. This might be a bank loan for unrestricted-use credit. The debtor is lent the money to do with as he pleases. A loan to pay off an existing debt is always a DCA.

23.6.2   Consumer hire

It may seem a little strange that a statute called the Consumer Credit Act should contain provisions relating to consumer hire, but there it is!

Since there is no purchase of property involved in a contract of hire, there is obviously no credit involved. However, the Act regulates many contracts of hire. This is thought to be based on the fact that many hire agreements have a great deal in common with hire-purchase agreements. For instance, a company might hire a fleet of cars for its executives. The company pays each month for the use of the cars. They never become the owners, but they may well keep the cars for virtually the whole of their useful lives.

Not all contracts of hire are included within the Act. Section 15 provides that:

> '(1) A consumer hire agreement is an agreement made by a person with an individual (the "hirer") for the bailment or (in Scotland) the hiring of goods to the hirer, being an agreement which –
>
> (a) is not a hire-purchase agreement, and
>
> (b) is capable of subsisting for more than three months, and

c) does not require the hirer to make payments exceeding £15,000.

(2) A consumer hire agreement is a regulated agreement if it is not an exempt agreement.'

Clearly not included in the definition, and therefore not affected by the CCA, are agreements with corporations, since they are not individuals for this purpose (although s 185(5) provides that if the agreement is made with more than one person, then if one is a corporation the CCA will still apply to it), agreements for less than three months (eg a car hired for the weekend trip to the seaside) and really large deals where the hiring charges would exceed £15,000 (this figure includes any deposit or other initial payment).

Hire-purchase agreements are not included either, because they come within the main category of consumer credit agreements.

Further, s 16(6) provides that the corporations which supply electricity, gas, water or telephones are not included here if the goods hired are meters or telephones.

Much of the regulations which affect consumer credit agreements also cover consumer hire agreements. This will be obvious from the use of the terms 'creditor or owner' and 'debtor or hirer' throughout the Act. As examples, s 87 (default notices), s 86 (effect of death), ss 76 and 98 (notice of intention to enforce).

Certain agreements, despite falling within the appropriate definitions have been expressly declared exempt from the provisions of the CCA by a convoluted and much amended section:

23.7   Exempt agreements

'16 (1) This Act does not regulate a consumer credit agreement where the creditor is a local authority ... or a body specified, or of a description specified, in an order made by the Secretary of State, being –

(a) an insurance company,

(b) a friendly society,

(c) an organisation of employers or organisation of workers,

(d) a charity,

(e) a land improvement company, ...

(f) a body corporate named or specifically referred to in any public general Act,

(ff) a body corporate named or specifically referred to in an order made under –

section 156(4), 444(1) or 447(2)(a) of the Housing Act 1985,

section 2 of the Home Purchase Assistance and Housing Corporation Guarantee Act 1978 or section 31 of the Tenants' Rights, &c (Scotland) Act 1980, or

Article 154(1)(a) or 156AA of the Housing (Northern Ireland) Order 1981, or

Article 10(6A) of the Housing (Northern Ireland) Order 1983; or

(g) a building society,

(h) an authorised institution or wholly-owned subsidiary (within the meaning of the Companies Act 1985) of such an institution.

(2) Subsection (1) applies only where the agreement is –

(a) a debtor-creditor-supplier agreement financing –

(i) the purchase of land, or

(ii) the provision of dwellings on any land,

and secured by a land mortgage on that land, or

(b) a debtor-creditor agreement secured by any land mortgage; or

(c) a debtor-creditor-supplier agreement financing a transaction which is a linked transaction in relation to –

(i) an agreement falling within paragraph (a), or

(ii) an agreement falling within paragraph (b) financing (aa) the purchase of any land, or

(bb) the provision of dwellings on any land, and secured by a land mortgage on the land referred to in paragraph (a) or, as the case may be, the land referred to in sub-paragraph (ii).

(3) The Secretary of State shall not make, vary or revoke an order –

(a) under subsection (1)(a) without consulting the Minister of the Crown responsible for insurance companies,

(b) under subsection (1)(b) ... without consulting the Chief Registrar of Friendly Societies,

(c) under subsection (1)(d) without consulting the Charity Commissioners,

(d) under subsection (1)(e), (f) or (ff)] without consulting any Minister of the Crown with responsibilities concerning the body in question or

(e) under subsection (1)(g) without consulting the Building Societies Commission and the Treasury or

(f) under subsection (1)(h) without consulting the Treasury and the Bank of England.

(4) An order under subsection (1) relating to a body may be limited so as to apply only to agreements by that body of a description specified in the order.

(5) The Secretary of State may by order provide that this Act shall not regulate other consumer credit agreements where –

(a) the number of payments to be made by the debtor does not exceed the number specified for that purpose in the order, or

(b) the rate of the total charge for credit does not exceed the rate so specified, or

(c) an agreement has a connection with a country outside the United Kingdom.

(6) The Secretary of State may by order provide that this Act shall not regulate consumer hire agreements of a description specified in the order where –

(a) the owner is a body corporate authorised by or under any enactment to supply electricity, gas or water, and

(b) the subject of the agreement is a meter or metering equipment,

or where the owner is a public telecommunications operator specified in the order.

(6A) This Act does not regulate a consumer credit agreement where the creditor is a housing authority and the agreement is secured by a land mortgage of a dwelling.

(6B) In subsection (6A) "housing authority" means –

(a) as regards England and Wales, the Housing Corporation, Housing for Wales and an authority or body within section 80(1) of the Housing Act 1985 (the landlord condition for secure tenancies), other than a housing association or a housing trust which is a charity;

(b) as regards Scotland, a development corporation established under an order made, or having effect as if made under the New Towns (Scotland) Act 1968, the Scottish Special Housing Association or the Housing Corporation;

(c) as regards Northern Ireland, the Northern Ireland Housing Executive.

(7) Nothing in this section affects the application of sections 137 to 140 (extortionate credit bargains).'

(Subsections 8 and 9 apply only to Scotland and Northern Ireland)

As an example, a DCSA to buy land or a house and land where the loan is secured by a mortgage of that land is exempt provided that the creditor is a local authority or building society, or other such body exempted by the Secretary of State. A list has been published (the Consumer Credit (Exempt Agreements) Order 1989). This list also includes various other exempt agreements. These include a DCSA where the credit is fixed and repayable by four instalments or less (eg newspaper bill), a DCSA where the loan is repaid by one payment (eg American Express and Diners Club where the account must be cleared each month), a DCA where the rate of interest (the annual percentage rate of total charge for credit) is less than a prescribed figure. This is currently 13% or 1% above the highest of the London and Scottish Clearing Banks' base rates 28 days before the agreement is made, whichever is higher. This exemption is designed to cover cheap loans extended by business to employees.

23.7 Small agreements

Section 17 provides that:

'17   (1) A small agreement is –

(a) a regulated consumer credit agreement for credit not exceeding £50, other than a hire-purchase or conditional sale agreement; or

(b) a regulated consumer hire agreement which does not require the hirer to make payments exceeding £50,

being an agreement which is either unsecured or secured by a guarantee or indemnity only (whether or not the guarantee or indemnity is itself secured).'

Small agreements are still generally regulated, that is, the mass of regulations apply to them, but they do escape some of the technicalities of formation if they are DCSAs for restricted-use credit.

It is not possible to make two small agreements instead of one large one to partly escape the CCA. If this is suspected, the CCA applies anyway:

'17 (3) Where –

(a) two or more small agreements are made at or about the same time between the same parties, and

(b) it appears probable that they would instead have been made as a single agreement but for the desire to avoid the operation of provisions of this Act which would have applied to that single agreement but, apart from this subsection, are not applicable to the small agreements, this Act applies to the small agreements as if they were regulated agreements other than small agreements.

(4) If, apart from this subsection, subsection (3) does not apply to any agreements but would apply if, for any party or parties to any of the agreements, there were substituted an associate of that party, or associates of each of those parties, as the case may be, then subsection (3) shall apply to the agreements.'

Often the main (principal) credit agreement is supplemented by other agreements, whether between the same parties or not. These are usually 'linked transactions' and are controlled by the CCA because, for example, the principal agreement might be perfectly reasonable and the linked transaction might be extortionate. When assessing whether or not a credit bargain is, taken overall, extortionate, linked transactions are taken into account. Further, the debtor's right of cancellation (if it exists, see below) applies to a linked transaction in the same way as it applies to the regulated agreement. Furthermore, a linked transaction entered into before the making of the principal agreement has no effect until such time (if any) as that agreement is made.

23.8   Linked transactions

Therefore a definition is necessary :

'19 (1) A transaction entered into by the debtor or hirer, or a relative of his, with any other person ("the other party"), except one for the provision of security, is a linked transaction in relation to an actual or prospective regulated agreement (the "principal agreement") of which it does not form part if –

(a) the transaction is entered into in compliance with a term of the principal agreement; or

(b) the principal agreement is a debtor-creditor-supplier agreement and the transaction is financed, or to be financed, by the principal agreement; or

(c) the other party is a person mentioned in subsection (2), and a person so mentioned initiated the transaction by suggesting it to the debtor or hirer, or his relative, who enters into it –

  (i) to induce the creditor or owner to enter into the principal agreement, or

  (ii) for another purpose related to the principal agreement, or

(iii) where the principal agreement is a restricted-use credit agreement, for a purpose related to a transaction financed, or to be financed, by the principal agreement.

(2) The persons referred to in subsection (1)(c) are –

(a) the creditor or owner, or his associate;

(b) a person who, in the negotiation of the transaction, is represented by a credit-broker who is also a negotiator in antecedent negotiations for the principal agreement;

(c) a person who, at the time the transaction is initiated, knows that the principal agreement has been made or contemplates that it might be made.

(3) A linked transaction entered into before the making of the principal agreement has no effect until such time (if any) as that agreement is made.

(4) Regulations may exclude linked transactions of the prescribed description from the operation of subsection (3).'

Note that an agreement to provide security for the principal agreement (eg a guarantee) is not a linked transaction.

So a linked transaction is an agreement between the debtor or hirer, or a relative of his (eg his wife) and anyone else, if it falls within one of three categories:

(a) the principal agreement stipulated that it should be made (eg the principal agreement is to hire a car. A term stipulates that comprehensive insurance must be taken out with a particular insurance company);

(b) the transaction is financed by a principal agreement which is a DCSA, eg when you use your Access card in a shop, the transaction is linked with the principal agreement you made with Access under which you hold the card. The principal agreement is a DCSA. You are the debtor, Access the creditor, the shop the supplier and there is a business arrangement between the shop and Access which is evidenced by the Access sign in the shop window;

(c) the transaction was suggested, for instance, by an agent, who may have said something like, 'If you were to agree to have the roof repaired, I'm sure that the building society would be prepared to lend you the money.'

23.9   Multiple agreements

The Act draws various distinctions between agreements: between regulated and exempt agreements, between DCAs and DCSAs, between restricted and unrestricted use agreements. There are free-standing notions such as consumer credit and consumer hire agreements too. Each of these attract different consequences from the terms of the Act and the many sets of regulations which have been made under it.

Life may seem complicated by these things, but it gets worse. There are other agreements which cannot be simply and neatly fitted into one category or another. These involve elements of various categories or they contain terms only some of which are caught by the Act. These are called 'multiple' agreements and are defined in Section 18:

'18   (1) This section applies to an agreement (a "multiple agreement") if its terms are such as –

>   (a) to place a part of it within one category of agreement mentioned in this Act, and another part of it within a different category of agreements so mentioned, or within a category of agreement not so mentioned, or

>   (b) to place it, or a part of it, within two or more categories of agreement so mentioned.

(2) Where a part of an agreement falls within subsection (1), that part shall be treated for the purposes of this Act as a separate agreement.

(3) Where an agreement falls within subsection (1)(b), it shall be treated as an agreement in each of the categories in question, and this Act shall apply to it accordingly.

(4) Where under subsection (2) a part of a multiple agreement is to be treated as a separate agreement, the multiple agreement shall (with any necessary modifications) be construed accordingly; and any sum payable under the multiple agreement, if not apportioned by the parties, shall for the purposes of proceedings in any court relating to the multiple agreement be apportioned by the court as may be requisite.'

So the Act treats multiple agreements as a number of separate agreements. Where a single agreement provides for credit or hire within differing categories within the Act, each is regarded as a separate agreement.

For example, the usual kind of plastic card that is carried by consumers these days facilitates both obtaining goods and services from suppliers and the withdrawal of cash from machines. The agreement under which they are issued is a multiple agreement. It is a DCA for the cash and a DCSA for the goods and services.

With an agreement for a normal bank account, to the extent that it regulates the day to day transactions while in credit, the

Act does not reach it. But once an overdraft facility is added, then it comes within the category of a DCA within the Act. The whole thing is, therefore, a multiple agreement.

The Consumer Credit Act 1974

This chapter considers the origins of the principal statute in this area – the Consumer Credit Act 1974.

Changing social habits and attitudes in the 1950s and 1960s led to a rapid growth in consumer credit. But existing legislation had developed in a rather piecemeal way within several distinct statutes, and concerns were expressed over the possible social and economic effects of credit as the so-called 'consumer society' grew during those decades.

In September 1968 a committee under the chairmanship of Lord Crowther was appointed to carry out a wide ranging review of consumer credit. The Crowther Report, published in March 1971, found that there was no justification for concerns about the economic and social effects of consumer credit, but recommended a new and comprehensive legal framework to regulate it including a licensing system.

The CCA is the legislature's implementation of many of the recommendations of the Crowther Committee on Consumer Credit.

The centrally important work of the Crowther Committee is considered, particularly in the light of the extensive consultation exercise on consumer credit reform carried out by the Office of Fair Trading in 1993. This OFT work considers the ways 'things have changed' since Lord Crowther and his committee considered the nature of the industry.

The scope of the Consumer Credit Act (CCA) is then considered, together with the impact it seems to have had upon credit laws across the European Union. The aims of the CCA are outlined, the most basic of which is to establish 'truth in lending'.

Then the rather complex terminology which pervades the CCA is introduced. The principal terms are defined and their importance is illustrated.

Chapter 24

Trading in Credit

The basic tenet of the CCA, 'truth in lending' is nowhere better exemplified than in the controls that are placed upon those who advertise for credit business.

In addition to a general prohibition on misleading advertising, there are detailed regulations which set out specific information which must be included in credit advertisements. The regulations are designed to prevent incomplete and potentially misleading advertising while at the same time preserving flexibility for advertisers.

24.1 CCA controls over those who seek credit business

Section 189, the definition section of the CCA, provides a definition of advertising that would have to be described as wide:

24.1.1 Advertising credit facilities

'"advertisement" includes every form of advertising, whether in a publication, by television or radio, by display of notices, signs, labels, showcards or goods, by distribution of samples, circulars, catalogues, price lists or other material, by exhibition of pictures, models or films, or in any other way, and references to the publishing of advertisements shall be construed accordingly'.

The CCA controls here are to be found in Part IV of the Act, s 43:

'43 (1) This Part applies to any advertisement, published for the purposes of a business carried on by the advertiser, indicating that he is willing –

(a) to provide credit, or

(b) to enter into an agreement for the bailment or (in Scotland) the hiring of goods by him.

(2) An advertisement does not fall within subsection (1) if the advertiser does not carry on

    (a) a consumer credit business or consumer hire business, or

    (b) a business in the course of which he provides credit to individuals secured on land, or

    (c) a business which comprises or relates to unregulated agreements where –

        (i) the law applicable to the agreement is the law of a country outside the United Kingdom, and

(ii) if the law applicable to the agreement were the law of a part of the United Kingdom it would be a regulated agreement.

(3) An advertisement does not fall within subsection (1)(a) if it indicates –

(a) that the credit must exceed £15,000, and that no security is required, or the security is to consist of property other than land, or

(b) that the credit is available only to a body corporate.

(4) An advertisement does not fall within subsection (1)(b) if it indicates that the advertiser is not willing to enter into a consumer hire agreement.

(5) The Secretary of State may by order provide that this Part shall not apply to other advertisements of a description specified in the order '

Broadly, regulations have exempted advertisements relating to agreements which are exempt agreements (see above).

It is noteworthy that, subject to s 43(3), the advertisement will be controlled under Part IV even if it does not relate to a regulated agreement.

Having established the target zones, what are these controls for and what do they consist of?

They are designed to secure 'truth in lending' (the basic policy behind the whole CCA), and they comprise the following sections:

'44 (1) The Secretary of State shall make regulations as to the form and content of advertisements to which this Part applies, and the regulations shall contain such provisions as appear to him appropriate with a view to ensuring that, having regard to its subject-matter and the amount of detail included in it, an advertisement conveys a fair and reasonably comprehensive indication of the nature of the credit or hire facilities offered by the advertiser and of their true cost to persons using them.

(2) Regulations under subsection (1) may in particular –

(a) require specified information to be included in the prescribed manner in advertisements, and other specified material to be excluded;

(b) contain requirements to ensure that specified information is clearly brought to the attention of persons to whom advertisements are directed, and that one part of an advertisement is not given insufficient or excessive prominence compared with another.'

Detailed regulations have been made using the powers within s 44(1): the Consumer Credit (Advertisements) Regulations 1989 (as amended).

They control the form and content of credit advertisements, dividing them into three distinct categories: 'simple', 'intermediate' and 'full'. They require advertisers to publish specified warnings in relation to loans secured on the prospective debtor's home. In particular the warning: 'Your home is at risk if you do not keep up repayments on a mortgage or other loan secured on it.'

This 'health warning', obviously, is designed to warn borrowers of the potentially dire consequences which can arise if they fail to repay a secured loan.

The Act makes further provision concerning certain misleading advertisements:

'45 If an advertisement to which this Part applies indicates that the advertiser is willing to provide credit under a restricted-use credit agreement relating to goods or services to be supplied by any person, but at the time when the advertisement is published that person is not holding himself out as prepared to sell the goods or provide the services (a the case may be) for cash, the advertiser commits an offence.'

and more generally:

'46 (1) If an advertisement to which this Part applies conveys information which in a material respect is false or misleading the advertiser commits an offence.

(2) Information stating or implying an intention on the advertiser's part which he has not got is false.'

Furthermore, the CCA casts its net wide when insisting upon advertising 'truth in lending':

'47 (1) Where an advertiser commits an offence against regulations made under section 44 or against section 45 or 46, or would be taken to commit such an offence but for the defence provided by section 168, a like offence is committed by –

(a) the publisher of the advertisement, and

(b) any person who, in the course of a business carried on by him, devised the advertisement, or a part of it relevant to the first-mentioned offence, and

(c) where the advertiser did not procure the publication of the advertisement, the person who did procure it.'

There are, of course, defences for those charged with offences within these sections:

'47 (2) In proceedings for an offence under subsection (1)(a) it is a defence for the person charged to prove that –

(a) the advertisement was published in the course of a business carried on by him, and

(b) he received the advertisement in the course of that business, and did not know and had no reason to suspect that its publication would be an offence under this Part.'

Further, there is the generalised defence mentioned above, in s 47(1):

'168 (1) In any proceedings for an offence under this Act it is a defence for the person charged to prove –

(a) that his act or omission was due to a mistake, or to reliance on information supplied to him, or to an act or omission by another person, or to an accident or some other cause beyond his control, and

(b) that he took all reasonable precautions and exercised all due diligence to avoid such an act or omission by himself or any person under his control.'

with the usual proviso:

'168 (2) If in any case the defence provided by subsection (1) involves the allegation that the act or omission was due to an act or omission by another person or to reliance on information supplied by another person, the person charged shall not, without leave of the court, be entitled to rely on that defence unless, within a period ending seven clear days before the hearing, he has served on the prosecutor a notice giving such information identifying or assisting in the identification of that other person as was then in his possession.'

Infringement does not affect the validity of any agreement subsequently entered into by the consumer:

'170 (1) A breach of any requirement made (otherwise than by any court) by or under this Act shall incur no civil or criminal sanction as being such a breach, except to the extent (if any) expressly provided by or under this Act.'

unless of course the advertisement constitutes a misrepresentation or misdescription.

24.1.2 Canvassing off trade premises

The Act contains provisions designed to control the doorstep selling of DCA credit. 'Canvassing' is defined, then 'trade premises', then the offence created by the Act:

'48 (1) An individual (the "canvasser") canvasses a regulated agreement off trade premises if he solicits the entry (as debtor or hire) of another individual (the "consumer") into the agreement by making oral representations to the consumer, or any other individual, during a visit by the canvasser to any place (not excluded by subsection (2)) where the consumer, or that other individual, as the case may be, is, being a visit –

(a) carried out for the purpose of making such oral representations to individuals who are at that place, but

(b) not carried out in response to a request made on a previous occasion.

(2) A place is excluded from subsection (1) if it is a place where a business is carried on (whether on a permanent or temporary basis) by –

(a) the creditor or owner, or

(b) a supplier, or

(c) the canvasser, or the person whose employee or agent the canvasser is, or

(d) the consumer.

49   (1) It is an offence to canvass debtor-creditor agreements off trade premises.

(2) It is also an offence to solicit the entry of an individual (as debtor) into a debtor-creditor agreement during a visit carried out in response to a request made on a previous occasion, where –

(a) the request was not in writing signed by or on behalf of the person making it, and

(b) if no request for the visit had been made, the soliciting would have constituted the canvassing of a debtor-creditor agreement off trade premises.'

So, 'canvassing off trade premises' involves making oral representations ('sales talk') during home visits made otherwise than in response to a previous request (an uninvited visit – a 'cold call').

The request should also be in writing and signed, otherwise the salesman commits the offence of soliciting debtor-creditor agreements during visits made in response to a previous oral request (s 49(2)). Section 49 does not apply to DCSA credit, so canvassing of such agreements off trade premises is permissible, but only if the supplier of the credit has the necessary licence.

The debtor will have a 'cooling-off' period when he signs a DCSA away from business premises.

24.1.3 Credit and children

The Act puts a particularly sharp focus upon dealings with minors in s 50:

'50 (1) A person commits an offence who, with a view to financial gain, sends to a minor any document inviting him to –

(a) borrow money, or

(b) obtain goods on credit or hire, or

(c) obtain services on credit, or

(d) apply for information or advice on borrowing money or otherwise obtaining credit, or hiring goods.

(2) In proceedings under subsection (1) in respect of the sending of a document to a minor, it is a defence for the person charged to prove that he did not know, and had no reasonable cause to suspect, that he was a minor.

(3) Where a document is received by a minor at any school or educational establishment for minors, a person sending it to him at that establishment knowing or suspecting it to be such an establishment shall be taken to have reasonable cause to suspect that he is a minor.'

24.1.4 Unsolicited credit-tokens

During the early 1970s it was not uncommon to find credit cards with the post. They were not requested. They were 'facilities' sent out by financial institutions as a 'service' to their customers. Credit cards are one form of 'credit token', and agreements involving them are regulated by the Act under s 14:

'14 (1) A credit-token is a card, check, voucher, coupon, stamp, form, booklet or other document or thing given to an individual by a person carrying on a consumer credit business, who undertakes –

(a) that on the production of it (whether or not some other action is also required) he will supply cash, goods and services (or any of them) on credit, or

(b) that where, on the production of it to a third party (whether or not any other action is also required), the third party supplies cash, goods and services (or any of them), he will pay the third party for them (whether or not deducting any discount or commission), in return for payment to him by the individual.

(2) A credit-token agreement is a regulated agreement for the provision of credit in connection with the use of a credit-token.'

The Act has tackled the perceived problem of the unrequested extension of such access to credit facilities in s 51:

'51 (1) It is an offence to give a person a credit-token if he has not asked for it.

(2) To comply with subsection (1) a request must be contained in a document signed by the person making the request, unless the credit-token agreement is a small debtor-creditor-supplier agreement.

(3) Subsection (1) does not apply to the giving of a credit-token to a person –

(a) for use under a credit-token agreement already made, or

(b) in renewal or replacement of a credit-token previously accepted by him under a credit-token agreement which continues in force, whether or not varied.'

The effect of this provision can be seen in *Elliott v DGFT* (1980) where the Divisional Court upheld the conviction under s 51(1) of footwear retailers who mailed to prospective customers an unrequested plastic card purporting to be a credit card valid for immediate use. The card was still a credit-token within s 14, notwithstanding that it was not capable of contractually binding the issuer.

The enterprising businessman may be asked to quote a price for credit facilities. Section 52 provides that:

24.1.5   Quotations

'52 (1) Regulations may be made –

(a) as to the form and content of any document (a "quotation") by which a person who carries on a consumer credit business or consumer hire business, or a business in the course of which he provides credit to individuals secured on land, gives prospective customers information about the terms on which he is prepared to do business;

(b) requiring a person carrying on such a business to provide quotations to such persons and in such circumstances as are prescribed.

(2) Regulations under subsection (1)(a) may in particular contain provisions relating to quotations such as are set out in relation to advertisements in section 44.'

So it is that we have the Consumer Credit (Quotations) Regulations 1989.

The regulations contain broadly similar provisions to those relating to the form and content of advertisements. The regulations also prescribe that a quotation must be provided in response to a request for written information made in writing, orally on the trader's premises or, in certain circumstances, by telephone.

Incidentally, under s 53, regulations could be made requiring a person who carries on a consumer credit or consumer hire business, or a business in the course of which he provides credit to individuals secured on land, to display certain information in a certain way about the business at any premises where the business is carried on and to which the public have access. But none have been made, yet!

24.2 Trading as, or dealing with, credit brokers and credit reference agencies

Once potential debtors have been attracted by the properly drafted and delivered credit advertisements, the next section of the credit industry with which they may come into contact are credit brokers and those whose business it is to provide credit references.

24.2.1 Credit brokers

Section 189, the definition section of the CCA is not as revelatory as it might be:

'"credit-broker" means a person carrying on a business of credit brokerage'

but then:

(2) Subject to section 146(5), credit brokerage is the effecting of introductions –

(a) of individuals desiring to obtain credit –

    (i) to persons carrying on businesses to which this sub-paragraph applies, or

    (ii) in the case of an individual desiring to obtain credit to finance the acquisition or provision of a dwelling occupied or to be occupied by himself or his relative, to any person carrying on a business in the course of which he provides credit secured on land, or

(b) of individuals desiring to obtain goods on hire to persons carrying on businesses to which this paragraph applies, or

(c) of individuals desiring to obtain credit, or to obtain goods on hire, to other credit-brokers.

(3) Subsection (2)(a)(i) applies to –

(a) a consumer credit business;

(b) a business which comprises or relates to consumer credit agreements being, otherwise than by virtue of section 16(5)(a), exempt agreements;

(c) a business which comprises or relates to unregulated agreements where –

    (i) the law applicable to the agreement is the law of a country outside the United Kingdom, and

(ii) if the law applicable to the agreement were the law of a part of the United Kingdom it would be a regulated consumer credit agreement.

(4) Subsection (2)(b) applies to –

(a) a consumer hire business;

(b) a business which comprises or relates to unregulated agreements where –

(i) the law applicable to the agreement is the law of a country outside the United Kingdom, and

(ii) if the law applicable to the agreement were the law of a part of the United Kingdom it would be a regulated consumer hire agreement.'

So, a consumer may approach a credit-broker for introduction to a source of credit – a kind of introduction agency.

As will be seen later, a credit broker needs a licence. By s 155 of the CCA, a credit-broker is only entitled to a nominal sum of £3 by way of fee or commission for his services if he fails to arrange the deal, that is, unless a 'relevant agreement' (which includes a regulated agreement) is entered into within six months of the broker introducing the consumer to the prospective source of credit.

During the process of negotiating an agreement a prospective creditor or owner is likely to check up on the credit rating of the prospective debtor or hirer with a credit reference agency. Section 145 provides:

24.2.2   Credit reference agencies

'145 (8) A credit reference agency is a person carrying on a business comprising the furnishing of persons with information relevant to the financial standing of individuals, being information collected by the agency for that purpose.'

As will be seen, credit reference agencies need to be licensed. They deal in information about consumers. It may be inaccurate. It is potentially damaging. It is therefore appropriate that consumers should have certain rights against those who hold information about them. Section 157 provides:

'157 (1) A creditor, owner or negotiator, within the prescribed period after receiving a request in writing to that effect from the debtor or hirer, shall give him notice of the name and address of any credit reference agency from which the creditor, owner or negotiator has, during the antecedent negotiations, applied for information about his financial standing.

(2) Subsection (1) does not apply to a request received more than 28 days after the termination of the antecedent

negotiations, whether on the making of the regulated agreement or otherwise.

(3) If the creditor, owner or negotiator fails to comply with subsection (1) he commits an offence.'

So, a creditor, owner or negotiator, at the request of a debtor or hirer received not more than twenty-eight days after the end of the antecedent negotiations, must disclose the name and address of any credit reference agency consulted about the debtor's or hirer's financial standing – and by virtue of the Consumer Credit (Conduct of Business) (Credit References) Regulations 1977 – this disclosure must take place within seven days.

Once the identity of any agency that has been consulted has been revealed, that agency is under a duty to disclose the file:

'158 (1) A credit reference agency, within the prescribed period after receiving,

(a) a request in writing to that effect from any individual (the "consumer") and

(b) such particulars as the agency may reasonably require to enable them to identify the file, and

(c) a fee of £1, shall give the consumer a copy of the file relating to him kept by the agency.

(2) When giving a copy of the file under subsection (1), the agency shall also give the consumer a statement in the prescribed form of his rights under section 159.

(3) If the agency does not keep a file relating to the consumer it shall give him notice of that fact, but need not return any money paid.

(4) If the agency contravenes any provision of this section it commits an offence.

(5) In this Act "file", in relation to an individual, means all the information about him kept by a credit reference agency, regardless of how the information is stored and "copy of the file", as respects information not in plain English, means a transcript reduced into plain English.'

The same 1977 Regulations provide that the 'prescribed period' within s 158(1) is seven days. The 'rights under s 159' mentioned in s 158(2) consist of the right to have a twisted thing set straight:

'159 (1) A consumer given information under section 158 who considers that an entry in his file is incorrect, and that if it is not corrected he is likely to be prejudiced, may give notice to the agency requiring it either to remove the entry from the file or amend it.

(2) Within 28 days after receiving a notice under subsection (1), the agency shall by notice inform the consumer that it has –

(a) removed the entry from the file, or

(b) amended the entry, or

(c) taken no action,

and if the notice states that the agency has amended the entry it shall include a copy of the file so far as it comprises the amended entry.

(3) Within 28 days after receiving a notice under subsection (2) or, where no such notice was given, within 28 days after the expiry of the period mentioned in subsection (2), the consumer may, unless he has been informed by the agency that it has removed the entry from his file, serve a further notice on the agency requiring it to add to the file an accompanying notice of correction (not exceeding 200 words) drawn up by the consumer and include a copy of it when furnishing information included in or based on that entry.

(4) Within 28 days after receiving a notice under subsection (3), the agency,unless it intends to apply to the Director under subsection (5), shall by notice inform the consumer that it has received the notice under subsection (3) and intends to comply with it.

(5) If –

(a) the consumer has not received a notice under subsection (4) within the time required, or

(b) it appears to the agency that it would be improper for it to publish a notice of correction because it is incorrect, or unjustly defames any person, or is frivolous or scandalous, or is for any other reason unsuitable, the consumer or, as the case may be, the agency may, in the prescribed manner and on payment of the specified fee, apply to the Director, who may make such order on the application as he thinks fit.

(6) If a person to whom an order under this section is directed fails to comply with it within the period specified in the order he commits an offence.'

The 'Director' referred to here is, of course, the DGFT. In 1994 50 applications were made for the DGFT to exercise his powers under s 159(5) above (18 fewer than in 1993). 40 were resolved by negotiation, without the need for the DGFT to make an order, as were the 10 applications outstanding at the end of 1993. That left 10 outstanding at the end of 1994.

The 1977 Regulations provide further protection for the consumer in that they require an agency that has been distributing incorrect material, and complied with a request or an order from the DGFT to amend the file, to notify, within ten working days, every enquirer that has approached them for information about the financial standing of the aggrieved consumer within the previous six months.

24.3 Trading in the consumer credit industry – licensing

In terms of establishing real consumer protection, the introduction of licensing all those who trade in this industry, making sure that they are 'fit and proper people', promised massive strides forward. It is at least arguable that the paces taken have been fewer and shorter than expected, but the system set up by Part III of the CCA cannot be described as anything short of genuine control over the trade. If a business needs a licence and operates without one, then a criminal offence is committed. Similarly, the threat to remove, revoke or even just modify a licence attracts the attention and focuses the mind of aberrant traders wonderfully. The scope of the system is as wide as the general sweep of the Act:

'21 (1) Subject to this section, a licence is required to carry on a consumer credit business or consumer hire business.

(2) A local authority does not need a licence to carry on a business.

(3) A body corporate empowered by a public general Act naming it to carry on a business does not need a licence to do so.

So, anyone who provides credit of up to £15,000 to individual consumers, sole traders or partnerships, or anyone who hires out goods to such persons, must hold a licence from the DGFT. Further, those who are involved in 'ancillary' businesses within the industry are also covered by s 147:

'147 (1) The provisions of Part III (except section 40) apply to an ancillary credit business as they apply to a consumer credit business.'

(Incidentally, s 40 concerns the enforcement of agreements made by unlicensed traders, because, in addition to amounting to a criminal offence to trade without a necessary licence, the transactions thus entered into are not enforceable in civil law unless the DGFT issues an appropriate order).

The Act expands the notion of an 'ancillary credit business' in s 145:

'145 (1) An ancillary credit business is any business so far as it comprises or relates to –

(a) credit brokerage,

(b) debt-adjusting,

(c) debt-counselling,

(d) debt-collecting, or

(e) the operation of a credit reference agency.'

Credit broking and the nature of the business of providing credit references were considered above. The Act defines the other 'ancillary' businesses. This is important. If an operation falls within these definitions, then a licence is required:

'145 (5) Subject to section 146(6), debt-adjusting is, in relation to debts due under consumer credit agreements or consumer hire agreements –

(a) negotiating with the creditor or owner, on behalf of the debtor or hirer, terms for the discharge of a debt, or

(b) taking over, in return for payments by the debtor or hirer, his obligation to discharge a debt, or

(c) any similar activity concerned with the liquidation of a debt.

(6) Subject to section 146(6), debt-counselling is the giving of advice to debtors or hirers about the liquidation of debts due under consumer credit agreements or consumer hire agreements.

(7) Subject to section 146(6), debt-collecting is the taking of steps to procure payment of debts due under consumer credit agreements or consumer hire agreements.'

Section 146 contains a number of finely detailed exceptions to the general categories explained in s 145.

There are two types of licence: standard and group. These are defined in s 22:

'22 (1) A licence may be –

(a) a standard licence, that is a licence, issued by the Director to a person named in the licence on an application made by him, which, during the prescribed period, covers such activities as are described in the licence, or

(b) a group licence, that is a licence, issued by the Director (whether on the application of any person or of his own motion), which, during such period as the Director thinks fit or, if he thinks fit, indefinitely, covers such persons and activities as are described in the licence.'

24.3.1   Types of licence

There were 17,751 applications for new standard licences in 1994. This represents a 6% fall on 1993, and it is the fourth successive year where the number has fallen. In the years to 1994 16,900 such licences have been issued.

Before June 1991 standard licences lasted 15 years. The 'prescribed period' for a standard licence is now five years. Then it is necessary to apply to have it renewed. During 1994 3,386 renewal applications were received by the DGFT and 3,154 renewal licences were issued. In the same year 17,233 licences lapsed. The Office of Fair Trading set up a survey late in 1994 in order to better understand the 'population' of licence holders. It is hoped that the information obtained will enable better predictions to be made about such matters as the renewal rate.

At the end of 1994 there were 16 group licences. They are held by such bodies as the Law Society, the National Association of Citizens' Advice Bureaux, Accountants' Professional bodies, some Higher Education Institutions, business enterprise organisations and Age Concern. A consultation exercise is being conducted on suggestions that the use of group licences might be extended to such bodies as trade associations who would hold them on behalf of their members. It seems unlikely that changes will be made in the very near future, but simplification of the overall regulatory framework is currently the favoured flavour of the legislature.

24.3.2   Application for licences

Licences are issued only if the DGFT thinks that the applicant is fit to hold one. Under s 25:

'25   (1) A standard licence shall be granted on the application of any person if he satisfies the Director that –

(a) he is a fit person to engage in activities covered by the licence, and

(b) the name or names under which he applies to be licensed is or are not misleading or otherwise undesirable.

(2) In determining whether an applicant for a standard licence is a fit person to engage in any activities, the Director shall have regard to any circumstances appearing to him to be relevant, and in particular any evidence tending to show that the applicant, or any of the applicant's employees, agents or associates (whether past or present) or, where the applicant is a body corporate, any person appearing to the Director to be a controller of the body corporate or an associate of any such person, has
–

(a) committed any offence involving fraud or other dishonesty, or violence,

(b) contravened any provision made by or under this Act, or by or under any other enactment regulating the provision of credit to individuals or other transactions with individuals,

(c) practised discrimination on grounds of sex, colour, race or ethnic or national origins in, or in connection with, the carrying on of any business, or

(d) engaged in business practices appearing to the Director to be deceitful or oppressive, or otherwise unfair or improper (whether unlawful or not).

(3) In subsection (2), "associate", in addition to the persons specified in section 184, includes a business associate.'

The DGFT can simply agree to issue a licence, but he cannot as easily refuse to do so. Section 27 provides that:

24.3.3   Issue of licences

'27 (1) Unless the Director determines to issue a licence in accordance with an application he shall, before determining the application, by notice –

(a) inform the applicant, giving his reasons, that, as the case may be, he is minded to refuse the application, or to grant it in terms different from those applied for, describing them, and

(b) invite the applicant to submit to the Director representations in support of his application in accordance with section 34.

(2) If the Director grants the application in terms different from those applied for then, whether or not the applicant appeals, the Director shall issue the licence in the terms approved by him unless the applicant by notice informs him that he does not desire a licence in those terms.'

Section 34, mentioned here, relates to the manner in which 'representations' are generally to be made to the DGFT:

'34 (1) Where this section applies to an invitation by the Director to any person to submit representations, the Director shall invite that person, within 21 days after the notice containing the invitation is given to him or published, or such longer period as the Director may allow –

(a) to submit his representations in writing to the Director, and

(b) to give notice to the Director, if he thinks fit, that he wishes to make representations orally, and where notice is given under paragraph (b) the Director shall arrange for the oral representations to be heard.

(2) In reaching his determination the Director shall take into account any representations submitted or made under this section.

(3) The Director shall give notice of his determination to the persons who were required to be invited to submit representations about it or, where the invitation to submit representations was required to be given by general notice, shall give general notice of the determination.'

Where an organisation trades within more than one category of business covered by the licensing system then an application to each category must be made. This is a little like the 'groups' within a driving licence.

Licences can be varied at the request of the holder (s 30), or compulsorily varied at the instance of the DGFT (s 31).

| 24.3.4 | Suspension or revocation of licence |

Plainly, if the 'fitness' of the licence holder becomes questionable, then the DGFT has the power to suspend or revoke the licence. However, bearing in mind that such an act might easily deprive the business of the ability to trade within the law, the process is staged. Section 32 provides that:

'32 (1) Where at a time during the currency of a licence the Director is of the opinion that if the licence had expired at that time he would have been minded not to renew it, and that therefore it should be revoked or suspended, he shall proceed as follows.

(2) In the case of a standard licence the Director shall, by notice –

(a) inform the licensee that, as the case may be, the Director is minded to revoke the licence, or suspend it until a specified date or indefinitely, stating his reasons, and

(b) invite him to submit representations as to the proposed revocation or suspension in accordance with section 34.

(3) In the case of a group licence the Director shall –

(a) give general notice that, as the case may be, he is minded to revoke the licence, or suspend it until a specified date or indefinitely, stating his reasons, and

(b) in the notice invite any licensee to submit to him representations as to the proposed revocation or suspension in accordance with section 34.

(4) In the case of a group licence issued on application the Director shall also –

(a) inform the original applicant that, as the case may be, the Director is minded to revoke the licence, or suspend it until a specified date or indefinitely, stating his reasons, and

(b) invite him to submit representations as to the proposed revocation or suspension in accordance with section 34.

(5) If he revokes or suspends the licence, the Director may give directions authorising a licensee to carry into effect agreements made by him before the revocation or suspension.

(6) General notice shall be given of the revocation or suspension of a group licence.

(7) A revocation or suspension under this section shall not take effect before the end of the appeal period.

(8) Except for the purposes of section 29, a licensee under a suspended licence shall be treated, in respect of the period of suspension, as if the licence had not been issued; and where the suspension is not expressed to end on a specified date it may, if the Director thinks fit, be ended by notice given by him to the licensee or, in the case of a group licence, by general notice.'

Naturally, there is a procedure within the Act for applying to have a suspension lifted (s 33).

These are very serious powers. The threat of their use presumably brings recalcitrant traders to heel very swiftly.

From time to time the DGFT issues 'warnings' which fall short of the exercise of his extensive powers over licences, but leave little doubt of his preparedness to do so:

- In March 1995 consumers were warned about 'in principle' loans. The OFT published this statement:

'Consumers have been warned to be wary of "in principle" loan offers operated by some moneylenders.'

The warning from the OFT followed complaints from consumers who were required to pay non-refundable commitment fees when they accepted 'in principle' secured loans. When the final loan offers were made they were substantially lower than the 'in principle' offers and consumers had little option but to reject them and lose their fees.

As a result, Sir Bryan Carsberg, the then Director General of Fair Trading, appointed an Adjudicating Officer to examine whether six associated moneylending businesses in the Manchester area were fit to continue to hold consumer credit licences.

The Adjudicating Officer concluded that potential borrowers were being misled into believing the 'in principle' offer would be the actual amount offered. The six businesses have now given undertakings to Sir Bryan that they have stopped the practice.

Peter Casey, OFT's acting Director of Consumer Affairs, warned: 'The companies kept their licences because they were able to prove that they had changed their procedures.

'But we will not hesitate to review the consumer credit licences of any other moneylenders who try to mislead consumers in this way ... It is improper to make any loan offer before an applicant's creditworthiness and the value of security have been checked ... At the application stage the lender should only indicate whether a loan will be considered not what the amount might be.'

- Similarly, on 14 December 1994 the DGFT 'warned' pawnbrokers. The OFT said:

'Pawnbrokers were today warned over disposing of unredeemed goods by internal sale unless they have agreed a price in advance with the person who pawned them.'

Sir Bryan Carsberg, Director General of Fair Trading, said: 'I will not hesitate to use my powers under the Consumer Credit Act to take action against pawnbrokers who engage in this practice, which I consider raises serious doubts as to their fitness to hold a consumer credit licence.' Alexanders the Jewellers Ltd, a jewellery retailer and pawnbroker in Farnham, Surrey, has given an undertaking to Sir Bryan about future practices in its pawnbroking business. Customers complained about Alexanders' selling unredeemed pawns to itself at what were said to be unfairly low prices. There were also complaints that Alexanders the Jewellers Ltd did not give information required by law as to the sale of customers' pawns.

A notice was issued under the Consumer Credit Act 1974 that the Director General was minded to revoke Alexanders' consumer credit licence following the complaints. An Adjudicating Officer, appointed by the Director General, has decided that he will not revoke the company's consumer credit licence. He was satisfied that Alexanders the Jewellers Ltd intended in future to conduct the pawnbroking side of its business fairly and therefore accepted an undertaking. Alexanders the Jewellers Ltd has agreed not to rely upon internal sale as a basis for calculating the proceeds of the sale unless the sale price has been agreed in advance with the pawnor. Sir Bryan said:

'The company has kept its licence because it has assured my Adjudicating Officer that it will provide full details to its customers of any sale, or any intended sale, of unredeemed pawns.

More importantly, it has ceased the practice of relying solely on an internal sale in calculating what sums, if any, are payable to a customer, the pawnor, who has failed to redeem a pawn, without prior negotiation with the customer to agree a sale price. This practice was open to abuse and potentially unfair.

If other pawnbrokers engage in such a practice, then I shall not hesitate to use my licensing powers against them.'

- Finally, and again in March 1995, a warning shot was fired towards debt collectors in general, action having been taken against two of their number. The OFT said:

'Debt collectors have been warned that they risk losing their credit licences if they use threatening or oppressive behaviour.'

The caution from the OFT came after two collectors had their licences revoked or refused.

Alan Hardy, trading as NNY Investigations, 17-19 Murton Street, Sunderland, was declared to be unfit to hold a licence after being convicted of sending a letter which was grossly offensive. One of his employees had also been convicted of perjury whilst working for the licensee. Other letters sent by the licensee were highly offensive and the OFT's Adjudicating Officer concluded, after hearing representations, that there would be serious risk to consumers if he was allowed to continue to hold his licence. Hardy did not appeal and his licence was revoked. He has also been prohibited from implementing agreements made before the revocation.

Ian Jackson, trading as GYM Business Services Bolton Enterprise Centre, Washington Street, Bolton, was declared, by an OFT Adjudicating Officer to be unfit to hold a consumer credit licence because he used intimidation and threatening behaviour when collecting debts. Jackson had also collected debts when not licensed to do so. One of his employees had been quoted in the local Press as saying: 'it's a case of intimidating people until they pay up'. Further evidence included another employee refusing to show any form of identification and harassing a debtor's wife by demanding payment on the spot 'or else' and having a business card with an offensive message which indicated that collection methods would be tough. The conduct of an employee can be taken into account by the Adjudicating Officer when assessing the fitness of an employer.

Peter Casey, acting Director of Consumer Affairs at the OFT said:

'Threatening and intimidating behaviour is not acceptable. It raises serious doubts about fitness to hold a consumer credit licence and will be dealt with by revocation or refusal of licences if necessary.'

Given the huge numbers of licences that are currently held, the number of instances when these powers have been used seems very small.

Between 1977 and the end of 1994 the DGFT has declared himself 'minded to' revoke, suspend or vary compulsorily the following numbers of traders in the following types of business. (This is not to say, of course that the 'minded to...' notices resulted in the threatened activity):

motor dealers 836

debt collectors and investigators 64

estate, insurance and mortgage agents 222

finance companies 460

retail traders and commercial leasing 318

building and home improvements companies 121.

Trading in Credit

This chapter is concerned with the ways in which the basic tenet of the CCA: 'truth in lending', is reflected in the statute itself and the regulations that have been made under it – with special regard to those who are traders in the credit industry.

The first section is concerned with credit advertising. In this context, according to the CCA, an 'advertisement':

'includes every form of advertising, whether in a publication, by television or radio, by display of notices, signs, labels, showcards or goods, by distribution of samples, circulars, catalogues, price lists or other material, by exhibition of pictures, models or films, or in any other way, and references to the publishing of advertisements shall be construed accordingly.'

Within this extraordinarily wide framework the CCA imposes a variety of disclosure requirements.

The chapter continues with a consideration of the regulation of other credit marketing activities, such as canvassing of trade premises, dealing with children, sending out unsolicited 'credit tokens' (usually credit cards), and the details required when a 'quotation' of credit terms is requested and supplied.

Having considered the ways in which potential debtors are attracted, the chapter goes on to deal with those who may be 'next in line', the credit broker and the credit reference agency. The detailed requirements that the CCA imposes upon such traders are considered.

Then the chapter deals with the extensive licensing system created by the CCA. In terms of establishing real consumer protection, the introduction of licensing all those who trade in this industry, making sure that they are 'fit and proper people', promised massive strides forward.

The system set up by Part III of the CCA cannot be described as anything short of genuine control over the trade. If a business needs a licence and operates without one, then a criminal offence is committed. Similarly, the threat to remove, revoke or even just modify a licence attracts the attention and focuses the mind of aberrant traders wonderfully. The scope of the system is as wide as the general sweep of the Act.

Having considered the nature and extent of the system, the chapter illustrates the ways in which the OFT has used the licensing system to regulate against various unacceptable trading practices.

Chapter 25

Regulated Agreements

The CCA regulates those who seek to do business in the consumer credit industry in a variety of ways. Licensing is supposed to weed out the undesirable participants, detailed regulations surround the display of advertising material, personal details about prospective customers can only be published within closely regulated parameters, and so on.

Supposing that parties to a prospective agreement eventually meet, the Act further regulates in great detail the manner in which they must trade together. At virtually every stage there are requirements made both in terms of the necessary procedure and the documentation used.

A failure to adhere to such requirements probably means that the transaction will be regarded as having been 'improperly executed'. Whilst that does not necessarily connote criminal activity, it does mean that the creditor or owner may well be prevented from enforcing his position in the civil law. There are those who argue that this seems to amount to the use of the civil law in a punitive manner.

When a regulated agreement is made, certain formalities are involved. These apply to virtually all regulated agreements, although they do not cover non-commercial agreements (those not made in the course of a business, such as the private sale of a car, where payment is made by instalments).

There is also a partial exception in the case of some 'small agreements' which involve £50 credit or less and are not hire purchase or conditional sale agreements.

A further illustration of the implementation of the 'truth in lending' policy behind the CCA is to be seen in the extensive range of formalities which are required, before, during and after the contract.

A regulated consumer credit agreement must be made in writing. Before such an agreement is signed the debtor must be given enough information to enable her to 'shop around' for the best deal. Whether or not she actually does, once the documentation has been produced, is not important. The CCA is designed to provide 'truth in lending' and this must be uttered at every stage.

25.1 The formation of a regulated agreement

25.2 The formalities

25.2.1 Disclosure of information

The precise requirements are to be found in the form of regulations. Section 60 of the Act provides:

'60 (1) The Secretary of State shall make regulations as to the form and content of documents embodying regulated agreements, and the regulations shall contain such provisions as appear to him appropriate with a view to ensuring that the debtor or hirer is made aware of –

(a) the rights and duties conferred or imposed on him by the agreement,

(b) the amount and rate of the total charge for credit (in the case of a consumer credit agreement),

(c) the protection and remedies available to him under this Act, and

(d) any other matters which, in the opinion of the Secretary of State, it is desirable for him to know about in connection with the agreement.

(2) Regulations under subsection (1) may in particular –

(a) require specified information to be included in the prescribed manner in documents, and other specified material to be excluded;

(b) contain requirements to ensure that specified information is clearly brought to the attention of the debtor or hirer, and that one part of a document is not given insufficient or excessive prominence compared with another.'

Accordingly, we have the Consumer Credit (Agreements) Regulations 1983 (as amended). They provide that the agreement must be easily legible and must state (*inter alia*):

(a) the amount of credit or credit limit

(b) the total charge for credit

(c) the amounts and timing of repayments

(d) the APR (Annual Percentage Rate)

(e) details of any security provided by the debtor.

The agreement must also contain details of the protection and remedies available to the debtor under the Act, chiefly in relation to cancellation, termination, and repossession, in so far as relevant to the type of agreement concerned.

Of course, detailed requirements such as these spawn standardised contractual documentation. All the major players have their standard forms. One of the clearest is that suggested by the 'Plain English Campaign'.

When presented with the proper documentation in the proper form, the prospective debtor or hirer may change his mind and revoke his offer. The common law here is that revocation is possible at any time up to acceptance, but that the decision to revoke must be communicated to the other party – here the prospective creditor or owner. This common law position is preserved by the Act in s 57:

25.2.2   Withdrawal from agreement

'57 (1) The withdrawal of a party from a prospective regulated agreement shall operate to apply this Part to the agreement, any linked transaction and any other thing done in anticipation of the making of the agreement as it would apply if the agreement were made and then cancelled under section 69.

(2) The giving to a party of a written or oral notice which, however expressed, indicates the intention of the other party to withdraw from a prospective regulated agreement operates as a withdrawal from it.

(3) Each of the following shall be deemed to be the agent of the creditor or owner for the purpose of receiving a notice under subsection (2) –

(a) a credit-broker or supplier who is the negotiator in antecedent negotiations, and

(b) any person who, in the course of a business carried on by him, acts on behalf of the debtor or hirer in any negotiations for the agreement.

(4) Where the agreement, if made, would not be a cancellable agreement, subsection (1) shall nevertheless apply as if the contrary were the case.'

Apart from being set out in the appropriate way, and containing the appropriate terms, in order to avoid the consequences of 'improper execution' the contract must be signed:

25.2.3   Signing the contract

'61 (1) A regulated agreement is not properly executed unless –

(a) a document in the prescribed form itself containing all the prescribed terms and conforming to regulations under section 60(1) is signed in the prescribed manner both by the debtor or hirer and by or on behalf of the creditor or owner, and

(b) the document embodies all the terms of the agreement, other than implied terms, and

(c) the document is, when presented or sent to the debtor or hirer for signature, in such a state that all its terms are readily legible.'

The regulations which expand this provision are the Consumer Credit (Agreements) Regulations 1983 and they set out a form of signature box for the different types of regulated agreements.

As an example, the 'prescribed' signature box in relation to hire-purchase agreements is:

> This is a Hire-Purchase Agreement regulated by the Consumer Credit Act 1974. Sign it only if you want to be legally bound by its terms.
>
> Signature(s) of Debtor(s)
>
> Date(s) of signature(s)
>
> The goods will not become your property until you have made all the payments. You must not sell them before then.

As was mentioned in s 57 above, some agreements are 'cancellable'. That is, the prospective debtor can sign a contract and later have a change of heart and cancel it. This surprisingly generous attitude of the law will be considered later, but if the agreement falls within this category, then the same Regulations require that immediately above, below or adjacent to the signature box there must appear a separate box containing a prescribed statement of protection:

> YOUR RIGHT TO CANCEL
>
> Once you have signed this agreement, you will have for a short time a right to cancel it. Exact details of how and when you can do this will be sent to you by post by the creditor.

The basis of all this is simply to ensure that the debtor or hirer knows exactly what she is letting herself in for when she makes the agreement. There is particular emphasis on the fact that he must be told the rate of charge for the credit.

Having signed the agreement, the same kind of consumer protection calls for at least one copy to be supplied to the debtor or hirer, as a reminder of what has been agreed.

The wording of the Act is complicated here. Before considering it, the general effect should be absorbed. The debtor or hirer will be entitled to at least one (and often two) copies of what he has agreed to. If the agreement is sent or given to him for signature, he should receive a copy then. If, when he signs, the agreement has still to be 'executed', ie signed by the other party, then within seven days of execution he must be sent another copy. So he will have two. He has only one if the agreement is not sent or given to him for signature, for example if he fills in a coupon in a newspaper. Here, he will only get the copy after execution.

However many copies of the agreement the debtor or hirer receives, he should also get copies of the documents referred to in it. With credit cards and trading checks the seven-day period is not so strict; it is sufficient if the copy arrives with the card or check. If there is a surety (eg a guarantor) then his agreement to act as such must also be in writing and he is entitled to a copy of the principal agreement, otherwise the security may be unenforceable:

'62 (1) If the unexecuted agreement is presented personally to the debtor or hirer for his signature, but on the occasion when he signs it the document does not become an executed agreement, a copy of it, and of any other document referred to in it, must be there and then delivered to him.

(2) If the unexecuted agreement is sent to the debtor or hirer for his signature, a copy of it, and of any other document referred to in it, must be sent to him at the same time.

(3) A regulated agreement is not properly executed if the requirements of this section are not observed.

63 (1) If the unexecuted agreement is presented personally to the debtor or hirer for his signature, and on the occasion when he signs it the document becomes an executed agreement, a copy of the executed agreement, and of any other document referred to in it, must be there and then delivered to him.

(2) A copy of the executed agreement, and of any other document referred to in it, must be given to the debtor or hirer within the seven days following the making of the agreement unless –

(a) subsection (1) applies, or

(b) the unexecuted agreement was sent to the debtor or hirer for his signature and, on the occasion of his signing it, the document became an executed agreement.

(3) In the case of a cancellable agreement, a copy under subsection (2) must be sent by post.

(4) In the case of a credit-token agreement, a copy under subsection (2) need not be given within the seven days following the making of the agreement if it is given before or at the time when the credit-token is given to the debtor.

(5) A regulated agreement is not properly executed if the requirements of this section are not observed.'

Another of the many sets of regulations that have been made under the CCA is the Consumer Credit (Cancellation Notices and Copies of Documents) Regulations 1983 (as amended in 1984 and 1989). These provide, in some considerable detail, requirements concerning the form and content of copies of the agreement.

Sections 77-79 give the debtor or hirer a general right during the currency of the agreement, on payment of a fee (now 50p), to a copy of the executed agreement and to information from the creditor or owner as to the state of the account between them.

The Consumer Credit (Prescribed Periods for Giving Information) Regulations 1983, and the Consumer Credit (Running-Account Credit Information) Regulations 1983 prescribe that the information must be provided within 12 working days after receipt of the written request by the debtor or hirer.

25.2.5   Notices of cancellation

Where the agreement is 'cancellable' then there are further documentary requirements made by s 64 and the Consumer Credit (Cancellation Notices and Copies of Documents) Regulations 1983 (as amended). These are designed to ensure that the debtor or hirer is informed about the right to cancel. All of the required copies must contain a notice in a prescribed form setting it out. If only one copy of the agreement is required, a separate notice of cancellation rights must be sent by post within seven days following the making of the agreement.

A notice of cancellation rights must indicate:

'64 (1) In the case of a cancellable agreement, a notice in the prescribed form indicating the right of the debtor or hirer to cancel the agreement, how and when that right is exercisable, and the name and address of a person to whom notice of cancellation may be given ... '

Some agreements involving consumer credit are not 'cancellable' within the meaning of the CCA, but for reasons perhaps connected with marketing, provide debtors or hirers with similar rights to cancel. Under the Consumer Credit (Cancellation Notices and Copies of Documents) (Amendment) Regulations 1984 these are to be treated as cancellable agreements for the purposes of giving copies under ss 62 and 63 of the Act.

As has been seen, the effect of not complying with the formalities is that the agreement is said to be 'improperly executed'. It cannot then be enforced by the creditor (or, in a contract of hire, the owner) without a court order. If the lapse was the lack of the debtor's signature, or if it concerned certain provisions relating to cancellable agreements, then it cannot be enforced at all by the creditor or owner. There is no impediment to the debtor or hirer enforcing it. (He may wish, for example, to complain about the quality of the goods.)

The debtor or hirer can cancel an agreement soon after it has been made. This incorporates the ideas found in the Hire Purchase Act 1964 which provided a 'cooling-off' period for people who had signed agreements on their doorsteps after having been subjected to fast-talking salesmen:

25.3   The debtor's or hirer's right to cancel

'67 A regulated agreement may be cancelled by the debtor or hirer in accordance with this Part if the antecedent negotiations included oral representations made when in the presence of the debtor or hirer by an individual acting as, or on behalf of, the negotiator, unless –

(a) the agreement is secured on land, or is a restricted-use credit agreement to finance the purchase of land or is an agreement for a bridging loan in connection with the purchase of land, or

(b) the unexecuted agreement is signed by the debtor or hirer at premises at which any of the following is carrying on any business (whether on a permanent or temporary basis) –

(i) the creditor or owner;

(ii) any party to a linked transaction (other than the debtor or hirer or a relative of his);

(iii) the negotiator in any antecedent negotiations.'

So the Act provides a right for the debtor or hirer to change her mind and undo the agreement, cancel it, where the deal was made after 'oral representations' (sales talk) in her presence (not on the telephone) and it was signed away from trade premises.

There are exceptions. Section 67(a) excludes certain transactions concerning land. Section 74 adds non-commercial agreements, small DCSAs for restricted-use credit (eg credit sales involving less than £50), DCAs concerned with the agreements after somebody dies and certain bank overdraft agreements.

But the right is restricted. The 'cooling off period' may not last long. Section 68 provides:

'68 The debtor or hirer may serve notice of cancellation of a cancellable agreement between his signing of the unexecuted agreement and –

(a) the end of the fifth day following the day on which he received a copy under section 63(2) or a notice under section 64(1)(b), or

(b) if (by virtue of regulations made under section 64(4)) section 64(1)(b) does not apply, the end of the fourteenth day following the day on which he signed he unexecuted agreement.'

The Act makes it easy to exercise the right to cancel the agreement, although there are a few detailed exceptions within s 69(2) and (3). When the agreement goes any linked transaction goes with it:

'69 (1) If within the period specified in section 68 the debtor or hirer under a cancellable agreement serves on –

(a) the creditor or owner, or

(b) the person specified in the notice under section 64(1), or

(c) a person who (whether by virtue of subsection (6) or otherwise) is the agent of the creditor or owner,

a notice (a "notice of cancellation") which, however expressed and whether or not conforming to the notice given under section 64(1), indicates the intention of the debtor or hirer to withdraw from the agreement, the notice shall operate –

(i) to cancel the agreement, and any linked transaction, and

(ii) to withdraw any offer by the debtor or hirer, or his relative, to enter into a linked transaction.'

'69 (4) Except as otherwise provided by or under this Act, an agreement or transaction cancelled under subsection (1) shall be treated as if it had never been entered into.'

The 'section 6' referred to here contains a list of those to whom an effective notice can be given, other than the creditor or owner:

'69 (6) Each of the following shall be deemed to be the agent of the creditor or owner for the purpose of receiving a notice of cancellation –

(a) a credit-broker or supplier who is the negotiator in antecedent negotiations, and

(b) any person who, in the course of a business carried on by him, acts on behalf of the debtor or hirer in any negotiations for the agreement.'

Incidentally, subsection (7) provides that posting the notice to the appropriate person is enough for it to be effective, even if it is not received in due time, or at all!

A recent illustration of the effect of exercising a right to cancel is *Global Marketing Europe v Berkshire County Council Department of Trading Standards* (1994), where a timeshare agreement, which would otherwise have been subject to the cancellation rights contained within The Timeshare Act 1992, was held to have constituted a 'linked transaction' to the credit agreement which financed it. Thus the exercise of the CCA cancellation rights effectively cancelled the timeshare agreement as well.

Once the agreement is cancelled there will be certain outstanding matters to be dealt with, such as the recovery of money paid by the debtor or hirer:

'70 (1) On the cancellation of a regulated agreement, and of any linked transaction –

(a) any sum paid by the debtor or hirer, or his relative, under or in contemplation of the agreement or transaction, including any item in the total charge for credit, shall become repayable, and

(b) any sum, including any item in the total charge for credit, which but for the cancellation is, or would or might become, payable by the debtor or hirer, or his relative, under the agreement or transaction shall cease to be, or shall not become, so payable, and

(c) in the case of a debtor-creditor-supplier agreement falling within section 12(b) any sum paid on the debtor's behalf by the creditor to the supplier shall become repayable to the creditor.'

Where credit has been paid to the debtor before the expiry of the 'cooling off' period it must be repaid, but if this is done promptly then, generally, no interest is payable:

'71 (1) Notwithstanding the cancellation of a regulated consumer credit agreement, other than a debtor-creditor-supplier agreement for restricted-use credit, the agreement shall continue in force so far as it relates to repayment of credit and payment of interest.

(2) If, following the cancellation of a regulated consumer credit agreement, the debtor repays the whole or a portion of a credit –

(a) before the expiry of one month following service of the notice of cancellation, or

(b) in the case of a credit repayable by instalments, before the date on which the first instalment is due,

no interest shall be payable on the amount repaid.'

Where goods have been supplied before the end of the 'cancellation period' then they should be returned (s 72). While the goods are in the possession of the debtor or hirer, before cancellation, then:

'72 (3) The possessor shall be treated as having been under a duty throughout the pre-cancellation period –

(a) to retain possession of the goods, and

(b) to take reasonable care of them.'

There are certain goods to which the obligation to return does not extend:

'72 (9) The preceding provisions of this section do not apply to –

(a) perishable goods, or

(b) goods which by their nature are consumed by use and which, before the cancellation, were so consumed, or

(c) goods supplied to meet an emergency, or

(d) goods which, before the cancellation, had become incorporated in any land or thing not comprised in the cancelled agreement or a linked transaction.'

From these provisions it is clear that the framers of the Act sought to discourage the provision of either credit or goods before the expiry of the right to cancel.

It is common, particularly in the motor car trade, for goods to be taken in part-exchange. If the agreement can be and is cancelled, then the goods must be returned. If this cannot be done, because perhaps the old wreck has already been sold 'down into the trade', then a sum equal to the part exchange allowance is payable:

'73 (2) Unless, before the end of the period of ten days beginning with the date of cancellation, the part-exchange goods are returned to the debtor or hirer in a condition substantially as good as when they were delivered to the negotiator, the debtor or hirer shall be entitled to recover from the negotiator a sum equal to the part-exchange allowance ... '

It had long been regarded as extraordinary that a policy to protect those who enter into 'doorstep agreements' on credit should not extend to those who enter cash agreements. The opportunity to extend this protection, indeed the obligation to do so, arose with the adoption by the EC of a Directive which was implemented by the UK by means of the 'Consumer Protection (Cancellation of Agreements Concluded away from Business Premises) Regulations 1987. The effect of these regulations is (broadly) to give the consumer a seven-day cooling off period if he agrees to a 'doorstep' sale for cash after an 'unsolicited' visit by the trader or his representative.

25.4   Extending the right of cancellation

A further extension of the right to change the mind and cancel the contract can be seen in the Timeshare Act 1992. This will be further extended as the European Directive on Timeshare is implemented.

The liability of the creditor depends upon the particular transactions that have been made.

25.5   The liability of the creditor

If the debtor has obtained credit from one source and with it she has contracted for goods or services from another then there are three distinct parties and two distinct contracts. One is for credit between the creditor and debtor. The other is a contract for the sale of goods and/or services between the debtor and the supplier. The liability of the creditor is confined to the terms of the contract for credit. She has no place in the other contract. She can derive no benefit from it. She incurs no obligations under it. If the supplier is in breach then the debtor can look for redress only to the supplier himself. He cannot stop paying the instalments to the creditor.

25.5.1   The debtor creditor agreement

An illustration of this is the unrestricted-use bank loan. The bank has no particular interest in where the money is spent, only in seeing it repaid with interest.

The position here is very different. If the transaction is a DCSA then s 75 generally applies:

25.5.2   The debtor-creditor-supplier agreement

'75 (1) If the debtor under a debtor-creditor-supplier agreement falling within section 12(b) or (c) has, in relation to a transaction financed by the agreement, any claim against the supplier in respect of a misrepresentation or breach of contract, he shall have a like claim against the creditor, who, with the supplier, shall accordingly be jointly and severally liable to the debtor.'

An understanding of this depends initially upon a grasp of the meaning of the term DCSA which was considered above. A DCSA arises where the creditor has his finger in the pie. Either he is himself the supplier (as in hire-purchase, conditional sale and credit sale agreements) or he has a business link with the supplier (as in transactions using credit cards). It seems right that the creditor in a DCA should not share the responsibility of the seller's breach since he has no connection with him. Conversely, it seems right that if such a connection does exist, as in a DCSA, then he ought to carry some of the burden of obligation. Section 75(1) sees to it that he does. If the supplier has committed some misrepresentation and misled the debtor into the contract, or if the supplier is in breach of contract (eg the goods are not of satisfactory quality), then s 75(1) provides that the two, the supplier and the creditor, shall be subject to a claim together ('jointly') and individually ('severally'). This protects the debtor if, for example, the supplier goes out of business.

However, the creditor is given a certain relief by the CCA in that she has a right to be indemnified:

'75(2) Subject to any agreement between them, the creditor shall be entitled to be indemnified by the supplier for loss suffered by the creditor in satisfying his liability under subsection (1), including costs reasonably incurred by him in defending proceedings instituted by the debtor.'

This means that if the creditor does have to pay compensation to the debtor in respect of a breach or a misrepresentation by the supplier, then he will be able to recover this from the supplier.

Section 75 does not apply to all DCSAs:

'75 (3) Subsection (1) does not apply to a claim –

(a) under a non-commercial agreement, or

(b) so far as the claim relates to any single item to which the supplier has attached a cash price not exceeding £100 or more than £30,000.

(4) This section applies notwithstanding that the debtor, in entering into the transaction, exceeded the credit limit or otherwise contravened any term of the agreement.

(5) In an action brought against the creditor under subsection (1) he shall be entitled, in accordance with rules of court, to have the supplier made a party to the proceedings.'

When considering the nature of a DCSA, we saw that hire purchase, conditional sale and credit sale agreements are generally included. However, s 75 does not apply to them either. The reason is obvious. If the creditor is also the supplier there is no need for separate claims. The creditor/supplier will answer for his own transgressions.

There is further protection for the debtor and liability for the creditor to be found in s 56. This section concerns the proud phrase 'antecedent negotiations'. This means the pre-contractual negotiations between the parties. The important issue here is that the other party to the negotiations may very well not be the creditor himself but the dealer or a credit broker of some kind. Section 56 is called the 'deemed agency' section since it provides that these people are speaking as if they were the creditor himself. They are deemed to be his agents. This is important because, if they commit any misrepresentation misleading the debtor into the agreement, then an action lies against the creditor for it. Furthermore, the statements which are later complained of may not have been made 'by word of mouth, but, for example, by means of a poster:

'56 (1) In this Act "antecedent negotiations" means any negotiations with the debtor or hirer –

(a) conducted by the creditor or owner in relation to the making of any regulated agreement, or

(b) conducted by a credit-broker in relation to goods sold or proposed to be sold by the credit-broker to the creditor before forming the subject-matter of a debtor-creditor-supplier agreement within section 12(a), or

(c) conducted by the supplier in relation to a transaction financed or proposed to be financed by a debtor-creditor-supplier agreement within section 12(b) or (c),

and "negotiator" means the person by whom negotiations are so conducted with the debtor or hirer.

(2) Negotiations with the debtor in a case falling within subsection (1)(b) or (c) shall be deemed to be conducted by the negotiator in the capacity of agent of the creditor as well as in his actual capacity.'

It was observed above that Schedule 2 of the Act contains a number of examples which serve as illustrations of some of the more complex concepts 'in action', as it were. Section 56 is illustrated in several of these, and in one example (Example 4) a variety of other terminology is set in context:

'EXAMPLE 4

Facts. Discussions take place and correspondence passes between a second-hand car dealer and a customer about a car, which is then sold by the dealer to the customer under a regulated conditional sale agreement. Subsequently, on a revocation of that agreement by consent, the car is resold by the dealer to a finance company introduced by him (with whom he has a business relationship), who in turn dispose of it to the same customer under a regulated hire-purchase agreement.

Analysis. The discussions and correspondence constitute antecedent negotiations in relation both to the conditional sale agreement and the hire-purchase agreement. They fall under section 56(1)(a) in relation to the conditional sale agreement, the dealer being the creditor and the negotiator. In relation to the hire-purchase agreement they fall within section 56(1)(b), the dealer continuing to be treated as the negotiator but the finance company now being the creditor. Both agreements are cancellable if the discussions took place when the individual conducting the negotiations (whether the "negotiator" or his employee or agent) was in the presence of the debtor, unless the unexecuted agreement was signed by the debtor at trade premises (as defined in section 67(b)). If the discussions all took place by telephone however, or the unexecuted agreement was signed by the debtor on trade premises (as so defined) the agreements are not cancellable.'

Section 56, it may be noted, overlaps with s 75 which also renders the creditor liable for misrepresentation by the supplier. It is an interesting overlap. There seems to be no reason why the debtor should need the right twice over. There is no limit (upper or lower) to the price of the goods involved in s 56 as there is in s 75. However s 56 does not create liability for breach of contract as does s 75. The debtor must be best advised to claim under both sections.

Conditional sale and credit sale agreements are sales of goods with time to pay the price, in the former with delayed transfer of ownership and in the latter without it. The Sale of Goods Act 1979 Act therefore applies to them. However, that Act does not cover hire-purchase agreements, since they are not sales of goods at all but a bailment of goods with an option to purchase. Hire-purchase contracts will be dealt with below.

25.5.3   Credit cards and s 75

Where a consumer purchases goods with a cash price of over £100 (but under £30,000!) using a credit card, the credit card company would, at first sight, be liable under s 75 were there any misrepresentation or breach of contract by the supplier of the goods. But the application of s 75 to credit cards can sometimes be, or at least appear to be, less straightforward.

First, certain credit cards (eg the American Express green card and Diners Club) are exempt from s 75 altogether because they require payment of the whole amount of the credit provided in each billing period to be made by a single payment. The agreements under which such cards are issued are thus 'exempt' agreements within s 16, as expanded in the 1989 Regulations. These cards (and some others) are often referred to as 'charge' cards.

The distinction is made between cards inside and outside s 75 by reference to the obligation to repay, not by the naming of the card. For example, some major high street stores call their in-house cards 'charge cards' whereas, as a matter of law, they are credit cards. Some say that the expression 'charge card' carries more 'cachet' than 'credit card'.

Secondly, s 75 came into operation on 1 July 1977, but only in relation to regulated agreements made on or after that day (Schedule 3, para 16). The effect of this seems to be that the statutory protection is not available to cardholders who first obtained their cards before 1 July 1977. There were several 'mailings' of 'credit tokens' before that date. After discussions with the Office of Fair Trading, however, Barclaycard and Access voluntarily agreed to accept liability to such cardholders in circumstances where s 75 would otherwise have applied. But this voluntary acceptance of liability is limited to the amount of the transaction charged to the cardholder's account. This could, in practice, reduce the cardholder's protection, since damage caused by defective goods (eg a microwave oven which bursts into flames) could well exceed their purchase price. Even if the cardholder should have recourse to s 56 (in cases involving misrepresentation, for example), there is still the problem that s 56 itself will probably not apply to cardholders who first obtained their cards before April 1977 (Schedule 3, para 1). There are, it seems, at least two 'classes' of credit card holders, each protected to a different extent.

It is thought that this situation will be neither addressed nor resolved, rather that, as the years go by, as consumers close and open accounts, it will recede.

There are alternative interpretations of the 'connected lender' liability under s 75. It could be that each use of the credit card creates a new contract in that it constitutes an acceptance of a standing offer of credit. Every couple of years or so new credit cards are issued. This might be the performance of a contract made long ago, as a result of which the first card was issued – or it could be that every time a card is renewed a new contract is made.

It is time that such matters were formally clarified. Indeed the Office of Fair Trading has conducted an extensive review of consumer credit, and reform may follow.

The UK government has been looking to 'deregulate' the framework within which business must operate. As part of this 'deregulation' process, the OFT conducted a series of public hearings to gather evidence, and reported in 1994. A large number of recommendations for change were made. These are detailed below.

The DGFT has broadly supported the 'deregulation' initiative, but with reservations.

There followed a further period of consultation. Then, as he was leaving office in the early summer of 1995, the then DGFT further pronounced upon his final proposals for reform in the area of 'connected lender liability':

(a) that joint liability, in the 's 75' sense, remain, but that the exposure of the creditor be limited to the amount of credit involved in the transaction;

(b) that the upper and lower financial limits within s 75 be related to the credit involved in the transaction and not to the cash price, as at present;

(c) that these limits be £100 at the lower end but only £15,000 at the upper end, that is, at the upper the limit for an agreement to be a 'regulated' agreement. This would be raised to £25,000 with the general limit, should a suggestion for that increase be adopted;

(d) he advised against the suggestion that creditors' liability be 'second-in-line' behind suppliers. That is, that there be an obligation on the aggrieved consumer to chase the supplier first;

(e) and he celebrated the agreement of the Association for Payment Clearing Services and the Credit Card Research Group (on behalf of the major card issuers) that claims arising from overseas transactions would be met (until 31 December 1996) on an *ex gratia* basis.

This is a little strange in the light of the contention of many, including the then DGFT himself, that this is a legal liability upon them anyway.

There is no doubt that 'deregulation' of commercial law will take place on a fairly massive scale over the next few years, but it is thought unlikely that very much will be done to the regulatory framework surrounding consumer credit. If nothing much is done we may celebrate the preservation of consumer protection, but we will be left with many of the areas of uncertainty which have developed since s 75 was implemented in 1977.

As examples:

(a) It has been argued that there should be no liability for finance companies where the particular dealer was not signed up by them but by 'merchant acquirers' on their behalf. This has been dismissed as ill-founded by the DGFT, and criticised by the Consumer and Commercial Law Committee of the Law Society as uncertain, but the point is still made;

(b) It is (probably correctly) argued, that in the increasingly common circumstances where an extra card is issued on an account, say for the use of a spouse, then the liability cannot attach to losses incurred by that second person because it only extends to the 'debtor', and further that if injury is caused to the debtor by defects in goods supplied to the extra cardholder then liability cannot extend that far either because the debtor was no part of the transaction! It is thought that where the goods are obviously for household or shared use then liability would be acknowledged, but it might be a difficult point to litigate;

(c) It has been (probably wrongly) argued, that once the credit has been paid off then the exposure to liability ceases. It is surely unacceptable that those who pay off early should be less protected than those who do not;

(d) It has been argued that liability is not extended to transactions effected abroad, say on holiday. Given the sales pitch that is used to attract cardholders, such an argument has a cynical ring. The OFT has asserted that it is wrong. The CCA makes no statement about geographical limitation. The Law Society has commented that 'there is significant backing for the view that the place where the card is used is irrelevant for the purposes of s 75'.

Directive 87/102 requires member states to implement 'connected lender' liability such that, as clause 1 of Article 11 states, a consumer should not be disadvantaged in relation to his or her rights against a supplier for defective goods and services merely by virtue of the fact that he/she has made a credit agreement which is used to finance the purchase of those goods or services.

25.5.4   'Connected lender liability' and Europe

The CCA already gives wider protection than this. Here the liability is restricted to that for breach whereas UK law extends to misrepresentation too. Here the extra target only arises after the consumer has unsuccessfully claimed against the supplier, whereas UK law provides joint and several liability. Consumers can claim against either or both the supplier and the finance company.

Implementation across the Member States has been uneven. In Holland it seems that creditor liability only arises where there has been no delivery at all. In Germany the debtor can simply refuse to pay the creditor if the dealer is in breach. In the UK the position is simple and clear, as was intended by the Crowther Committee in 1971.

As to the implementation of the DGFT's revised proposals on s 75 and 'connected lender liability', he said in his report:

'I have been considering how my recommendations might be implemented with the minimum delay (and therefore, ideally without primary legislation). I understand that, because legislation of some kind is necessary in this area to fulfil the United Kingdom's obligations under the Consumer Credit Directive, it may be possible to make Regulations under the European Communities Act 1972. These would set out the whole of the rules for connected lender liability including both the existing provisions for the traditional case and those I recommend above for credit cards. The existing section 75 would then be revoked by an Order under the Deregulation and Contracting Out Act 1994. This would be a particularly attractive route because it would allow the new provisions to appear in one place as a coherently-drafted whole, and to deal expressly with four-party and overseas transactions.'

25.5.5   The Hire Purchase Agreement

The CCA defines such agreements in s 189:
'189 "hire-purchase agreement" means an agreement, other than a conditional sale agreement, under which

(a) goods are bailed or (in Scotland) hired in return for periodical payments by the person to whom they are bailed or hired, and

(b) the property in the goods will pass to that person if the terms of the agreement are complied with and one or more of the following occurs –

(i) the exercise of an option to purchase by that person,

(ii) the doing of any other specified act by any party to the agreement,

(iii) the happening of any other specified event';

The consumer, the prospective debtor, approaches a trader with a view to acquiring goods by means of a hire-purchase agreement. These days the goods are more likely than not to be motor vehicles. Just about everything else that is bought on credit within the scope of the CCA is bought using credit cards of one kind or another.

Now, the retailer may finance the hire-purchase agreement himself, but usually the arrangement is a tripartite (or 'triangular') one. That is, the retailer sells the goods to a finance house and the finance house lets the goods out on hire-purchase terms to the consumer (the debtor). The finance house has, in effect, made a secured loan to the debtor. Two sets of documents will be used. One will propose the sale of the goods by the trader to the finance house and the other set will propose the hire-purchase agreement between the finance house and the prospective debtor. There may even be a third agreement, or at least a term in the contract for the sale of goods, whereby the trader 'indemnifies' the finance house against the prospective debtor's default. This amounts to a kind of guarantee.

The finance house will then decide whether or not to take on the whole transaction, probably never seeing the goods, but nevertheless acquiring ownership of them and keeping it until, usually, the debtor pays in accordance with the terms of the agreement and then exercises the option to purchase.

The deal between the finance house and the debtor is not a sale of goods. The goods are hired with an option (which arises later) to purchase them. This differs importantly from a conditional sale and both differ from a credit sale.

The 'examples' within Schedule 2 of the Act include:

'EXAMPLE 10

Facts. C (in England) agrees to bail goods to D (an individual) in return for periodical payments. The agreement provides for the property in the goods to pass to D on payment of a total of £7,500 and the exercise by D of an option to purchase. The sum of £7,500 includes a down-payment of £1,000. It also includes an amount which, according to regulations made under section 20(1), constitutes a total charge for credit of £1,500.

Analysis. This is a hire-purchase agreement with a deposit of £1,000 and a total price of £7,500 (see definitions of "hire-purchase agreement", "deposit" and "total price" in section 189(1)). By section 9(3), it is taken to provide credit amounting to £7,500 − (£1,500 + £1,000), which equals £5,000. Under section 8(2), the agreement is therefore a consumer credit agreement, and under sections 9(3) and 11(1) it is a restricted-use credit agreement for fixed-sum credit. A similar result would follow if the agreement by C had been a hiring agreement in Scotland.'

Now a 'conditional sale' according to s 189 is:

'189 "conditional sale agreement" means an agreement for the sale of goods or land under which the purchase price or part of it is payable by instalments, and the property in the goods or land is to remain in the seller (notwithstanding that the buyer is to be in possession of the goods or land) until such conditions as to the payment of instalments or otherwise as may be specified in the agreement are fulfilled.'

The definition of a 'credit sale agreement' is:

'189 "credit-sale agreement" means an agreement for the sale of goods, under which the purchase price or part of it is payable by instalments, but which is not a conditional sale agreement.'

The important distinctions to be drawn here are concerned with whether there is an agreement at all under which one party has bought or agreed to buy the goods (not in a hire-purchase agreement) and whether there is to be any delay in the movement of the 'property in' (ownership of) the goods from one party to the other (not in a credit sale agreement).

As far as the use of terms implied by statute in order to protect the consumer is concerned, there is little difference in objective or substance, although there are differences in detail.

In much the same way, and to much the same extent, statute law implies terms into contracts of hire-purchase as it does into contracts for the sale of goods by means of the Sale of Goods Act 1979.

With hire-purchase the relevant Act is the Supply of Goods (Implied Terms) Act 1973 (as amended). The terms cannot be excluded at all in a consumer hire-purchase agreement and only as far as it is fair and reasonable to allow exclusion in contracts other than those with consumers (in exactly the same way as we saw as being applicable to contracts for the sale of goods). It may be remembered that the relevant statute here is the Unfair Contract Terms Act 1977.

Briefly glancing at the terms themselves, s 8 of the 1973 Act implies a condition as to the title of the creditor (as per s 12 of the 1979 Act, with the obvious alterations in wording to relate to contracts of hire-purchase). Section 8(1)(b) of the 1973 Act implies warranties of quiet possession and freedom from encumbrance (as per s 12(2) of the 1979 Act).

The common law adds a point here. There is a condition implied that the creditor must have title when the debtor takes delivery. Obviously, the debtor does not actually take ownership until he has exercised his option to buy, usually after having paid all the instalments. Thus until then the creditor need not have title to pass as far as the 1973 Act is concerned. However, the common law insists that when delivery is made, the creditor shall have title. This is to protect the debtor from being bothered by the true owner. If the true owner does turn up before the exercise of the option to buy, the creditor is in breach of the implied warranty of quiet possession under the 1973 Act and of the condition implied by the common law. The overall effect is that the debtor can cancel the whole contract and recover what he has paid. He would not be able to do so for breach of warranty but the common law, in effect, allows the debtor to cancel his agreement with the creditor if he finds that someone else has the ownership which he hoped to acquire from the creditor. If, of course, the creditor can acquire ownership after the agreement is made but before delivery to the debtor, then all will be well. Further, if the creditor acquires ownership before the debtor repudiates the contract, this will remove the right to repudiate.

Section 9 of the 1973 Act implies a condition that the goods shall correspond with description (as per s 13 of the 1979 Act). Section 10 of the 1973 Act implies conditions that the goods shall be of satisfactory quality and reasonably fit for a purpose made known to the creditor or his agent, who is called a 'negotiator in antecedent negotiations' (as per s 14 of the 1979 Act). Section 11 implies three conditions relating to sale by sample (as per s 15 of the 1979 Act).

At common law, though not by statute, the debtor must collect the goods, the creditor need not transport them, but he must be prepared to hand possession over in return for the debtor's willingness to pay. The consequent rights of the parties are much the same as with the sale of goods. The one point worth noting as being substantially different is that, once accepted, goods cannot be rejected under a sale of goods. That is, the buyer cannot cancel; he is left with a remedy in damages alone. With hire-purchase the position is different. The obligations are continuous throughout the period of hire and at the point of exercise of the option to purchase. It follows from this that if the goods are of less than satisfactory quality the debtor can reject them at any time. The fact that he has retained them cannot deprive him of his right to cancel, as it could if it were a sale of goods.

Regulated Agreements

This long chapter deals with the detailed formal requirements imposed by the CCA and the regulations made under it of all those who are involved in consumer credit transactions.

First is the pre-contractual disclosure. A regulated consumer credit agreement must be made in writing. Before such an agreement is signed the debtor must be given enough information to enable him or her to 'shop around' for the best deal. Whether or not he or she actually does, once the documentation has been produced, is not important. All the pertinent information must be provided, and clearly, and early.

Because the initial documentation amounts (usually) only to an offer on the part of the prospective debtor, there are formal provisions made for withdrawal (revocation) from the deal.

The agreement must be made by a signed document. There are strict requirements here.

Copies must be provided, and this requirement dovetails with the right to cancel once the agreement has been made.

This right to cancel arises in defined circumstances, and appears extraordinary in the light of the normal attitude of the law of contract, whereby the parties are held to the binding nature of their signatures. Here one party can cancel and walk away if the right is exercised in accordance with the regulations.

One of the key advances achieved by the CCA was the extension of the liability of a supplier of goods to the creditor by virtue of whose activity the transaction was financed. This has proved particularly important in the context of credit cards.

The position here has been closely and recently reviewed. Proposals for change have been made, and these are considered, together with the imminent impact of the EU and another of its 'directives'.

The chapter concludes with a section dealing with a particular form of regulated agreement – the Hire Purchase contract. This has been developed in order to render the 'consumer', the debtor someone who has not 'bought or agreed to buy' goods. This avoids the impact of the Sale of

Goods Act, although, as the chapter outlines, the legislation does provide similar protection for the debtor in such contracts. Terms are incorporated by the Supply of Goods (Implied Terms) Act 1973. A comparison is drawn between hire purchase, conditional sale and credit sale contracts.

Chapter 26

The Rights of the Parties

Both parties to consumer credit agreements as these have rights, at common law and by virtue of the legislation. The creditor may wish to enforce the agreement, seize security, or recover what (after all are his) goods. The debtor may wish to terminate the agreement, whether or not he is in arrears, or he may wish to complain that the deal is unconscionably expensive.

The rights of the creditor to enforce the agreement will vary, dependent upon whether or not the debtor has kept his side of the bargain.

26.1 The creditor's or owner's right to enforce the agreement

(a) Where the debtor or hirer is in breach

Section 87 of the CCA seeks to prevent the creditor or owner from taking precipitate action in order to force the debtor or hirer into performing his side of the bargain. He must first serve a 'default notice' and then give the debtor or hirer a week to put his house in order:

'87 (1) Service of a notice on the debtor or hirer in accordance with section 88 (a "default notice") is necessary before the creditor or owner can become entitled, by reason of any breach by the debtor or hirer of a regulated agreement –

(a) to terminate the agreement, or

(b) to demand earlier payment of any sum, or

(c) to recover possession of any goods or land, or

(d) to treat any right conferred on the debtor or hirer by the agreement as terminated, restricted or deferred, or

(e) to enforce any security.'

These are the actions which the creditor or owner cannot take without notice following a breach by the debtor or hirer, but the creditor can stop further lending.

Section 88 provides that the notice must be in a prescribed form:

'88 (1) the default notice must be in the prescribed form and specify –

(a) the nature of the alleged breach;

(b) if the breach is capable of remedy, what action is required to remedy it and the date before which that action is to be taken;

(c) if the breach is not capable of remedy, the sum (if any) required to be paid as compensation for the breach, and the date before which it is to be paid.

(2) A date specified under subsection (1) must not be less than seven days after the date of service of the default notice, and the creditor or owner shall not take action such as is mentioned in section 87(1) before the date so specified or (if no requirement is made under subsection (1)) before those seven days have elapsed.

(3) The default notice must not treat as a breach failure to comply with a provision of the agreement which becomes operative only on breach of some other provision, but if the breach of that other provision is not duly remedied or compensation demanded under subsection (1) is not duly paid, or (where no requirement is made under subsection (1)) if the seven days mentioned in subsection (2) have elapsed, the creditor or owner may treat the failure as a breach and section 87(1) shall not apply to it.

(4) The default notice must contain information in the prescribed terms about the consequences of failure to comply with it.

(5) A default notice making a requirement under subsection (1) may include a provision for the taking of action such as is mentioned in section 87(1) at any time after the restriction imposed by subsection (2) will cease, together with a statement that the provision will be ineffective if the breach is duly remedied or the compensation duly paid.'

What these sections mean is that for a breach the creditor or owner can refuse extra credit but do little else until the debtor-hirer has been given seven days' notice of his intention.

The prescribed form and content for default notices will be found in the Consumer Credit (Enforcement, Default and Termination Notices) Regulations 1984. A default notice might look like this:

1.   <u>IMPORTANT – YOU SHOULD READ THIS CAREFULLY</u>

2.   This is a default notice served under section 87(1) of the Consumer Credit Act 1974.

3.   It relates to a hire-purchase agreement dated the 20th day of June 1994 between Fleecem Finance Company PLC of 1 Tower Place, London EC9 6ZX (the Creditor) and Kylie Sharon Penberthy of 13 Kynance Close, Bishops Tipple, Blankshire BT17 8SJX (the Debtor)

4.   Under this agreement the Debtor agreed to take on hire-purchase terms a video recorder from the Creditor and to make payments of £25 per month to the Creditor for a period of 12 months.

5.   The instalments for the months of August, September and October 1994 have not been paid.

6.   The outstanding instalments totalling £75 in all must be paid by the 14th day of November 1994.

7.   IF THE ACTION REQUIRED BY THIS NOTICE IS TAKEN <u>BEFORE THE DATE SHOWN</u> NO FURTHER ENFORCEMENT ACTION WILL BE TAKEN IN RESPECT OF THE BREACH.

8.   IF YOU DO <u>NOT</u> TAKE THE ACTION REQUIRED BY THIS NOTICE <u>BEFORE THE DATE SHOWN</u> THEN THE FURTHER ACTION SET OUT BELOW MAY BE TAKEN AGAINST YOU.

9.   If the arrears of £75 are not paid by the 14th day of November 1994 the creditor will commence court proceedings seeking an order that:-

> a) You return the goods which are the subject of the agreement to the creditor and
>
> b) You make such further payments to the creditor as the court thinks fit not exceeding a sum bringing your payments up to one-half of the total payments due under the agreement.

10. BUT IF YOU HAVE PAID AT LEAST ONE-THIRD OF THE TOTAL AMOUNT PAYABLE UNDER THE AGREEMENT SET OUT BELOW (OR ANY INSTALLATION CHARGE PLUS ONE-THIRD OF THE REST OF THE AMOUNT PAYABLE), THE CREDITOR MAY NOT TAKE BACK THE GOODS AGAINST YOUR WISHES UNLESS HE GETS A COURT ORDER (IN SCOTLAND HE MAY NEED A COURT ORDER AT ANY TIME). IF HE DOES TAKE THEM WITHOUT YOUR CONSENT OR A COURT ORDER, YOU HAVE THE RIGHT TO GET BACK ALL THE MONEY YOU HAVE PAID UNDER THE AGREEMENT SET OUT BELOW.

11. The total amount payable under the agreement is £300.

12. The total amount you have paid under the agreement is £125.

13. IF YOU HAVE DIFFICULTY IN PAYING ANY SUM OWING UNDER THE AGREEMENT OR TAKING ANY OTHER ACTION REQUIRED BY THIS NOTICE, YOU CAN APPLY TO THE COURT WHICH MAY MAKE AN ORDER ALLOWING YOU OR ANY SURETY MORE TIME.

14. IF YOU ARE NOT SURE WHAT TO DO, YOU SHOULD GET HELP AS SOON AS POSSIBLE. FOR EXAMPLE YOU SHOULD CONTACT A SOLICITOR, YOUR LOCAL TRADING STANDARDS DEPARTMENT OR YOUR NEAREST CITIZENS ADVICE BUREAU.

If the defaulting debtor does get his house in order in time then the whole sorry thing is to be forgotten:

'89 If before the date specified for that purpose in the default notice the debtor or hirer takes the action specified under section 88(1)(b) or (c) the breach shall be treated as not having occurred.'

The agreement may permit the creditor or owner to do the things listed in s 87(1) if the debtor or hirer dies. However, despite what the agreement may say about the creditor or owner's rights, s 86(1) provides that if the regulated agreement is 'fully secured' then nothing of the kind listed in s 87(1) can be done. The creditor or owner is running no risk and the debtor or hirer's personal representatives will take his place. If, however, the agreement is not 'fully secured' then the actions listed in s 87(1) can be taken if the county court orders it. This will be done if the court is satisfied that the rights of the creditor or owner are at risk; for instance, if it is clear that nobody who survives the debtor or hirer is prepared to take on the agreement. The term 'fully secured' here is not defined in the CCA, but it presumably means that the security which was provided by the deceased was sufficient to cover all the obligations which remained to be performed when he died.

There are certain exceptions to s 86. An agreement that the debt be repaid out of life assurance payments escapes, as does the right to prevent further borrowing, and to end an agreement which had no fixed duration.

Generally, however, s 86 is designed to inhibit the creditor or owner from ending the agreement or demanding immediate repayment simply because the other party to the agreement has died.

(b) Where the debtor or hirer is not in breach

The creditor or owner may be entitled under the agreement to do one or other of the things in s 87 (1) even if the other party is not in breach, eg if another creditor is destraining upon the debtor's goods. If the agreement is of a fixed duration, then, despite the immediate right conferred by the agreement, s 76 applies:

'76 (1) The creditor or owner is not entitled to enforce a term of a regulated agreement by –

(a) demanding earlier payment of any sum, or

(b) recovering possession of any goods or land, or

(c) treating any right conferred on the debtor or hirer by the agreement as terminated, restricted or deferred, except by or after giving the debtor or hirer not less than seven days' notice of intention to do so.'

This restriction of the creditor or owner's rights does not apply to stopping further lending.

A contractual right to terminate the agreement, as opposed to enforcing a term within it, where the debtor or hirer is not in breach, is not restricted by s 76, but it is by s 98:

'98 (1) The creditor or owner is not entitled to terminate a regulated agreement except by or after giving the debtor or hirer not less than seven days' notice of the termination.

(2) Subsection (1) applies only where –

(a) a period for the duration of the agreement is specified in the agreement, and

(b) that period has not ended when the creditor or owner does an act mentioned in subsection (1),

but so applies notwithstanding that, under the agreement, any party is entitled to terminate it before the end of the period so specified.'

So the creditor or owner must, generally, give a week's notice of his intention to enforce the agreement. If the right arises through the debtor or hirer's breach, then the chance to remedy the situation must be given. If it arises otherwise, there is nothing much that the debtor or hirer can do but seek to delay the action. He has a week. He can ask for longer. Under ss 129 and 135, a county court can give extra time to the debtor or hirer to pay outstanding instalments and/or delay the enforcement intended by the creditor or owner.

As was discussed above, security can take a number of forms. Broadly, it consists of the measures taken by the creditor or owner in order to protect against the risk of being left unpaid.

26.2   The creditor's or owner's right to enforce security

Section 189 of the Act contains this definition:

'189 "security", in relation to an actual or prospective consumer credit agreement or consumer hire agreement, or any linked transaction, means a mortgage, charge, pledge, bond, debenture, indemnity, guarantee, bill, note or other right provided by the debtor or hirer, or at his request (express or implied), to secure the carrying out of the obligations of the debtor or hirer under the agreement.'

The right of the creditor or owner to call on the person providing the security (the 'surety') or otherwise to realise it to cover the loss incurred by the debtor or hirer's breach is subject to restrictions.

The security is enforceable only by court order if the surety has not received a copy of any default notice sent to the debtor or hirer:

'111 (1) When a default notice or a notice under section 76(1) or 98(1) is served on a debtor or hirer, a copy of the notice shall be served by the creditor or owner on any surety (if a different person from the debtor or hirer).

(2) If the creditor or owner fails to comply with subsection (1) in the case of any surety, the security is enforceable against the surety (in respect of the breach or other matter to which the notice relates) on an order of the court only.'

A mortgage of land is only ever enforceable by court order (s 126). With pledges, the rights of the pawnbroker (the pawnee) are restricted, as has been seen above, by ss 114-122.

A general attitude within the CCA is visible in s 113:

'113 (1) Where a security is provided in relation to an actual or prospective regulated agreement, the security shall not be enforced so as to benefit the creditor or owner, directly or indirectly, to an extent greater (whether as respects the amount of any payment or the time or manner of its being made) than would be the case if the security were not provided and any obligations of the debtor or hirer, or his relative, under or in relation to the agreement were carried out to the extent (if any) to which they would be enforced under this Act.'

This means, broadly, that the creditor or owner cannot get more out of the surety than she could have got out of the debtor or hirer. Security is essentially a secondary thing. Thus, if the agreement is only enforceable by court order, so is the security. If the agreement is 'improperly executed' the security may be unenforceable, and so on. The section also prevents evasion of certain restrictions in the CCA. For example, if a hire-purchase agreement is terminated, the creditor may be entitled to 50% of the total price. She cannot enforce the security so as to get more than this.

26.3 The creditor's right to recover 'protected goods'

There is a further restriction placed upon the creditor's rights in regulated hire-purchase and conditional sale agreements by Section 90:

'90 (1) At any time when –

(a) the debtor is in breach of a regulated hire-purchase or a regulated conditional sale agreement relating to goods, and

(b) the debtor has paid to the creditor one-third or more of the total price of the goods, and

(c) the property in the goods remains in the creditor, the creditor is not entitled to recover possession of the goods from the debtor except on an order of the court.'

So, where the debtor has paid one-third or more of the total price of the goods (excluding installation charges) and is then found to be in breach of the agreement, the ownership of the goods not having passed to him, the creditor cannot recover possession of the goods without a court order. These goods are called 'protected goods'.

This would not apply if the debtor terminates (by exercising his right to do so). Here recovery is always allowed, no matter how much has been paid. Further, recovery is possible if it is done with the consent of the debtor. Generally, recovery will be possible from a third party.

It will also be possible if the goods have been abandoned by the debtor: in *Bentinck v Cromwell Engineering* (1971) the car was left without comment at a garage for nine months.

The restriction does, however, continue to apply after the debtor's death, until probate or administration is granted to his personal representatives (s 90(6)).

If the creditor ignores these provisions, the consequences for him will be severe: the agreement is automatically brought to an end, all liabilities of the debtor are discharged and all the payments that have been made under the agreement must be returned (s 91).

26.4 The debtor's or hirer's right to terminate

The debtor or hirer normally ends the agreement by paying all the instalments due. He has a right to do this early under s 94:

'94 (1) The debtor under a regulated consumer credit agreement is entitled at anytime, by notice to the creditor and the payment to the creditor of all amounts payable by the debtor to him under the agreement (less any rebate allowable under section 95), to discharge the debtor's indebtedness under the agreement.

(2) A notice under subsection (1) may embody the exercise by the debtor of any option to purchase goods conferred on him by the agreement, and deal with any other matter arising on, or in relation to, the termination of the agreement.'

So the debtor or hirer must give written notice to the creditor or owner. He must pay all the money due, although since the creditor or owner will gain his benefits early, the debtor or hirer will be entitled to a rebate. The extent of the rebate is subject to the Consumer Credit (Rebate on Early Settlement) Regulations 1983 which give detailed formulae for calculating the rebate.

Actually, many finance companies operated a rebate scheme for early settlement for years before the regulations were made. Section 173(1) provides that any term which purports to exclude this right is void.

The right to a statutory rebate is all very well, provided that the state of the account, particularly the amount outstanding, is known by the debtor or hirer. Accordingly, the creditor is placed under a duty, on receipt of a written request, to give the debtor a statement indicating the amount of payment required to discharge his indebtedness under the agreement (s 97). Under the Consumer Credit (Settlement Information) Regulations 1983, the creditor must provide the settlement information in the prescribed form within 12 working days after receiving the written request. The information given must include, in particular, details of any rebate to which the debtor is entitled.

A repayment statement might look like this:

1. This statement relates to a hire-purchase agreement dated the 20th day of June 1994 between Fleecem Finance Company PLC of 1 Tower Place, London EC9 6ZX (the Creditor) and Kylie Sharon Penberthy of 13 Kynance Close, Bishops Tipple, Blankshire BT17 8SJX (the Debtor).

2. The total amount to be paid to discharge the hire-purchase debt is £175.

3. Under the terms of the agreement if the hire-purchase debt is paid off by the settlement date the Debtor will be entitled to a rebate of £25.

4. If the hire-purchase debt is paid off by the settlement date the Debtor will have to pay £150.

5. The settlement date is 1 December 1994 and has been ascertained in accordance with Regulation 3 of the Consumer Credit (Settlement Information) Regulations 1983.

6. The amount of the rebate in paragraph 3 was calculated having regard to the Consumer Credit (Rebate on Early Settlement) Regulations 1983.

7. General information about the operation of the Consumer Credit Act and the regulations made under it can be obtained from the Office of Fair Trading, Field House, Breams Buildings, London EC4 1PR.

You may obtain advice from your local Trading Standards Department or the nearest Citizens Advice Bureau.

The creditor should take care that the information given is accurate. In *Lombard North Central plc v Stobart* (1990) the creditor informed the purchaser of a car (orally and in writing) that £1,003 was required to settle his account. Relying upon this, the car was sold for £5,100. In fact the settlement figure had been understated by £4,710. The Court of Appeal refused to over-rule a county court judgment rejecting the creditor's claim for the rest of the money. The reliance was shown to have been honest. There is, it seems, no requirement that it be reasonable.

If the right of early settlement is exercised, then there will be no future liability under a linked transaction (s 96).

The debtor under a regulated hire-purchase or conditional sale agreement is (subject to minor exceptions) entitled to terminate the agreement at any time (ss 99 and 100). He does this by means of written notice to anyone entitled to receive the payments.

The consequences can be dire. He must pay any arrears. Further, he may pay over enough money to bring his total payments up to half of the total cost under the agreement. This does not include any installation costs, and is subject to any reduction allowed by the agreement itself or by a court. Further, he must compensate for any damage to the goods caused by his negligence, and he must hand the goods back.

The debtor may be unaware of the consequences of telling the creditor he wants to give up the deal. If the court recognises this in him, it will ignore what he said and regard the case as one of arrears of payments giving rise to the creditor having terminated the agreement. Then the further sum would not be payable.

Generally, a hirer under a regulated consumer hire agreement can also terminate (s 101), giving notice, provided the agreement is 18 months old and the annual payments are no greater than £900 (there are several minor exceptions).

When the right to terminate has been validly exercised, the debtor or hirer is entitled (except in a non-commercial agreement) to a termination statement which declares that his indebtedness has been discharged (s 103).

26.5 The debtor's or hirer's right to cancel

This was considered above. Sections 67-73 provide that there are certain agreements, broadly, those which are signed away from trade premises after 'sales talk' where the debtor has a 'cooling off' period within which she can have a change of mind and cancel the contract, generally, putting the parties back into a position as if the contract had not been made at all.

26.6 The right to have an extortionate credit bargain re-opened

Sections 137-140 give the court the power to re-open any credit bargain. It needs to be stressed that this does not mean just those agreements regulated by various other parts of the CCA, any credit bargain at all is subject to this jurisdiction (the only exception is where the debtor is a corporation):

'137 (1) If the court finds a credit bargain extortionate it may reopen the credit agreement so as to do justice between the parties.'

The power can be exercised on the application of a debtor or a surety either in proceedings for this purpose or any proceedings related to the bargain (eg enforcement by the creditor or owner).

The bargain as a whole is considered. This means that linked transactions are considered together with the principal agreement in order to assess whether the bargain is 'extortionate'. This strong word is defined, and the factors to be used in assessing its quality are listed in s 138:

'138 (1) A credit bargain is extortionate if it –

(a) requires the debtor or a relative of his to make payments (whether unconditionally, or on certain contingencies) which are grossly exorbitant, or

(b) otherwise grossly contravenes ordinary principles of fair dealing.

(2) In determining whether a credit bargain is extortionate, regard shall be had to such evidence as is adduced concerning –

(a) interest rates prevailing at the time it was made,

(b) the factors mentioned in subsections (3) to (5), and

(c) any other relevant considerations.

(3) Factors applicable under subsection (2) in relation to the debtor include –

(a) his age, experience, business capacity and state of health; and

(b) the degree to which, at the time of making the credit bargain, he was under financial pressure, and the nature of that pressure.

(4) Factors applicable under subsection (2) in relation to the creditor include –

(a) the degree of risk accepted by him, having regard to the value of any security provided;

(b) his relationship to the debtor; and

(c) whether or not a colourable cash price was quoted for any goods or services included in the credit bargain.

(5) Factors applicable under subsection (2) in relation to a linked transaction include the question how far the transaction was reasonably required for the protection of debtor or creditor, or was in the interest of the debtor.'

Section 171(7) places the burden of proof on the creditor. This means that the debtor must raise the issue by illustrating what he believes is extortion, and thereafter it will be for the creditor to prove on a balance of probabilities that the bargain is not extortionate.

In assessing an alleged 'extortion', the court has a variety of powers. The policy that was noted above, whereby in defined circumstances, a debtor can change his mind and cancel a contract reappears here in the sense that the court can reopen a credit bargain (no matter how much credit is involved) and change the figures and hold both sides bound by the new numbers:

'139 (1) A credit agreement may, if the court thinks just, be reopened on the ground that the credit bargain is extortionate –

(a) on an application for the purpose made by the debtor or any surety to the High Court, county court or sheriff court; or

(b) at the instance of the debtor or a surety in any proceedings to which the debtor and creditor are parties, being proceedings to enforce the agreement, any security relating to it, or any linked transaction; or

(c) at the instance of the debtor or a surety in other proceedings in any court where the amount paid or payable under the credit agreement is relevant.

(2) In reopening the agreement, the court may, for the purpose of relieving the debtor or a surety from payment of any sum in excess of that fairly due and reasonable, by order –

(a) direct accounts to be taken, or (in Scotland) an accounting to be made, between any persons,

(b) set aside the whole or part of any obligation imposed on the debtor or surety by the credit bargain or any related agreement,

(c) require the creditor to repay the whole or part of any sum paid under the credit bargain or any related agreement by the debtor or a surety, whether paid to the creditor or any other person,

(d) direct the return to the surety of any property provided for the purposes of the security, or

(e) alter the terms of the credit agreement or any security instrument.'

26.7   Unjust credit transactions

In 1991, at the request of the then Parliamentary Under Secretary of State for Industry and Consumer Affairs, the then DGFT published a report on 'unjust credit transactions' putting forward proposals for changes in the law relating to extortionate credit deals. Introducing the report, he said

> 'most credit, for most consumers, most of the time, causes no problems, but there is continuing concern about a minority of activities, mainly on the margins of the market, which can be described as socially harmful lending.'

In his report he pointed out that the provisions on extortionate credit in the Consumer Credit Act 1974 have not been as effective as originally intended.

For instance, although there are powers for the courts to reopen extortionate credit agreements 'so as to do justice between the parties', the Office of Fair Trading could discover only four court cases since 1977 in which this had been done.

> 'The people mainly affected are those who believe – or are persuaded – that borrowing, or further borrowing is the solution to their financial difficulties. Such borrowers, often on low incomes, may face a limited choice of lender and have little or no option. They may be faced with misleading or oppressive practices, especially those which obscure the terms and conditions of loans.'

In the report he pointed to 'particular concerns', including:

(a) loans marketed explicitly to people in debt with poor creditworthiness, but with some equity in their homes, often involving high brokers' fees and very high interest rates and granted with little or no consideration of ability to repay;

(b) 'topping-up' or 'rolling-over' arrangements – a series of short-term cash loans to pay off existing debts to the same lender;

(c) a variety of other undesirable activities including brokers breaching their duty to act in the best interests of the borrower, lenders illegally keeping benefit books as security for a loan, irregular documentation and misrepresentation, increasing interest rates without reference to general interest rates movements, and high pressure selling techniques.

The report recommended:

(a) that the courts should have the power to re-open an 'unjust credit transaction'. Replacing the concept of an 'extortionate credit bargain', the new approach is as much concerned with unacceptable lending practices as with the cost of credit;

(b) a finding that a transaction involved excessive payments – a wider test than 'grossly exorbitant' should be a factor pointing towards an unjust credit transaction, but not necessarily conclusive one way or the other;

(c) further factor should be whether the transaction involved business activity which was deceitful, oppressive, unfair or improper;

(d) other factors in determining an 'unjust' credit transaction should remain, as in the current legislation, but with one addition – consideration should be given to the lender's care and responsibility in granting a loan, including steps taken by the lender to check creditworthiness and ability to make repayments;

(e) the court should be empowered to re-open a credit transaction of its own motion – without the need for an application by the debtor;

(f) in cases involving the public interest, the Director General and local authority trading standards officers should be able to apply to the courts to have a particular credit transaction or any particular aspect of it declared unjust;

(g) tougher penalties for unlicensed (and therefore illegal) money lenders.

The DGFT concluded:

'my main concern is with a minority of credit deals which involve an element of exploitation. There is no sort of mechanistic APR or other cost threshold to identify these which would be practicable or desirable for the UK market. My proposals therefore focus attention on all the circumstances of a loan, but involve a less restrictive approach than at present. I am confident that their effect will be to improve credit traders' behaviour and to reduce the incidence of socially harmful lending.'

As part of the report, examples of 'unjust' credit transactions were included.

A consumer borrowed £400. Credit charges of £399.92 were made, and the total amount repayable was £799.92 in 12 monthly instalments at £66.66. The consumer had a weekly income of £51. The APR was 320%.

26.7.1   Excessively high cost and high risk loans

26.7.2	Secured loans to consolidate existing debts	A couple were in arrears with a building society mortgage and also had a second mortgage (these totalled £14,800). They responded to a broker's advertisement. He arranged a four month bridging loan at 4% per month interest, for £22,400. The brokerage fee of £4,000 and interest of £3,584 were deducted from the advance. The couple were left with £16. No remortgage was arranged by the broker and the couple had to sell their home in order to pay off £25,000 on the bridging loan, interest on which continued to accrue. In effect they exchanged two mortgages totalling £14,800 for one of £26,000.
26.7.3	'Roll-over' or 'top-up cash' loans	A man borrowed £30 with £12 interest, making £42 to be repaid in 14 weekly instalments of £3. The APR was 1068%. After six weeks he borrowed another £30 on the same terms. He only received £6 as the remainder of the £30 loan was retained to pay off the outstanding £24 on the initial loan. No rebate of interest was given to reflect the early settlement of the first loan. The APR on the first loan would have been 2515% had the original terms required repayment after six weeks. The effect of the second loan was that in return for £6 in cash he increased his indebtedness from £24 to £42.

26.8 Consumer credit and deregulation

The UK government has been looking to 'deregulate' the framework within which business must operate. This is obviously intended to stimulate economic recovery, but there is a danger that consumer protection may be whittled away as sets of regulations are repealed.

During 1993 and 1994 the OFT carried out an extensive review of the Act. Two consultation documents were issued, on the working and enforcement of the Consumer Credit Act 1974, in August 1993, and on the treatment of business consumers under the Act, in September 1993, which were followed by three public hearings in October and November 1993 and March 1994.

On the 7 June 1994 the DGFT published his report, containing his proposals for reform. Introducing the report, he said:

> 'The key issue is to have strong powers in the main areas where regulation is clearly necessary. The licensing system provides this and it should continue. This makes it possible to limit detailed regulations to those that are really cost effective: when the need to avoid technical breaches of the law produces a mass of small print the main purpose can become obscured and compliance costs can be large. There is also the risk of losing sight of what is really serious, oppressive or misleading.

The Consumer Credit Act has provided a good basis for consumer protection and I attach the highest importance to maintaining this. My proposals are in the nature of a spring-clean, not a wholesale clearing-out of the cupboard.

There are areas where I have concluded that the rules are too detailed and compliance unnecessarily onerous. But there are others where I judge that new rules are desirable in order to provide better protection with equitable results for the consumer.

In some cases I feel that the rules as currently set out, while reflecting sound motives, fail to meet their objectives, with results that can either be misleading, for example in some cases with APRs, or inequitable for consumers as in the case of early settlement terms. In these cases I have proposed modification or tightening of the rules.'

The main proposals, listed in an annex to the report, amount to a formidable agenda for reform. What we have here is either a checklist for progress over the next few years, or another wedge of proposed reform that may lie to gather dust on a shelf somewhere. Perhaps the reality lies between these extremes!

- The main recommendations

    'The government's proposal to remove all business lending and hiring from the scope of the Consumer Credit Act should be implemented, save that lending and hiring to individuals as defined in the Act (which includes unincorporated businesses such as sole traders and partnerships) and related ancillary credit activity should continue to be licensable activities.

    My existing discretionary power under section 74(3) to exempt bank overdrafts and certain other agreements from the provisions of Part V of the Act (entry into credit or hire agreements) should be extended to permit the exemption, on application by named businesses, of specified types of agreement from some or all of Part V, subject to my being satisfied that exemption would be consistent with the interests of debtors or hirers and to any other conditions I considered should be imposed in a given case.

    The upper limit for a regulated credit or hire agreement should be increased from £15,000 to £25,000 to reflect inflation since 1974, together with similar adjustments to most of the other monetary limits in the Act to reflect inflation over the same period. The lower cash price limit for connected lender liability under section 75 should be increased to £150 and the upper limit reduced to £25,000.'

(These figures were amended in his 'second report' in 1995, after further consultation. The later version was considered above.)

'The obligation to show an APR for small credit agreements up to £150 should be removed.

The regulations relating to credit and hire quotations should be revoked. Separately from this, if and when there is a suitable legislative opportunity, the existing offence of conveying credit or hire information that is false or misleading in a material respect in advertisements should be extended to include responses to requests for information from prospective customers.

The regulations relating to credit and hire advertisements should be replaced by new, much simpler, regulations.

The alternative formulas for calculating APRs in regulations 7 and 8 of the Consumer Credit (Total Charge for Credit) Regulations 1980 should be revoked, leaving just the formula in regulation 9. The latter should be adjusted so that it is identical to the single formula in the Directive.

APRs for all types of running account credit should be based only upon the interest charge element of the total charge for credit, with separate disclosure of fees and any other fixed charges. (This is subject to an amendment to the Directive, which the UK should actively promote.)

Pending the change proposed above, calculations, for advertising purposes, of APRs for credit card accounts where an annual fee is payable should assume an average outstanding balance of £500 rather than the notional credit limit of £1,000 currently agreed by credit card issuers as a representative example.

APRs for mortgages where the initial rate of interest differs, for a period at the start of the mortgage, from a lender's current standard variable rate (whether the initial rate of interest is variable but at a constant discount from the latter, or is fixed), should take into account only that initial rate and relate only to the initial period. The current level of the later, variable rate should also be given in advertisements, expressed as an APR relating to the later period. This should be given less prominence than the APR for the initial period and be accompanied by a short statement of its applicability. Mortgage lenders should be encouraged, preferably by means of a code of practice, to provide good information about the cash flow implications and the APRs of given variations in rates of interest.

My determination under section 74(3) should be amended to require interest rates for overdrafts to be presented, in all cases, as compound annual rates. All compound annual rates should be as APRs.

The number of copies of documents concerning regulated agreements secured on land (other than loans for, or bridging loans connected with, the purchase of land) that have to be sent to consumers should be reduced from three to two.

Cancellation rights under section 67 should not apply to credit agreements where antecedent negotiations take place on trade premises but the agreement is signed subsequently by the consumer on his own away from trade premises.

There should be a simplified procedure for modifying credit or hire agreements where this is at the request of the customer.

The regulations governing the calculation of early settlement rebates on fixed-sum loans should be revised so that they are more equitable for borrowers. The 'Rule of 78' formula should be replaced by an actual reducing balance formula. The provisions permitting certain deferments of the settlement date and thus the charging of *ad valorem* settlement fees should be revoked, lenders being permitted instead, if they wish, to charge an appropriate early settlement fee subject to a monetary ceiling of about £100 (this figure to be subject to confirmation in the light of any comments). The regulations on the form and content of credit agreements should be revised so that, if any early settlement fee is to be charged, it must be disclosed at the start of an agreement.

Section 36 of the Act should be amended to replace the obligation for a licensee to notify the Director General of all changes in the officers of its business and its controllers by a requirement to notify only where there are convictions or other matters raising a question of fitness to hold a licence.'

(This proposal has already been published.)

'Consumer credit licences should normally be issued to cover all categories of credit and hire trading rather than it leaving it to the applicant to have to decide which categories are applicable to his business and for which he should thus apply.'

(This proposal has already been published and the necessary administrative changes are now being developed.)

'Subsections (1) – (3) of section 104 of the Courts and Legal Services Act 1990 should be implemented forthwith by statutory instruments made under section 105 of that Act. The objectives of section 104(4) can be achieved through revised regulations on credit advertisements.'

The Rights of the Parties

Both parties to consumer credit agreements have rights, at common law and by virtue of the legislation. This chapter considers the restrictions that the CCA imposes upon the powers of the parties to enforce their rights.

The rights of the creditor to enforce the agreement vary, dependent upon whether or not the debtor has kept his side of the bargain. Where the debtor or hirer is in breach, the CCA seeks to prevent the creditor or owner from taking precipitate action in order to force the debtor or hirer into performing his side of the bargain. He must first serve a 'default notice' and then give the debtor or hirer a week to put his house in order, and there is a 'prescribed form' for such notices.

Where the debtor or hirer is not in breach the creditor or owner may be entitled under the agreement to take action in defined circumstances, eg if another creditor is destraining upon the debtor's goods. If the agreement is of a fixed duration, then, despite the immediate right conferred by the agreement, the CCA provides that the creditor or owner must, generally, give a week's notice of his intention to enforce the agreement. There is nothing much that the debtor or hirer can do but seek to delay the action. He has a week. He can ask for longer. Under ss 129 and 135, a county court can give extra time to the debtor or hirer to pay outstanding instalments and/or delay the enforcement intended by the creditor or owner.

The right to enforce security is restricted, as is the right of the creditor or owner to call on the person who may be providing the security (the 'surety') to cover the loss incurred by the debtor or hirer's breach.

Broadly, the creditor or owner cannot get more out of the surety than he could have got out of the debtor or hirer. Security is essentially a secondary thing. Thus, if the agreement is only enforceable by court order, so is the security. If the agreement is 'improperly executed' the security may be unenforceable, and so on.

Sometimes the goods will have become 'protected', so that where the debtor has paid one-third or more of the total price of the goods (excluding installation charges) and is then found to be in breach of the agreement, the ownership of the goods not having passed to him, the creditor cannot recover possession of the goods from the debtor without a court order unless he consents, or upon his termination of the agreement, or abandoning the goods or (generally) where they are in the hands of a third party.

On the other hand, the debtor has rights too, eg terminate the agreement: the debtor or hirer normally ends the agreement by paying all the instalments due. He has a right to do this early, paying all the money due and (probably) obtaining a rebate on his interest liability.

If all the money is not paid, the agreement can still be terminated, but the consequences can be dire.

The chapter points to the important distinction between termination and cancellation, referring back to 'the right to cancel'.

The chapter concludes with an examination of the right of the debtor to have an 'extortionate' credit bargain re-opened and the recent Report and Recommendations for change from the Director General of Fair Trading.

Index